BIBLICAL
imagination
SERIES

MATTHEW

The Gospel of Identity

MICHAEL CARD

IVP Books

An imprint of InterVarsity Press
Downers Grove, Illinois

InterVarsity Press
P.O. Box 1400, Downers Grove, IL 60515-1426
World Wide Web: www.ivpress.com
Email: email@ivpress.com

InterVarsity Press® is the book-publishing division of InterVarsity Christian Fellowship/USA®, a movement of students and faculty active on campus at hundreds of universities, colleges and schools of nursing in the United States of America, and a member movement of the International Fellowship of Evangelical Students. For information about local and regional activities, write Public Relations Dept., InterVarsity Christian Fellowship/USA, 6400 Schroeder Rd., P.O. Box 7895, Madison, WI 53707-7895, or visit the IVCF website at <www.intervarsity.org>.

Scripture quotations, unless otherwise indicated, are taken from the Holman Christian Standard Bible, *copyright ©1999, 2000, 2002, 2003 by Holman Bible Publishers, Nashville, Tennessee. Used by permission HCSB Holman Bible Publishers. All rights reserved.*

Design: Cindy Kiple
Images: Healing of the Leper from the manuscript "The Four Gospels" at Mount Athos Monastery, Iberon, Greece.
Erich Lessing/Art Resource, NY

ISBN 978-0-8308-3812-7 (print)
ISBN 978-0-8308-8441-4 (digital)

Printed in the United States of America ∞

Library of Congress Cataloging-in-Publication Data

Card, Michael, 1957-
  Matthew : the gospel of identity / Michael Card. pages cm. — (The biblical imagination series ; Volume 3)
  Includes bibliographical references.
  ISBN 978-0-8308-3812-7 (pbk. : alk. paper)
1. Bible. Matthew—Commentaries. I. Title
BS2575.52.C37 2013
226.1'077—dc22
2013003880

P	20	19	18	17	16	15	14	13	12	11	10	9	8	7	6	5	4	3
Y	35	34	33	32	31	30	29	28	27	26	25	24	23	22	21			

CONTENTS

THE BIBLICAL IMAGINATION

*T*his is the third volume in the Biblical Imagination Series. The first two examined the Gospels of Luke and Mark. Our approach is to "engage the text at the level of the informed imagination." This method takes seriously the impact of the fall on every dimension of human experience, including the fragmented and fallen way we listen to the Bible.

On one side are those who study Scripture with their minds. They engage intellectually, puzzling over the text as if it were only a cipher to be solved. They tend to gravitate toward theology. They revel in being "right." On the other side are those who engage the Bible predominately with the heart. They lean toward the emotional, even mystical understanding of the Scripture. Rather than theological, I would describe them as devotional in their approach. Neither approach is wrong, but both are incomplete. God has given us hearts with which to feel and minds for reasoning. He longs to recapture them both with the truth of the Word.

"*Listen*, Israel: The LORD our God, the LORD is One. *Love* the LORD your God with all your heart, with all your soul, and with all your strength." When the Shema (Deut 6:4-5) calls us to "hear" or "listen," it goes on to say that we are to love the Lord our God with all that we are—all our heart, soul and strength.

"*Listen*, Israel: the LORD our God, the Lord is One. *Love* the LORD your God." Listening and loving—these two imperatives demand that we learn to engage the Scriptures with all we can muster, for to listen to God is at the same moment to love him.

How do we reconnect this rift between the heart and mind that was caused by the fall? As I understand it, only the imagination can bridge the gap. This is why the Bible reaches out primarily to our imaginations, for by doing so, the heart and mind become reengaged. We hear the poetry of the Psalms or the music of the Prophets, we listen to the parables of Jesus. As we do, the recaptured imagination engages both heart and mind. Our listening becomes an expression of love. We are made whole and the Living Word comes to life in us.

Imagine the possibilities if we could bring more of ourselves to the task of listening to the Bible. How many new connections might be made, and how many new insights might come to the surface, all as a result of loving God by listening to him with all that we are—all our hearts and all our minds.

Thanks

*E*ven though there may be one person pushing the pen on a project like this, it is nonetheless the product of a community of friends, too many to count.

I would like to thank Aaron Gale for his book *Redefining the Ancient Borders* and J. Andrew Overman for his *Matthew's Gospel and Formative Judaism*. Both of these works provided key backgrounds for the approach to Matthew as a scribal work that was initially focused on the synagogue community of Galilee. I also owe much to Stanley Hauerwas's commentary on Matthew for the power of his images and the beauty of his language.

When I first proposed that Matthew is the Gospel of identity, I shared the idea with three brothers who gave me deep encouragement to follow that line of thought: my new friends Michael Wilkins and Craig Keener, and George Guthrie, a very old and good friend and brother. They are all top-notch servants and scholars.

The Wednesday night Bible study at Christ Community helped test many of these ideas. Thank you all for your faithfulness, week after week.

In the final week of writing, Mark and Stephen at Sandy Cove Retreat Center provided me a place and some space to finish the rough draft. Thanks, brothers.

Without the encouragement and support of InterVarsity Press, you would not be holding this book in your hands. Thanks to the entire team, especially Bob Fryling, Jeff Crosby and Al Hsu. Cindy Kiple has provided the rich designs for the covers.

The team at Harvest Productions in Kansas City makes all of this possible, including concerts and Biblical Imagination Conferences. Thanks, Ron Davis, Holly Benyousky, Susan Surman, Whitney Smith and Shelby Turner.

Thanks especially to my best friend, Scott Roley, for listening to my endless wanderings on the various ideas in this book and for giving me the space to talk through even the stupid ideas.

Finally, blessings to my family, to my wife, Susan, and to our kids, Kate, Will, Maggie and Nate, for putting up with so much time away, not just for the writing of books, but for all of it, for so many years.

Please receive this book from all of us as a gift to the church.

LEARNING
TO LISTEN TO
MATTHEW

*T*he voice we hear in Matthew, perhaps his own, perhaps not, has been for me the least distinct of all the Gospel writers. Mark, clearly speaking for Peter, reflects Peter's intensity, his simplicity of focus, his absence of agenda. It is a disciple's voice that has embraced the personality of his "discipler." Luke's voice is different, but no less distinct. It is an articulate, educated voice, which is just what we would expect from a well-educated slave/doctor. John's voice is an elderly voice, as we will see in a later book in this series. His sophisticated themes are what we would expect to hear sitting at the feet of the last living disciple of Jesus, one who has been preaching and teaching about Jesus for decades.

But Matthew's voice is different. His does not appear to be the voice of a tax collector, a reformed traitor to his people. We might expect a preoccupation with tax collectors, but we have only one unique story involving tax collection (Mt 17:24-27), and it concerns a completely different sort of tax than Matthew collected. Only occasionally Jesus will mention in an aside, "even the tax collectors and sinners."

We would also expect a focus on traitors to Judaism, as Matthew had betrayed his own people, but such is not the case. In fact, we find the opposite voice—a concern for the Old Testament and its fulfillment, for Judaism redeemed and reborn, and the triumph of the new reality over the old orthodoxy. It has been described as the voice of a Christian scribe, and we will see that Matthew is a scribal work that represents more than one voice.

The facts we know about Matthew himself are few; most of them come from Matthew 9. His name was Levi. "Matthew" may very well be a nickname Jesus had given him. It means "gift of God." There is a good chance that James (not the brother of John) was the brother of Matthew, since they are both described as "sons of Alpheus" (Mk 2:14; 3:18; Lk 6:15). This would mean that half of the twelve disciples were composed of three pairs of brothers.

That Matthew was a tax collector speaks the most about him as a person. Without question, he would have been banned from the synagogue and looked upon as a traitor by his own people (Lk 18:9-14). Even though this experience might have provided a bridge to his first readers, we will see that the writer of Matthew makes no mention of it. His tax office, in Capernaum, would have been a choice location, because it was on a major road from Damascus and close to the Via Maris, one of the oldest trade routes in the ancient world. As a tax collector, he would have been an efficient record keeper, familiar with keeping track of family genealogies. He would have worked under the authority of Herod Antipas, collecting taxes for Rome.

It does not compute that his Gospel, the most Jewish of the four Gospels, should have been written by the least Jewish of all Jesus' disciples. Yet dependable tradition attributes the Gospel to Matthew or at least establishes a vital connection to him.

When we look at the evidence that comes to us from the church fathers, a light begins to dawn. The earliest word concerning Matthew comes from Papias, Bishop of Hierapolis (A.D. 130), who says that Matthew composed oracles (*logia*) of Jesus in the Hebrew tongue.[1]

The Gospel of Matthew as a collection of sayings of Jesus compiled by a tax collector, that makes sense. This becomes even clearer when we return to the text of Matthew's Gospel and discover there are five large blocks of Jesus' sayings, which occasionally seem to reflect an unconnected list of *logia*. This may very well be Matthew's fingerprint on the Gospel. I suggest that someone else, whom some scholars describe as a "Christian scribe," who was a part of Matthew's community, took those original *logia* and, using the Gospel of Mark as a template, wrote what we have come to know as the Gospel of Matthew.

As we work our way through the Gospel again and again, we will see the mind and hear the voice of a scribe at work, sometimes seemingly unaware of connections being made to great teachers like Hillel, who had come before Jesus. As we become mindful of his original audience, sitting in the synagogue, listening to his various lessons from the life of Jesus, the Gospel of Matthew will come to life.

MAJOR THEMES

THE CRISIS IN GALILEE

What sets Matthew apart is the focus on a place and a crisis. The place is Galilee, to which Matthew refers some sixteen times. The ministry of Jesus begins and ends in Galilee (Mt 4:12-16; 28:16, 26). That Jesus lives there is a fulfillment of two Old Testament prophecies (Mt 2:23; 4:14). It is the hub of his ministry. He flees there for comfort and perspective when his cousin John is arrested (Mt 4:12). Most of Jesus' ministry involves canvasing Galilee (Mt 4:23, 25; 17:22). The women who accompany him throughout his ministry and to the cross and the empty tomb are Galilean women (Mt 27:55). His ministry will come to its climax on a hilltop in Galilee (Mt 28:7, 10, 16). Matthew could be described as the Gospel of Galilee.

The Galilee of Jesus' day was a land in crisis. Major trade routes intersected there, where two continents join. Though the population was primarily Jewish, the influence of many nations impacted the culture, not always for good. Even Matthew refers to it as "Galilee of the Gentiles" (Mt 4:15).

Josephus, who had once been governor of Galilee, estimated the population at three million.[2] Revolts frequently ignited there (see Acts 5:37). Far from the bucolic collection of villages many of us nurtured in Sunday school, Galilee in Jesus' day was crowded and frequently the center of conflict between the Romans and the Jews, and among the Jews themselves.

The people of Galilee, Jesus' people, were no less conflicted. The statement of Nathanael regarding Nazareth, a city in Galilee, says it all: "Can anything good come out of Nazareth?" (Jn 1:46). In John 7:41, the crowd echoes, "Surely the Messiah doesn't come from Galilee, does He?" Their statement reflects the consensus of opinion that a lowly place like Galilee could never produce the Messiah. In response to Nicodemus, the Pharisees mistakenly conclude, "No prophet arises from Galilee" (Jn 7:52; they were in error, since the prophets Jonah and Nahum were both from Galilee).

The Talmud describes the Galileans as "quarrelsome and ignorant." One famous rabbi, Yohanan ben Zakkai, later lamented, "O Galilee, Galilee, thou hatest the Torah."[3]

More religious Jews from Judea criticized Galileans for eating meat along with dairy products. The Galileans typically passed through the unclean territory of Samaria on their way to Jerusalem, something a strictly pious Jew would never do (Jn 4:3). Jewish congregations in Judea, south of Galilee, forbid Galileans to recite prayers in their synagogues due to their distinctive accent, the accent that gave Peter away in Caiaphas's courtyard during Jesus' trial (Mt 26:73). Only Matthew, the Gospel of Galilee, gives us the detail. Finally, in Judea, Galilean olive oil was considered unclean and could not be used for ritual purposes.

Galilee was a crowded place with a mixed population with customs often at odds with one another—a people who were contentious and looked down on, a place where poor tenant farmers were commonly abused by wealthy landowners from Judea, a country at war with the Romans and with itself. Into this turmoil of mid-first-century Galilee, Jesus and his movement were born, and the first community of his followers, all Galileans, was set on a collision course with crisis.

As we enter into that world, we need to unlearn our old picture of the Judaism of Jesus' day. It was not the monolithic religion we usually imagine but one rife with pluralism. The Gospels clearly portray a variety of divisions within Judaism: Sadducees, Herodians, followers of John the Baptist, scribes, priests, Levites and, of course, the Pharisees. But even these groups were divided internally and often at odds with one another. As the followers of Jesus of Nazareth came together, they were universally considered by both the Jews and the Romans as simply another division, another subset within the matrix of first-century Judaism.

The growing crisis between the Jews and the Jewish followers of Jesus was experienced by and large within the walls of the synagogue. The problems and persecutions of the Jewish community were experienced equally by the followers of Jesus who were still predominantly Jewish, still attended synagogue and considered themselves part of the community.

When the insane Emperor Caligula ordered a statue of himself to be erected in the temple in Jerusalem in A.D. 40, the followers of Jesus shared in the outrage. The writ of tolerance Claudius issued to the Jews in A.D. 41 included the Christian community. And when he expelled the Jews from Rome because of riots over someone mistakenly identified by the slave name Chrestus (*Christos*) in A.D. 52, the Christians were evicted from the city as well (Acts 18:1).[4] When the first Jewish war began in A.D. 66, the followers of Jesus fought alongside their compatriots from the synagogue. And when Jerusalem fell in A.D. 70, many Jewish Christians died, though some apparently heeded Jesus' apocalyptic warning and fled to the city of Pella.[5]

After the temple was destroyed, the Romans permitted a diverse group of scribes and Pharisees to settle in the city of Jamnia (Yavneh) near the Mediterranean coast, west of Jerusalem. The temple was gone, burned to the ground, its stones pried apart by soldiers seeking the gold that had lined the walls. The destruction of the temple marked the end of priest, Levite and Sadducee in Israel. The Pharisees were effectively the only major group left standing.

There the Torah scholars were tasked with remaking and reforming Judaism itself. What does Jewish observance look like now that there is no temple, no sacrifice? Together these scholars reconstructed the essence of the Judaism we know today, based not on sacrifice but on diligent study of the Torah. Here they codified the prayers and practices of synagogue observance, a rich collection of petitions and blessings. Here they began to collect the sayings of the Mishnah—next to the Torah, the most sacred book of Judaism.

The Talmud, a twenty-volume commentary on the Mishnah, describes how, during that process, a cotton dealer named Simeon arranged eighteen benedictions in the presence of Rabbi Gamaliel II, the grandson of Paul's famous teacher.[6] These prayers, recited two to three times a day, would be known as the Amidah (the Hebrew word for "standing," since the prayers were recited while standing) or simply as the Shemonah Esreh (Eighteen Benedictions). They would become the centerpieces of Jewish liturgy. It was said that, during the recitation of the eighteen benedictions, the worshiper could erase all worldly matters from the mind.

As the benedictions were being formulated, Gamaliel asked if someone could word a benediction relating to the *mînîm* (heretics). Samuel the Small composed a new benediction that was inserted into the twelfth slot. This "blessing" was in fact a curse. Its insertion into the list of prayers that would become a key to Orthodox observance marked a shift in the relationship between Jews and Jewish Christians that can hardly be underestimated. In the future, suspected heretics would be watched closely as they recited the Amidah. If anyone made an error while reciting benediction twelve, they could be excluded from the synagogue as heretics, since it was believed no one would curse themselves. The blessing that was a curse became a litmus test for exposing the followers of Jesus, a tool used to ban them from the synagogue.[7]

> For the apostates, let there be no hope
> And let the arrogant government [Rome]
> Be speedily uprooted in our days.
> Let the Nazarenes [Christians] and the Mînîm [heretics]
> Be destroyed in a moment.
> And let them be blotted out of the Book of Life
> And not be inscribed together with the righteous.
> Blessed art thou, O Lord, who humbles the proud.[8]

The exact date of the compilation of the eighteen benedictions is debated among scholars. Clearly, it occurred sometime after A.D. 70. Its direct relation to Matthew's Gospel is also a matter of debate. However, regardless of the exact date of its composition, the existence of benediction twelve establishes the tone of the life situation of Matthew's first listeners. Even if the benedictions were authored after Matthew's Gospel, it is an indicator of the tension that was growing in the synagogue between the followers of Jesus and the other members of the congregation. Clearly, they are about to be shown the door.

So, within the preexisting turmoil that was Galilee, another crisis was brewing. Amid the growing conflict between the Romans and the Jews that would result in the destruction of the temple and the rebirth of Judaism as we know it, a small group of Jews was coming together. They had found the Messiah, Jesus of Galilee. To the best of their ability, they carried on with their daily work, Sabbath observance and synagogue attendance (see the disciples observing the hours of prayer in the temple, Acts 3:1; 10:30). The crisis that loomed on the horizon would destroy what fragile identity they had left. They were Christians who did not yet know they were Christians. Matthew's Gospel is written in the face of this growing crisis. His portrayal of Jesus and his word will provide for this conflicted congregation the one thing they most badly need: identity.

THE GOSPEL OF IDENTITY

Perhaps the most fundamental human question is, "Who am I?" Our peace rests in finding the answer to this question. The greatest moments of emotional stress and upheaval occur when our self-understanding is challenged or violated, when we don't know who we are.

We seek to define ourselves in many ways: where we are from, our ethnicity, our occupation, our religion, even our gender. I am from Tennessee, a white male, songwriter, Protestant. But none of these labels taken alone or as a whole answer the basic question of who I am. What inevitably must happen, if I hope to be able to answer the ultimate question, is that all these incomplete identities must be stripped away in what is most often a painful process. Only after we arrive at the end of our incomplete and false identities are we ready to receive the final and conclusive answer to the question of who we really are. The first listeners to the Gospel of Matthew were on the brink of that experience.

The crisis in Galilee will strip those first followers of Jesus of their identity. Many of them will lose their jobs. They will be betrayed by their families. Their fundamental Jewish identities will be stripped away. Eventually they will be banned from the synagogue, which means being excluded from Jewish life altogether (see Jn 9:22; 12:42). The organizing principle of identity pulls together all the unique threads of the life situation of the first recipients of the Gospel of Matthew, the Gospel of identity.

To those who were being stripped of their identity as children of Israel, Matthew's Gospel speaks repeatedly of the kingdom of God. More than any other Gospel, it portrays the kingship of Jesus and the radical uniqueness of his kingdom. Only in Matthew do we hear Jesus tell his followers that they are the light of the world and the salt of the earth (Mt 5:13-14; see Jn 8:12).

Jesus will redefine his followers, whose identities were rooted in the occupation of fishing, as fishers of people (Mt 4:19). The Beatitudes of Matthew 5 will forever redefine the identities of the followers of Jesus; they are the poor, mourning, gentle, hungry, merciful peacemaking ones who, above all, are persecuted. According to this radical new identity, they will possess the new kingdom of which Jesus is the king. The unclean leper, the bleeding woman, the blind and the lame will all discover a new healed identity in Jesus. The Twelve will be redefined as "apostles" when they are sent out on mission, bearing Jesus' authority.

But most of all, it is Jesus' identity that is revealed in the Gospel of Matthew. He is the king who is worshiped by the "king-making" magi in Matthew 2. He is the one who identifies with sinners in need of a baptism of repentance in chapter 3. He is the one who finds his identity with the Father in the face of the temptation in the wilderness in chapter 4. He is the Lord of the Sabbath and God's chosen servant in chapter 12. He is the new Moses, providing manna in the wilderness in chapters 14 and 15. He is defined by his friend Peter as the Christ in chapter 16. His true, luminous identity is unveiled before the Three on the Mount of Transfiguration in chapter 17. He is the returning Son of Man in chapter 24. He is the wine and bread of chapter 26. He is the suffering servant on the cross in chapter 27. And finally, in chapter 28, He is the Risen One.

Matthew's Gospel is about identity, about discarding the old, incomplete identities that enslave us and receiving a radical new identity. It is not your Jewish or rabbinic self, or your tax-collecting self. You are not defined by the old orthodoxy, but by the new reality. All of the old, false, incomplete identities must go and be swallowed up in a new organizing principle. It is about surrendering whatever citizenship you define your identity by and becoming a citizen of the new kingdom, whose king is Jesus.

Matthew is primarily about the identity of Jesus and the often-painful process of subsuming our identities in his (see Gal 3:28). As we come to the Gospel of Matthew with that most fundamental question, "Who am I?" the writer responds by telling us who Jesus is. The entire Gospel might be summed up in the plea "Jesus, tell me who you are, so I can know who I am." In this light the question "Who am I?" is transformed into the penultimate question as it becomes servant to the ultimate question, "Who is Jesus?"

MATTHEW 1

THE MESSIAH'S PEDIGREE

A DREAM COME TRUE

THE MESSIAH'S PEDIGREE

[1]*The historical record of Jesus Christ, the Son of David, the Son of Abraham:*

[2]*Abraham fathered Isaac,*

Isaac fathered Jacob,

Jacob fathered Judah and his brothers,

[3]*Judah fathered Perez and Zerah by Tamar,*

Perez fathered Hezron,

Hezron fathered Aram,

[4]*Aram fathered Amminadab,*

Amminadab fathered Nahshon,

Nahshon fathered Salmon,

[5]*Salmon fathered Boaz by Rahab,*

Boaz fathered Obed by Ruth,

Obed fathered Jesse,

[6]*and Jesse fathered King David.*

Then David fathered Solomon by Uriah's wife,

[7]*Solomon fathered Rehoboam,*

Rehoboam fathered Abijah,

Abijah fathered Asa,

[8]*Asa fathered Jehoshaphat,*

Jehoshaphat fathered Joram,

Joram fathered Uzziah,

[9]*Uzziah fathered Jotham,*

Jotham fathered Ahaz,

Ahaz fathered Hezekiah,

[10]*Hezekiah fathered Manasseh,*

Manasseh fathered Amon,

Amon fathered Josiah,

[11]*and Josiah fathered Jechoniah and his brothers*
at the time of the exile to Babylon.

[12]*Then after the exile to Babylon*
Jechoniah fathered Shealtiel,

Shealtiel fathered Zerubbabel,

[13]*Zerubbabel fathered Abiud,*

Abiud fathered Eliakim,
Eliakim fathered Azor,
[14] Azor fathered Zadok,
Zadok fathered Achim,
Achim fathered Eliud,
[15] Eliud fathered Eleazar,
Eleazar fathered Matthan,
Matthan fathered Jacob,
[16] and Jacob fathered Joseph the husband of Mary,
who gave birth to Jesus who is called the Messiah.
[17] So all the generations from Abraham to David were 14 generations; and
from David until the exile to Babylon, 14 generations; and from the exile to
Babylon until the Messiah, 14 generations.

The "book of the origin of Jesus Christ" is a more literal translation of the opening phrase of the Gospel of Matthew. The phrase
contains a precise echo of Genesis, the original book of origins. In
fact, the ancient Greek translation of Genesis 2:4 contains those exact
words, only in reference to the "book of the origins" of the heavens
and the earth.

Unlike Luke, who tucks his genealogy in chapter 3 of his Gospel,
after the baptism of Jesus, the author of Matthew opens his book with
the genealogy, a record of the pedigree of Jesus. To the first hearers of
the Gospel, it would have been both reassuring and alarming.

Genealogies were nothing new. The Old Testament is filled with
them (Gen 5:1-32; 10:1-32; 11:10-32; 25:12-18; 36:1-43; 46:8-27; Ex
6:14-25; 1 Chron 1–9). The first hearers of Matthew would have nod-
ded, name by name, when the list of Jesus' descendants were read to
them in the synagogue. Many of the names would have been familiar,
since much of the list contains a roll call of famous men: Abraham,
Isaac and Jacob, the founding fathers of the Jewish people; David, the
great king; his wise son, Solomon; Uzziah, the great reformer; and even
Coniah, the king who was cursed (Jer 22:24-30).

Four of those named in the genealogy would have caused a momentary distraction, not simply because there are references to women, who were normally not listed in genealogical records, but primarily because of who these women were. Tamar (Mt 1:3) deceived her father-in-law, Judah, who, thinking she was a prostitute, slept with her (Gen 38:11-18). Rahab (Mt 1:5), though she helped Joshua's spies in Jericho, actually was a prostitute (Josh 2:1-24). Ruth (Mt 1:5) was the Moabite who married the kind and elderly Boaz. And though she is only referred to in the genealogy as "Uriah's wife" (Mt 1:6), Bathsheba was the beautiful Hittite whom David seduced.

Often the commentaries try to make the case that these four women were somehow infamous and their presence in the pedigree of Jesus demonstrates his association with sinners. But certainly Ruth is presented as a paradigm in the Old Testament book named for her, and Rahab helped the Israelite spies. Though Tamar tricked Judah, he was the person who approached her and instigated their illicit affair. And was it not Bathsheba who was victimized by David?

More to the point, what these four women have in common is their non-Jewish descent and the fact that they all married Jewish men. The presence of these women, the only female names that appear in the list, hints at a theme that will appear throughout this Gospel. Though Matthew is the most Jewish of the Gospels, the writer is still aware that there is a place for the Gentiles in the future God has planned for his people. They have a part in the future because, according to the genealogy, they had a part in the past.

The genealogy has been shaped by the author. He has been selective in listing Jesus' ancestors in three specific groups of fourteen generations (Mt 1:17). The first group begins with Abraham, whose son Isaac he was willing to sacrifice. The second group begins with David, the great king whose throne and name are connected with Jesus, the "Son of David" (Mt 9:27; 12:23; 15:22; 20:30; 21:9, 15). The final group is not connected to a person, but to an event: the Babylonian exile. What was done in the exile will ultimately be undone in Jesus. He will establish a new kingdom, fulfilling a promise made to David of an eternal throne (1 Kings 2:45; 9:5; Is 9:7; see also Lk 1:32-33). Abraham was promised innumerable descendants,

David an eternal throne. Jesus will perfectly fulfill these promises within Matthew's major theme of the kingdom.

A DREAM COME TRUE

18 The birth of Jesus Christ came about this way: After His mother Mary had been engaged to Joseph, it was discovered before they came together that she was pregnant by the Holy Spirit. 19 So her husband Joseph, being a righteous man, and not wanting to disgrace her publicly, decided to divorce her secretly.

20 But after he had considered these things, an angel of the Lord suddenly appeared to him in a dream, saying, "Joseph, son of David, don't be afraid to take Mary as your wife, because what has been conceived in her is by the Holy Spirit. 21 She will give birth to a son, and you are to name Him Jesus, because He will save His people from their sins."

22 Now all this took place to fulfill what was spoken by the Lord through the prophet:

> *23 See, the virgin will become pregnant*
> *and give birth to a son,*
> *and they will name Him Immanuel,*

which is translated "God is with us."

24 When Joseph got up from sleeping, he did as the Lord's angel had commanded him. He married her 25 but did not know her intimately until she gave birth to a son. And he named Him Jesus.

*T*he birth of Jesus comes to us from Joseph's point of view. Mary does not open her mouth. In fact, she appears only in verse 11, and this is a fleeting appearance. (Luke gives us the story from Mary's point of view.) We are told the couple was engaged to be married. In Judaism, an engagement was binding and required a divorce (*get*) to break. The violation of an engagement was literally a matter of life and death (Deut 22:23-29).

The Gospels tell us virtually nothing about Joseph. We know that he was a builder (Mt 13:55). He was a descendent of David (Lk 2:4).

Though Joseph is present in Luke 2:41-52, when the twelve-year-old Jesus is lost and found in the temple, he does not utter a word. He is as silent in Luke as Mary is in Matthew. The vast majority of what we see of and know about Joseph we learn from the Gospel of Matthew.

Like his Old Testament namesake, Joseph was a dreamer (see Gen 37:5; 40:8-16; 41:15-17, 25). In Luke's Gospel, Mary is communicated to by means of direct angelic messengers. Somehow Joseph was the sort of person who could more easily believe a dream than a real-life encounter with an angel.[9] In Matthew 1:20-21, the angel of the Lord, referring to Joseph as "son of David," communicates the impossible to him. His virgin fiancée is pregnant through the Holy Spirit. The baby's name will be Jesus (*Yēšûa*). The angel provides an etymology of the name: "He will save His people from their sins." *Yēšûa* literally means "Yahweh saves."

In Matthew 1:22 we have the first example of what is referred to as a "fulfillment formula" in Matthew's Gospel. Again and again, the author of Matthew will return to the Old Testament to show how the coming of Jesus of Nazareth has perfectly fulfilled something that was spoken long ago in the Old Testament Scriptures.

When Joseph awakes, he immediately obeys the angelic message. There is no hint of internal emotional struggle on his part. He takes Mary to his home but denies himself the privileges of a husband by not having union with her until Jesus is born. The actual birth takes place offstage in the Gospel. The next time we see Jesus, he is a toddler living in a house.

We know so little of Joseph, yet as the Scripture always does, we are told everything we need to know about him. The most important information comes to us from Matthew 1:19. Joseph is described as a "righteous" (*dikaios*) man. He does not want to publicly humiliate Mary. And so he decides to divorce her quietly. (The word translated "divorce" can also mean "dismissed.") The point is, *before* the angel came to Joseph in the dream and explained the true cause of Mary's pregnancy, Joseph had already decided not to harm her, not to take full advantage of his legal rights. In fact, it seems Joseph was willing to take upon himself the guilt that he thought was Mary's guilt. This is all we know about the heart of Joseph. But it is all we need to know.

Joseph would have been the first character in the Gospel with whom

its first hearers in Matthew's community would resonate. His predicament is a parable of theirs. Like them, he faces a difficult decision: to
maintain the status quo of the old orthodoxy or to follow a new and
wonderful dream from God at an enormous personal cost. Joseph, the
namesake of a dreamer, clearly follows the dream. Though his life is
made vastly more difficult as a result, on every hand he is protected by
God. Matthew's first hearers have reason to embrace the same hope.

MATTHEW 2

THE WORLD'S WISDOM BOWS DOWN

2:1–12 The magi.

THE ESCAPE

2:13–23 The flight to Egypt.

THE WORLD'S WISDOM BOWS DOWN

¹After Jesus was born in Bethlehem of Judea in the days of King Herod, wise men from the east arrived unexpectedly in Jerusalem, ²saying, "Where is He who has been born King of the Jews? For we saw His star in the east and have come to worship Him."

³When King Herod heard this, he was deeply disturbed, and all Jerusalem with him. ⁴So he assembled all the chief priests and scribes of the people and asked them where the Messiah would be born.

⁵"In Bethlehem of Judea," they told him, "because this is what was written by the prophet:

> *⁶And you, Bethlehem, in the land of Judah,*
> *are by no means least among the leaders of Judah:*
> *because out of you will come a leader*
> *who will shepherd My people Israel."*

⁷Then Herod secretly summoned the wise men and asked them the exact time the star appeared. ⁸He sent them to Bethlehem and said, "Go and search carefully for the child. When you find Him, report back to me so that I too can go and worship Him."

⁹After hearing the king, they went on their way. And there it was—the star they had seen in the east! It led them until it came and stopped above the place where the child was. ¹⁰When they saw the star, they were overjoyed beyond measure. ¹¹Entering the house, they saw the child with Mary His mother, and falling to their knees, they worshiped Him. Then they opened their treasures and presented Him with gifts: gold, frankincense, and myrrh. ¹²And being warned in a dream not to go back to Herod, they returned to their own country by another route.

> An ancient superstition was current
> in the East, that out of Judea at this time
> would come one of the rulers of the world.[10]
> Suetonius

*I*t has been roughly two and a half years since the close of Matthew 1. After that chapter of the story of Jesus, recorded for us in Luke 2, the author of Matthew takes up the thread of Jesus' life.

It is roughly the last year of Herod the Great's tumultuous reign. He is sickly, dying of gonorrhea and possibly also cancer. He has spent his entire reign protecting his precarious throne. His appointment first came in 40 B.C. through his patron Mark Antony. He weathered the split between Antony and Augustus and was able to deftly change sides and preserve his power. In time he would build temples and name cities for Caesar, further cementing his title as *rex socius* (a client king).

In the latter years of his reign, their relationship will begin to break down. At one point Augustus said of Herod, "It is better to be Herod's pig than Herod's son," owing to the fact that Herod had killed so many of his own but maintained the appearance of keeping kosher.[11] He barely survived a plot by none other than Queen Cleopatra of Egypt to seduce and blackmail him. He executed his beloved wife, Mariamne, and her mother, Alexandra, as well as his three older sons. As he lay dying in Jericho in 4 B.C., he ordered a number of well-loved Jewish leaders to be held in the hippodrome in Jericho to be executed upon his death so that there would be "mourning in Israel." His tomb in the Herodium has only recently been discovered by archaeologists.

That the magi come from the East would have been interpreted as a particular threat. Herod had built several fortresses along his eastern borders in anticipation of a threat coming from Persia. Masada is the best known and most imposing of these forts. He also constructed the fortresses known as the Herodium and Machaerus, where John would later be beheaded by Herod's son, Antipas.

Herod had degenerated into a sickly, spent force. Driven mad by decades of stress, not to mention the long-term neurological effects of gonorrhea, he was pathologically paranoid. With this as background, we can begin to imagine the impact the magi's message would have had on the fragile king. The greatest threat he could imagine had reared its head once more, only this was a very real threat, not an imagined one.

The bearers of the message of the newborn king represented an even greater threat to Herod. The magi were an elite political and spiritual force that had exercised authority since before the time of Daniel, who was appointed as one of their number (Dan 2:48; 5:11). They were the interpreters of dreams (Dan 2:2; 4:7) and possessors of secret knowledge of the planets and the stars (see Esther 1:13). Owing to the presence of the exiled Jewish community in Babylon during the captivity, the Jewish Scriptures had become part of the magi's vast accumulation of knowledge. Though the passage is not quoted, the most likely reason for their journey was the prophecy of the wicked prophet Balaam in Numbers 24:17:

> I see him, but not now;
> I perceive him, but not near.
> A star will come from Jacob,
> and a scepter will arise from Israel.

The magi appear from the East, presumably with their entourage of Persian cavalry announcing they have come to "worship" the newborn king of the Jews. The word describing Herod's response can also be translated "terrified," "troubled" or even "intimidated." From what we know of Herod the Great, he most likely experienced this entire range of emotions.

The two groups of advisers he calls together—the chief priests and the teachers of the law—represent the two groups that will in time band together in an attempt to destroy the newborn king. The chief priests were primarily Sadducees, and the teachers of the law were mostly Pharisees. It seems common enough knowledge, from Micah 5:2, that the king will be born in the city of David's birth: Bethlehem. Just why the magi didn't notice the passage before we are left to wonder.

Herod's secret meeting with them to determine the exact time of the guiding star's appearance is actually a ruse to allow him to calculate the age range of the boys in Bethlehem he will order to be executed (see Mt 2:16). This number also indicates the probable length of their journey, two years.

As they resumed their journey, the star reappears and guides the weary troop to a house where the young child is waiting. Their joy at seeing the familiar star once more and finding the goal of their long trek is difficult for us to imagine. What, to me, is most significant about the magi occurs in Matthew 2:11. There is a doubled statement: they fall to their knees and worship him. When we take into consideration the vast knowledge base possessed by the magi, and the fact that they were willing to undertake such a long journey, indicates one simple startling fact: in all their sacred wisdom, in all their vast learning, they had not yet found the wisdom their hearts were longing for. Why else would they have taken such an arduous trip if not for an aching need to satisfy a hunger that all of the world's wisdom had not yet satisfied?

We must rid ourselves of the notion that because there were three gifts, there must have been only three magi. Perhaps there were dozens of them. Gold is a gift for kings. Frankincense was the only incense allowed on the altar in the temple (Ex 30:9, 34-38). Myrrh was primarily used as a perfume but also in the process of embalming (Jn 19:39). They were the perfect gifts for a king who was also a priest who had come to die.

The simple fact that they worshiped the toddler king indicates that in him they apparently found all they had been looking for. This wordless one, who was the Word, was at the same time the wisdom of God. The wisest men in the world recognize it and fall to their knees.

The Persian dreamers are warned by one final dream to go home by another route, to avoid the insane Herod, who by this time was surely furious.[12]

THE ESCAPE

[13]After they were gone, an angel of the Lord suddenly appeared to Joseph in a dream, saying, "Get up! Take the child and His mother, flee to Egypt, and stay there until I tell you. For Herod is about to search for the child to destroy Him." [14]So he got up, took the child and His mother during the night, and escaped to Egypt. [15]He stayed there until Herod's death, so that what was spoken by the Lord through the prophet might be fulfilled: Out of Egypt I called My Son.

[16]Then Herod, when he saw that he had been outwitted by the wise men, flew into a rage. He gave orders to massacre all the male children in and around Bethlehem who were two years old and under, in keeping with the time he had learned from the wise men. [17]Then what was spoken through Jeremiah the prophet was fulfilled:

> *[18]A voice was heard in Ramah,*
> *weeping, and great mourning,*
> *Rachel weeping for her children;*
> *and she refused to be consoled,*
> *because they were no more.*

[19]After Herod died, an angel of the Lord suddenly appeared in a dream to Joseph in Egypt, [20]saying, "Get up! Take the child and His mother and go to the land of Israel, because those who sought the child's life are dead." [21]So he got up, took the child and His mother, and entered the land of Israel. [22]But when he heard that Archelaus was ruling over Judea in place of his father Herod, he was afraid to go there. And being warned in a dream, he withdrew to the region of Galilee. [23]Then he went and settled in a town called Nazareth to fulfill what was spoken through the prophets, that He will be called a Nazarene.

Once more we turn to Joseph, the dreamer. The angel warns him to flee to Egypt and remain there until further instructions are given. Herod is going to seek to kill the child.

The journey from Bethlehem to Alexandria, where a sizable Jewish population dwelled, was roughly three hundred miles. I have always imagined their journey primarily as a trip to the south, but the map indicates that it was almost due west. The small family would have hugged the coast of the Mediterranean, gone across the vast delta of the Nile and then on to Alexandria.

For the second time, in Matthew 2:15, the fulfillment formula appears. Hosea 11:1—"When Israel was a child, I loved him, and out of Egypt I called My son"—originally referred to the sonship of Israel. But now it applies to the solitary Son of God, who like Israel was forced to flee to the wilderness of Egypt.

In what is essentially a flashback, Matthew 2:16 recounts the story of the slaughter of all the infant boys of Bethlehem and the surrounding area, a number that modern scholars estimate to have been around thirty to forty. Herod had once slaughtered forty-five eminent and wealthy citizens in Jerusalem,[13] but this atrocity never made it into the secular histories.

The response in Matthew 2:17 is another fulfillment formula, this one from Jeremiah 31:15. The prophet is describing the seizure and forced march from Israel to Babylon. "Rachel" is used as a figurehead for all the women of Jerusalem who are grief stricken and beyond all comfort.

Finally, in Matthew 2:19, another dream directs Joseph back home. On the way he learns that Archelaus, Herod's eldest son and another monster so cruel he was eventually deposed by Augustus for his atrocities, is reigning in Judea. In one last dream, Joseph is directed to Galilee and the obscure village of Nazareth—one final dream and one last fulfillment formula, in this, the opening chapter of Matthew's remarkable narrative.

It is striking that Matthew even interprets this final move as a fulfillment of Old Testament Scripture. Scholars have puzzled about the exact verse to which the text is referring. The literal phrase "he will be called a Nazarene" appears nowhere in the Old Testament. So far the best guess is Isaiah 11:1, which speaks of a branch growing from the root of Jesse. The Hebrew word for "branch" is *nēṣer*.

At the opening of Matthew 2 we experienced a gap of some two and a half years. Now at the end of that chapter, we enter into a significantly longer "dark" period in the life of Jesus, lasting some thirty years. Except for one small window in the book of Luke when Jesus was twelve years old, the entire span of his growing-up years is left untouched in the Gospels. If they were meant simply to be biographies, this would be a serious failure. But the Gospels aren't meant to be biographies; they are testimonies, perfect testimonies.

As the first hearers of Matthew's Gospel sat listening in the synagogue, once again the theme has been touched upon that the Gentiles have a stake in the ministry of Jesus from the very beginning. The magi, who had come so far risking their very lives, are the first to recognize the dignity of Jesus and to offer him worship. Though the priests and experts in the Law know the facts about where the Messiah would be born, they missed out on the reality of who he was. Matthew's first hearers are being encouraged not to miss out on who Jesus is, even though they, as Jews, know all the facts as well.

MATTHEW 3

THE VOICE OF ONE IN THE WILDERNESS

3:1–12 John the Baptist.

THE PERFECT WORDS OF THE FATHER

3:13–17 The baptism of Jesus.

THE VOICE OF ONE IN THE WILDERNESS

[1]*In those days John the Baptist came, preaching in the Wilderness of Judea* [2]*and saying, "Repent, because the kingdom of heaven has come near!"* [3]*For he is the one spoken of through the prophet Isaiah, who said:*

> *A voice of one crying out in the wilderness:*
> *Prepare the way for the Lord;*
> *make His paths straight!*

[4]*John himself had a camel-hair garment with a leather belt around his waist, and his food was locusts and wild honey.* [5]*Then people from Jerusalem, all Judea, and all the vicinity of the Jordan were flocking to him,* [6]*and they were baptized by him in the Jordan River as they confessed their sins.*

[7]*When he saw many of the Pharisees and Sadducees coming to the place of his baptism, he said to them, "Brood of vipers! Who warned you to flee from the coming wrath?* [8]*Therefore produce fruit consistent with repentance.* [9]*And don't presume to say to yourselves, 'We have Abraham as our father.' For I tell you that God is able to raise up children for Abraham from these stones!* [10]*Even now the ax is ready to strike the root of the trees! Therefore, every tree that doesn't produce good fruit will be cut down and thrown into the fire.*

[11]*"I baptize you with water for repentance, but the One who is coming after me is more powerful than I. I am not worthy to remove His sandals. He Himself will baptize you with the Holy Spirit and fire.* [12]*His winnowing shovel is in His hand, and He will clear His threshing floor and gather His wheat into the barn. But the chaff He will burn up with fire that never goes out."*

In all of the Gospels, the ministry of Jesus begins with John the Baptist. His is the first voice we hear in Mark's Gospel (Mk 1:7). Luke devotes a lengthy passage to his miraculous birth, telling it in parallel structure to the more miraculous birth of Jesus (Lk 1:5-25, 57-80). And in John's Gospel, after his beautiful opening sermon on the Word,

John's testimony is the first we hear, insisting (as he will over and over again) that he is not the Messiah (Jn 1:20-28).

John's ministry is in contrast to Jesus', although their central message, "Repent for the kingdom is near," appears identical. John remains in the wilderness, calling men and women to come out to him. Jesus seems to seek out crowded cities and synagogues. John sternly requires his followers to repent and to be baptized. While Jesus' disciples were known to baptize his followers, the stridency of John's demand is softened in Jesus'. The focus of his call is simply to "follow Me."

Some have recognized similarities between John and the Essenic community of Qumran. In fact, Luke's statement that John was "in the wilderness" (Lk 1:80) has been taken as a hint that perhaps after the death of his elderly parents, John joined the Qumran community. His self-understanding as the "voice of one calling in the wilderness" (Is 40:3) was a virtual motto of the Essenes. They considered themselves to be the ones who were preparing the way in the wilderness. Likewise, John's command to be baptized at first sounds Essenic, although his is not a periodic ritual cleansing but more a mode of entering into a new community through repentance done apparently once for all. Some scholars have even tried to demonstrate that John was the legendary "teacher of righteousness" spoken of again and again in the Qumran scrolls. However, his clothing of camel hair would have been looked upon as unclean by the Essenes, who dressed only in white priestly garments.

Whether John is an Essene or not, clearly he and his message had been impacted by the Essene separatist way of thinking. His primary mission was to make the Israelites aware of their personal sin and to urge them to respond in repentance and baptism. That is how one prepares the way for the Lord. Again and again in Jesus' ministry, we encounter repentant people (see, for example, Peter in Lk 5:8) who were no doubt exposed to the preaching of John. He is clearly the fulfillment of Malachi's closing promise that in the last days Elijah would come (Mal 4:5-6).

In Matthew 2:7, we see the twofold group we last encountered in Herod's palace thirty years and two chapters ago: the Pharisees and the Sadducees. John's response to their presence is direct and burning with prophetic zeal. He calls them a brood of vipers, an epitaph his cousin Jesus will echo in Matthew 12:34 and 23:33. The challenge he has confronted all his hearers with—to repent—is now issued to the religious elite whose response is centered more on personal righteous acts than on repentance.

Next John confronts the confidence they had simply by being Abraham's descendants. Their Jewishness is not what will save them, according to John. His image of the ax laid at the root of the tree comes straight from the prophets (Jer 45:22; Ezek 31:3, 11-12). You can almost sense the water around him steaming from the prophetic heat from his conflict with the Jewish leaders.

In the history of the interpretation of Matthew's Gospel, it has unfortunately been the conclusion of many scholars that Matthew is "anti-Jewish." What this point of view fails to consider is that John, and more so Jesus, criticized Judaism as *insiders*. Only in Matthew does Jesus tell us he has come not to destroy the law but to fulfill it (Mt 5:17). Likewise many of us have shortsightedly viewed the Sadducees and especially the Pharisees as a monolithic group that became the object of Jesus' scorn. We fail to realize that those Jesus confronted were almost certainly a smaller group who had focused their attention on him and his ministry. We know from the Gospels that men like Joseph of Arimathea and Nicodemus, both Pharisees, became followers of Jesus even before the crucifixion. Likewise we have stories in Luke's Gospel of two congenial meals between Jesus and the Pharisees (Lk 7:36-50; 14:1-6). And certainly we should not forget Paul, who though a part of the pharisaic party that violently opposed Jesus, became his most articulate and zealous follower.

THE PERFECT WORDS OF THE FATHER

¹³Then Jesus came from Galilee to John at the Jordan, to be baptized by him. ¹⁴But John tried to stop Him, saying, "I need to be baptized by You, and yet You come to me?"

¹⁵Jesus answered him, "Allow it for now, because this is the way for us to fulfill all righteousness." Then he allowed Him to be baptized.

¹⁶After Jesus was baptized, He went up immediately from the water. The

heavens suddenly opened for Him, and He saw the Spirit of God descending
like a dove and coming down on Him. [17]*And there came a voice from heaven:*
> *This is My beloved Son.*
> *I take delight in Him!*

*N*otice that Jesus has come "from Galilee" to see John at the Jordan.
Always true to his character, Jesus acts in an unexpected way, asking
John to baptize him. From the beginning, John seems to have understood Jesus' superiority, if not his divinity. He is understandably confused by the request and so protests that Jesus should be baptizing him.

These are Jesus' first words in the Gospel of Matthew: "Allow it
[Jesus' baptism] for now, because this is the way for us to fulfill all righteousness" (Mt 3:15). In fact, they are his first words in the New Testament. The first words of any character in any piece of literature are
important. How much more the first words of God's Son in the pages
of the New Testament! Jesus is asking John to do something out of the
ordinary, outside the confines of his understanding, outside the boundaries of the old orthodoxy. Jesus is asking John to take part in "fulfilling
all righteousness," though he does not completely understand at the
moment. These are important first words, because they can be understood as his first words to you and me, inviting us into a world that is
beyond our understanding, asking us to become a part of a new reality
that lies far beyond our old orthodoxy.

What was it in Jesus' tone that convinced John that any further protest was useless? Jesus' desire to "fulfill all righteousness" implies that,
for him, it is the right thing to do, identifying himself with the sinful
men and women he had come to rescue. If it is a cause for momentary
confusion, so be it.

As Jesus is coming out of the water, he sees heaven open and the
Spirit descending and resting on him. This is the inauguration of his
ministry. Present there is the Trinity, in whose name his future followers will all one day be baptized: Jesus, the Son; the Father's voice; and
the Spirit, in the form of a dove.

As the luminous moment unfolds, Jesus hears from the Father those words every child longs to hear. They are the two sentiments that will carry him on into his difficult ministry: They will strengthen him and reinforce his unique identity.

I love you.

I am pleased with you.

MATTHEW 4

THE TEMPTATION IN THE WILDERNESS

4:1–11

PREACHING IN GALILEE

4:12–17

THE FIRST DISCIPLES, THE FIRST MISSION

4:18–25

THE TEMPTATION IN THE WILDERNESS

↳ Right of passage

¹Then Jesus was led up by the Spirit into the wilderness to be tempted by the Devil. ²After He had fasted 40 days and 40 nights, He was hungry. ³Then the tempter approached Him and said, "If You are the Son of God, tell these stones to become bread."

⁴But He answered, "It is written:

> *Man must not live on bread alone*   *What works are*
> *but on every word that comes*   *you living on?*
> *from the mouth of God."*

⁵Then the Devil took Him to the holy city, had Him stand on the pinnacle of the temple, ⁶and said to Him, "If You are the Son of God, throw Yourself down. For it is written:

> *He will give His angels orders concerning you,*
> *and they will support you with their hands*
> *so that you will not strike*
> *your foot against a stone."*

⁷Jesus told him, "It is also written: Do not test the Lord your God."
⁸Again, the Devil took Him to a very high mountain and showed Him all the kingdoms of the world and their splendor. ⁹And he said to Him, "I will give You all these things if You will fall down and worship me."
¹⁰Then Jesus told him, "Go away, Satan! For it is written:

> *Worship the Lord your God,*
> *and serve only Him."*

¹¹Then the Devil left Him, and immediately angels came and began to serve Him.

*T*he same Spirit that descends on Jesus at his baptism now leads him into the wilderness to be tempted. The two events are always linked in the Gospels: baptism and temptation. As Jesus comes up out of the water, the Father speaks, announcing Jesus' ultimate and definitive identity. He is the beloved Son. Now that identity will be severely tested in the wilderness. The situation is just the same with us, whose identities are rooted in Jesus. Precisely at those moments when we best understand our true identities as sons and daughters of God and as brothers and sisters of Jesus, the evil one seeks to distort or destroy that identity.

Note the attack on who Jesus is. At the baptism, God had pronounced him to be Son. In Matthew 4:3, Satan makes his premiere appearance in the New Testament. "If You are . . . ," he hisses. For those of us who rarely go for hours without eating, it is difficult, if not impossible, to imagine the level of Jesus' hunger after forty days in the wilderness. The first attack on his identity comes via his physical body.

Jesus responds, "It is written . . . " In every case, he quotes the book of Deuteronomy in his defense; here he quotes 8:3. Life is derived, not from physical bread, but from God's Word. Jesus had feasted on that Word forty days before as he stood waist deep in the cool Jordan. He had been fed with the words "this is My beloved Son" (Mt 3:17).

In a flash, Satan shifts his plan of attack. If Jesus is responding, "It is written," he will try that approach as well. "If" Jesus is who the Father said he was back in the Jordan, then the twelve legions of angels who attend him will protect him if he throws himself off the pinnacle of the temple (see Mt 26:53).

Again Jesus turns to Deuteronomy for clarity. This time it is 6:16. God is not to be put to the test. To do so would reveal a fundamental flaw of mistrust in their relationship. Jesus does not need to test the Father's loving protection to know its bedrock reality. This second temptation should be understood as yet another attempt on Jesus' life. The first was the slaughter of the innocents.

With the final temptation, Jesus is transported to an ethereal place Matthew describes as a very high mountain. But this is a mountain from which you can see the entire world. Satan's attack on Jesus' hunger had failed, as had the temptation to put his Father to the test. Now Satan exposes his hand and reveals the goal he has had all along. He wants Jesus to worship him. He promises Jesus the wealth and splendor of the world if he will only bow down in worship.

Though this would seem to be the least tempting of the three temptations, it only makes sense that Satan would escalate the force of each of his attacks. Perhaps if we could imagine the transcendental sight of all the wealth and splendor of the kingdoms of the world, we would see that this was the greatest of the temptations. Jesus uses the same command here that he will speak in Matthew 8:32 to the demon-possessed men of Gadara: "Go!" And then his final haymaker, "it is written" that only the Lord God is to be worshiped and served.

Though Jesus is starving and emotionally exhausted, the authoritative command to go must be heeded by the tempter. Jesus might have commanded him to depart from the very beginning, but then the victory he had just won would never have occurred. The angels, who exist both to fight and to feed, appear to serve the one who has been fighting for forty days, all alone.

To a community that was in the process of transitioning from sacrifice to Torah study as a central focus of observance, Jesus' formula "It is written" would have been empowering.

PREACHING IN GALILEE

12When He heard that John had been arrested, He withdrew into Galilee. 13He left Nazareth behind and went to live in Capernaum by the sea, in the region of Zebulun and Naphtali. 14This was to fulfill what was spoken through the prophet Isaiah:

> *15Land of Zebulun and land of Naphtali,*
> *along the sea road, beyond the Jordan,*
> *Galilee of the Gentiles!*
> *16The people who live in darkness*
> *have seen a great light,*
> *and for those living in the shadowland of death,*
> *light has dawned.*

17From then on Jesus began to preach, "Repent, because the kingdom of heaven has come near!"

*J*esus leaves the wilderness of Judea, which is as desolate as the moon, and goes north, back to the green comfort of Galilee. Somehow he has heard that his cousin John has been arrested. Even now John is languishing in one of Herod's fortresses. In Matthew 4:13 we are told Jesus relocates from the small village of Nazareth to the much larger Capernaum, the center of the Jewish community in northern Galilee. This is the second move of Jesus that Matthew understands as a fulfillment of Old Testament prophecy (see Mt 2:23).

Before he has chosen a single disciple, Jesus begins the ministry all alone. Though the words of his message are identical with those of his cousin John (Mt 3:2), it is a different message altogether. John was preparing the way for the kingdom by seeking the repentance of the people. In Jesus, that kingdom has come. The proper response to John's message was to repent. The only response to Jesus' call is to follow.

THE FIRST DISCIPLES, THE FIRST MISSION

18As He was walking along the Sea of Galilee, He saw two brothers, Simon, who was called Peter, and his brother Andrew. They were casting a net into the sea, since they were fishermen. 19"Follow Me," He told them, "and I will make you fish for people!" 20Immediately they left their nets and followed Him.

21Going on from there, He saw two other brothers, James the son of Zebedee, and his brother John. They were in a boat with Zebedee their father, mending their nets, and He called them. 22Immediately they left the boat and their father and followed Him.

23Jesus was going all over Galilee, teaching in their synagogues, preaching the good news of the kingdom, and healing every disease and sickness among the people. 24Then the news about Him spread throughout Syria. So they brought to Him all those who were afflicted, those suffering from various diseases and intense pains, the demon-possessed, the epileptics, and the paralytics. And He healed them. 25Large crowds followed Him from Galilee, Decapolis, Jerusalem, Judea, and beyond the Jordan.

*I*f we had only the Synoptic Gospels, we would believe this is their first meeting. But John 1:40 tells us they had met before, perhaps months earlier. Jesus is walking along the rough shore of the lake when he sees two brothers, Andrew and Peter. It appears they are wading close to the shore and casting their nets. We will see them deep-draft fishing (Lk 5:4) as well as casting single hook on a hand line (Mt 17:27).

"Follow me" is not an invitation but a command. It is to be responded to immediately in obedience, not weighed or considered among other invitations. There is no hint that they have seen this coming, that for weeks or months they have been waiting and hoping or perhaps dreading the call. Dietrich Bonhoeffer says the call makes everything possible, even the courage to leave everything and follow. Andrew and Peter respond immediately and their world is changed forever—and ours as well.

Further down the shore, two more brothers are waiting. Perhaps it is morning, and they are preparing their nets for the day's work. Or maybe it is late afternoon, and they have just come in. We are told that Zebedee, their father, is with them in the boat. Peter and Andrew simply walk away from their nets; James and John leave their father. Months from this moment, Jesus will proclaim that anyone who loves his father or mother more than him is not worthy of him (Mt 10:37). Later still he will comfort the Twelve by assuring them that anyone who has left his father will receive a hundred times more in this life as well as in eternal life (Mt 19:29). But those words are months away from being spoken. For now there are only two nets floating beside the shore, and farther down a dumbstruck father watching the five of them walking away, down the shoreline.

Jesus has been baptized, identifying himself with the sinners he has come to save. He has survived the first assault on his identity in the wilderness. He has found the core of his message and begun calling his first disciples. Now the ministry can begin in earnest. Josephus speaks of over two hundred separate villages in the region of Galilee (of which he was governor). Now the five of them move out, initially focusing on the synagogue communities. Here Jesus will teach and preach the good news. Here he will exercise his authority to heal and cast out demons. There is a predictable result: the crowd begins to grow, from a radius of roughly sixty miles.

Matthew 4 has prepared us to hear the first of the five blocks of Jesus' teaching (see appendix A). In Matthew 5:1, when Jesus goes up on the mountain to present the first large block of teaching, we must never forget that he is the one who was baptized and tempted, and that he knows his cousin is even now rotting in Herod's prison. He had returned to Galilee (Mt 4:12), walked beside the Sea of Galilee (Mt 4:18) and carried out his first mission in Galilee (Mt 4:23). Now he will climb one of the green Galilean hillsides and begin turning the world upside down.

MATTHEW 5

JESUS' NINE BENEDICTIONS

¹When He saw the crowds, He went up on the mountain, and after He sat down, His disciples came to Him. ²Then He began to teach them, saying:

> *³"The poor in spirit are blessed,*
> *for the kingdom of heaven is theirs.*
> *⁴Those who mourn are blessed,*
> *for they will be comforted.*
> *⁵The gentle are blessed,*
> *for they will inherit the earth.*
> *⁶Those who hunger and thirst for righteousness are blessed,*
> *for they will be filled.*
> *⁷The merciful are blessed,*
> *for they will be shown mercy.*
> *⁸The pure in heart are blessed,*
> *for they will see God.*
> *⁹The peacemakers are blessed,*
> *for they will be called sons of God.*
> *¹⁰Those who are persecuted for righteousness are blessed,*
> *for the kingdom of heaven is theirs.*

¹¹"You are blessed when they insult and persecute you and falsely say every kind of evil against you because of Me. ¹²Be glad and rejoice, because your reward is great in heaven. For that is how they persecuted the prophets who were before you."

*E*verything is in place: the first disciples have been chosen, and Jesus has been baptized and endured the temptation. The ministry has begun in the synagogues of Galilee. His message, rooted in the kingdom, has spread to Syria, the Decapolis and all the way south to Jerusalem itself. The time has come for his inaugural message, the first of five large blocks of Jesus' teaching in Matthew's Gospel (see appendix A). If these blocks represent Matthew's unique contribution to the Gospel, it helps us understand why, of all the Gospels, we get the most "face time" with Jesus in Matthew. If you simply time yourself reading the words of Jesus (the red letters) in each Gospel, you will discover that in Matthew you spend the most time listening to Jesus speak: roughly an hour and twelve minutes.[14]

The text hints that perhaps Jesus is drawn to the crowd. When he sees them, he moves up onto the mountain and sits down. This has been called the Sinai moment of the New Testament. Jesus goes up on the mountain to deliver the first of five blocks, his own unique and radical Pentateuch.

Remembering that the life situation of Matthew's first hearers might have involved the eighteen benedictions, it is striking that here Jesus is pronouncing nine benedictions, none of which is a curse. Luke includes a section of curses in 6:24-26, which Matthew significantly chooses to omit for the sake of his first readers. Their form is rooted in the Psalms (see Ps 1:1; 32:1-2; 40:4; 119:1; 128:1). In Hebrew they are known as *berakoth*, or blessings. But these blessings have a strikingly unexpected character. If we keep in mind the fact that Matthew was written to a community that was experiencing persecution and eventual expulsion from the synagogue, the benedictions of Jesus come into focus. They are a virtual description of his earliest followers in Galilee. But, at the same time, they announce a radical reversal that takes place only with the coming of the kingdom. In fact, the bookends of the poetry of the nine benedictions is a promise of the kingdom itself (Mt 5:3, 10b).

The term "poor in spirit" actually referred to the persecuted people of God in the Qumran literature.[15] In the upside-down kingdom, a new identity is granted each group of individuals: the poor in spirit will become kingdom possessors; those who mourn will become the comforted; those who are gentle will become the inheritors of the earth; those who are hungry for righteousness will become the satisfied.

The fifth benediction (Mt 5:7), the central benediction, marks a shift. It is a blessing focused not on one of the suffering groups but on the merciful. The concept of mercy, *hesed* in Hebrew, is the defining characteristic of God in the Old Testament. It is the word God uses to define himself (see Ex 20:6; 34:6; Deut 5:10; Num 14:18-19). Only in Matthew will Jesus confront the Pharisees twice with the words of

Hosea 6:6. In Matthew 9:13 and 12:7, he challenges them to go and discover what this means: "I desire mercy and not sacrifice." The first occurrence happened in Matthew's house. Ḥesed is always reciprocal; if you are shown mercy, you are expected to respond with mercy (see Mt 18:21-35). Here, in Jesus' core benediction, the promise is made that the reciprocity goes both ways. Those who show ḥesed in the kingdom will become the recipients of ḥesed.

The next two benedictions of Jesus' poem of blessing are also directed at the positive qualities of those who are pure in heart and makers of peace. For both, God himself is their reward. The eighth blessing (the ninth and final blessing lies outside the poetic structure) returns to the prospect of suffering. Once more we are reminded of the first hearers huddled together in a Galilee synagogue. The blessing is also the other bookend that promises the kingdom. It mentions those who are persecuted for righteousness, not simply those who are hungry and thirsty for it. Their identity will not be shaped by persecution, but by the kingdom itself.

In verse 11, the poem ends. The final benediction lies outside the poem. The picture of Matthew's first hearers comes into the sharpest focus. They will be insulted and persecuted, and they will have all sorts of evil things said about them because of their relationship to Jesus. But the radical reversal of the first eight benedictions overflows here in the final blessing. Insults and persecutions are an occasion for rejoicing and gladness because the reward is waiting, a reward that is the goal of the kingdom. Their identity is not their present precarious persecution, not their mourning, not the insults they bear for Jesus' sake. They are citizens of the kingdom of which Jesus is the king. The persecuted prophets have led the way before them. Their new identity is linked to the prophets!

JESUS, TELL US WHO WE ARE

13 "You are the salt of the earth. But if the salt should lose its taste, how can it be made salty? It's no longer good for anything but to be thrown out and trampled on by men.

14 "You are the light of the world. A city situated on a hill cannot be hidden. 15 No one lights a lamp and puts it under a basket, but rather on a lampstand,

*and it gives light for all who are in the house. [16] In the same way, let your light
shine before men, so that they may see your good works and give glory to your
Father in heaven."*

Some forty years after Jesus' time, Pliny the Elder wrote in his massive
Natural History, "There is nothing more useful than salt and sunshine."[16]
As Jesus proceeds with his inaugural manifesto of new identity, he becomes even more direct. The two things most useful to the world, salt
and light, describe the character of the new identity of his followers.

Salt preserves food and also lends its flavor. In the new upside-down
kingdom, Jesus' disciples will flavor the world by means of his mercy
and wisdom. As his authoritative representatives, they will preserve
and serve the world through the message of the kingdom that has come.
In time they will bear the message of the saving provision of his cross.

But this piece of their new identity comes with a solemn warning.
Salt from the Dead Sea contains impurities that sometimes cause it to
become rancid. As the salt of the earth, his followers can lose their
flavor to compromise, and losing their flavor, they lose their identity
and purpose.

Next he bestows upon them an aspect of his own identity; even as he
is the light of the world (Jn 8:12), so they are the light. As the purpose
of the salt is to flavor and preserve, the purpose and nature of light is
simply to shine. It is his encouragement to become what they already
are. Confronted with persecution, they might be tempted to hide their
light, but that goes against the very nature of life itself. As the light of
the world, Jesus always wins praise for the Father. Whenever he performs a miracle, the crowd responds with praise to God; never do they
praise Jesus. It is just the same with his followers. If they will simply
shine, people will praise the Father.

AN UNEXPECTED FULFILLMENT

[17] *"Don't assume that I came to destroy the Law or the Prophets. I did not
come to destroy but to fulfill. [18] For I assure you: Until heaven and earth pass
away, not the smallest letter or one stroke of a letter will pass from the law*

until all things are accomplished. [19] Therefore, whoever breaks one of the least of these commands and teaches people to do so will be called least in the kingdom of heaven. But whoever practices and teaches these commands will be called great in the kingdom of heaven. [20] For I tell you, unless your righteousness surpasses that of the scribes and Pharisees, you will never enter the kingdom of heaven."

*W*henever we encounter a passage that is unique to one of the Gospels, we must always ask ourselves why the author included it. Most often the answer to its uniqueness is found in the life situation of the author or his audience. Matthew will make it clear that the religious leaders consider Jesus to be a lawbreaker (see Mt 12:1-10). That charge will stick to his followers in the decades to come (Acts 6:13; 18:13; 25:8). If indeed the Gospel of Matthew was written to Galilean Jews who were experiencing the first waves of persecution in their own synagogues, this unique word of Jesus took on a new significance.

Jesus insists that he has come to fulfill, not to abolish, the law. He solemnly speaks an "amen" in Matthew 5:18-19 as he declares it is the nature of the law to accomplish its divine purposes, and those who seek to stand in the way of the law will suffer the consequences in the kingdom. Note that Jesus does not conclude that lawbreakers will be barred from the kingdom, but only that breaking the law will affect their position in the kingdom. Eligibility for the kingdom is based solely on the new identity that Jesus grants by his grace.

Matthew 5:18 is a purposely unsettling statement designed to draw in and focus listeners. In his kingdom of commandment keepers, Jesus demands a new, unheard-of level of righteousness—a righteousness that exceeds even the Pharisees' minute observances. That, says Jesus, will be the determining factor for entry into the kingdom.

We must imagine the shock wave that moves through the crowd upon hearing Jesus' final statement. They are on pins and needles, waiting to hear him explain more about this new supra-pharisaic righteousness. And this is exactly what his sermon will take up in verses 21-48.

A NEW RIGHTEOUSNESS

[21]*"You have heard that it was said to our ancestors, Do not murder, and whoever murders will be subject to judgment.* [22]*But I tell you, everyone who is angry with his brother will be subject to judgment. And whoever says to his brother, 'Fool!' will be subject to the Sanhedrin. But whoever says, 'You moron!' will be subject to hellfire.* [23]*So if you are offering your gift on the altar, and there you remember that your brother has something against you,* [24]*leave your gift there in front of the altar. First go and be reconciled with your brother, and then come and offer your gift.* [25]*Reach a settlement quickly with your adversary while you're on the way with him, or your adversary will hand you over to the judge, the judge to the officer, and you will be thrown into prison.* [26]*I assure you: You will never get out of there until you have paid the last penny!*

[27]*"You have heard that it was said, Do not commit adultery.* [28]*But I tell you, everyone who looks at a woman to lust for her has already committed adultery with her in his heart.* [29]*If your right eye causes you to sin, gouge it out and throw it away. For it is better that you lose one of the parts of your body than for your whole body to be thrown into hell.* [30]*And if your right hand causes you to sin, cut it off and throw it away. For it is better that you lose one of the parts of your body than for your whole body to go into hell!*

[31]*"It was also said, Whoever divorces his wife must give her a written notice of divorce.* [32]*But I tell you, everyone who divorces his wife, except in a case of sexual immorality, causes her to commit adultery. And whoever marries a divorced woman commits adultery.*

[33]*"Again, you have heard that it was said to our ancestors, You must not break your oath, but you must keep your oaths to the Lord.* [34]*But I tell you, don't take an oath at all: either by heaven, because it is God's throne;* [35]*or by the earth, because it is His footstool; or by Jerusalem, because it is the city of the great King.* [36]*Neither should you swear by your head, because you cannot make a single hair white or black.* [37]*But let your word 'yes' be 'yes,' and your 'no' be 'no.' Anything more than this is from the evil one.*

[38]*"You have heard that it was said, An eye for an eye and a tooth for a tooth.* [39]*But I tell you, don't resist an evildoer. On the contrary, if anyone slaps you on your right cheek, turn the other to him also.* [40]*As for the one who wants to*

sue you and take away your shirt, let him have your coat as well. ⁴¹*And if anyone forces you to go one mile, go with him two.* ⁴²*Give to the one who asks you, and don't turn away from the one who wants to borrow from you.*

⁴³*"You have heard that it was said, Love your neighbor and hate your enemy.* ⁴⁴*But I tell you, love your enemies and pray for those who persecute you,* ⁴⁵*so that you may be sons of your Father in heaven. For He causes His sun to rise on the evil and the good, and sends rain on the righteous and the unrighteous.* ⁴⁶*For if you love those who love you, what reward will you have? Don't even the tax collectors do the same?* ⁴⁷*And if you greet only your brothers, what are you doing out of the ordinary? Don't even the Gentiles do the same?* ⁴⁸*Be perfect, therefore, as your heavenly Father is perfect."*

*A*n inaugural sermon opening with nine unexpected benedictions, a preliminary picture of their own new identity as salt and light, a compelling statement concerning a new and impossible level of righteousness—although bits and pieces of what follows is found scattered throughout the other Gospels, only Matthew brings together Jesus' words within this unique framework. Again, the material is structured into five blocks of teaching, each set off with the phrases like "you have heard that it was said" and "but I tell you."

Jesus redefines the new righteousness by redefining sin itself: beyond the concrete act, sin begins with the intention of the heart. Sin begins not in dark alleyways but in a darkened imagination.

First, Jesus redefines murder. Clearly Exodus 20:13 states that to murder is to break the law. But Jesus has come to perfect and fulfill the law, to introduce a new righteousness that is the fabric of the new kingdom. He goes on: "But I tell you" anger itself is the seed of murder; the expression of anger through abusive name calling, will result in judgment. To be angry is to violate the perfected and fulfilled law. This new level of righteousness impacts our ability to present our offerings. We have no place at the altar, says Jesus, if we are aware that anyone is holding something against us. Note that Jesus' statement is based on the presupposition that his followers will continue to make offerings at the temple (Mt 8:4).

Next comes the law concerning adultery (Ex 20:14). Once more Jesus redefines adultery as an act of the imagination: lust. According to the new righteousness, it is better to lose an eye or hand than to forfeit a place in the new kingdom for one in hell. His language is stark and disturbing, including gouged out eyes and severed hands. The horror of such images is nothing compared to the horrific prospect of being cut off from the kingdom.

The new righteousness required to enter his kingdom demands a purity of heart that gives no place to lustful glances. Anticipating an argument on divorce recorded in Matthew 19, Jesus expands the new unheard-of righteousness to include divorce. If a lustful look represents a violation of the seventh commandment, then according to the new and impossible righteousness, divorce is not allowed either.

In Matthew 5:33-37, Jesus explains the taking of oaths in light of this new righteousness. The structure remains the same: "You have heard that it was said," he begins. In the ancient world, the taking of an oath was serious business. During that time before well-developed and structured courts and the due process of law, the weight of an oath was significant. Throughout the law, the seriousness of oaths was reiterated (Lev 19:12; Num 30:2; Deut 23:23). Stanley Hauerwas says that "oaths are a sign that we live in a world of lies."[17]

But Jesus' kingdom is no world of lies, so even the taking of oaths will not be tolerated. Nor will the nonsense of swearing by heaven or earth or Jerusalem itself, as if such pledges might make our words more binding. For the followers of Jesus, who live within the context of the new righteousness, a casual word is as serious as a binding oath. Our words simply mean what they say. Nothing less will be expected of those who are salt to the earth and light to the world.

Next we come to the law of reciprocity (Ex 21:24; Lev 24:20; Deut 19:21). This law demands that a lawbreaker suffer a reciprocal punishment that suits the crime. If, in the commission of the crime, an eye was lost or a tooth knocked out, the punishment should be in kind. This is also known as retributive justice; in essence, you should get the punishment you deserve.

But that is not so in a perfected and fulfilled understanding of the law. The citizens of Jesus' kingdom will not seek retribution or reciprocity. If struck, they will offer the other cheek. When sued, they will render more than the judge decreed. If forced to carry a burden one mile, they will go two. (Behind this statement is the Roman law of impressment. According to the Julian code, a Roman soldier had the legal right to require anyone to carry his burden for one mile. We see this law in effect when Simon is forced by the soldiers to carry the cross of Jesus [Mt 27:32].)

The followers of Jesus, the citizens of his kingdom, will learn that their citizenship is based precisely on *not* getting what they deserve. His mercy, his *ḥesed*, makes their citizenship possible. Once they realize all that his *ḥesed* has made possible, they are obliged to respond to the world with the same *ḥesed*. We do not give people the punishment they deserve, because we did not receive the punishment we deserved. We love our enemies because God loves his enemies.

Jesus' final mandate in this manifesto of the new righteousness might be said to embrace all the previous mandates. "You have heard," he states for the last time, "love your neighbor." This is a clear reference to Leviticus 19:18. What follows is not so clear. The notion of a legal requirement to hate our enemies is not a biblical one but rather an idea that developed later. One place it is reflected is in the rule of the community from Qumran.[18] This statement reveals that it is not a monolithic, developed Judaism that Jesus is confronting but a divided, multilayered, complex religious culture that is often not rooted in the Old Testament.

In the kingdom, enemies are to be loved and prayed for, says Jesus. The new righteousness, without which no one will enter the kingdom, demands that we extend forgiveness and love, since those who need forgiveness the most deserve it the least. The Father loves both the evil and the good by lavishing upon them his sun and rain. The new righteousness demands nothing less than perfection: perfect control of our thoughts, our tongues, our tempers. The command to perfection is the straw meant to break the camel's back. We hear not a single word of response from the crowd, because they are speechless, stunned by Jesus' impossible demands.

MATTHEW 6

A SECRET RIGHTEOUSNESS

[1]"Be careful not to practice your righteousness in front of people, to be seen by them. Otherwise, you will have no reward from your Father in heaven. [2]So whenever you give to the poor, don't sound a trumpet before you, as the hypocrites do in the synagogues and on the streets, to be applauded by people. I assure you: They've got their reward! [3]But when you give to the poor, don't let your left hand know what your right hand is doing, [4]so that your giving may be in secret. And your Father who sees in secret will reward you.

[5]"Whenever you pray, you must not be like the hypocrites, because they love to pray standing in the synagogues and on the street corners to be seen by people. I assure you: They've got their reward! [6]But when you pray, go into your private room, shut your door, and pray to your Father who is in secret. And your Father who sees in secret will reward you. [7]When you pray, don't babble like the idolaters, since they imagine they'll be heard for their many words. [8]Don't be like them, because your Father knows the things you need before you ask Him.

[9]"Therefore, you should pray like this:

> *Our Father in heaven,*
> *Your name be honored as holy.*
> *[10]Your kingdom come.*
> *Your will be done*
> *on earth as it is in heaven.*
> *[11]Give us today our daily bread.*
> *[12]And forgive us our debts,*
> *as we also have forgiven our debtors.*
> *[13]And do not bring us into temptation,*
> *but deliver us from the evil one.*
> *[For Yours is the kingdom and the power*
> *and the glory forever. Amen.]*

[14]"For if you forgive people their wrongdoing, your heavenly Father will forgive you as well. [15]But if you don't forgive people, your Father will not forgive your wrongdoing.

[16]"Whenever you fast, don't be sad-faced like the hypocrites. For they make

their faces unattractive so their fasting is obvious to people. I assure you: They've got their reward! [17]*But when you fast, put oil on your head, and wash your face,* [18]*so that you don't show your fasting to people but to your Father who is in secret. And your Father who sees in secret will reward you."*

*M*atthew 6 continues the presentation of the new kingdom and its unique approach to righteousness. In the opening verses, Jesus looks at fasting, prayer and giving to the poor—the three pillars of Jewish piety. His instruction is manifestly simple and focused: all of these observances should be done in secret. Verse 1 is the thesis: Acts of righteousness are not to be done so that others will see them. If they are, any reward from the Father will be forfeited.

In verses 2-4 the idea is applied to the concept of giving to the poor. Today charity is unfortunately looked upon as being optional, but in the Judaism of Jesus' day almsgiving was as natural a part of worship as prayer and study of the Torah. Note that Jesus observes that "in the synagogue" some hypocritical people apparently make a show of their giving. There is no concrete historical reference that explains the reference to sounding "a trumpet" (Mt 6:2). There were thirteen trumpet-shaped collection boxes in the temple, but this hardly explains Jesus' words. Most likely it is a figure of speech referring to those who make a spectacle when they give to the poor. Jesus says that whatever adulation they might have received in public is all they are ever going to get.

In contrast to those who give to be seen, Jesus' followers are to give in secret. The figure of speech "don't let your left hand know what your right hand is doing" does not appear in any of the ancient sources and is thought to be an original statement of Jesus.

Jesus goes on to apply the same thought and structure to the topic of prayer. Again, prayer was not a matter of personal observance, an option that some chose and others did not. There were regular hours of prayer and even, at least in later years, formula prayers like the Qaddish that were a part of everyone's daily life. One more reference is specifically made to those who pray for a show "in the synagogue," and in parallel form Jesus says these hypocritical people have received all their reward in the present.

Rather than praying in the open synagogue or the public street corner, Jesus' listeners are to seek out a private room, or "inner room" (*tameion*). Matthew uses this word again in 24:26 to describe an inner or secret room. Luke uses it twice to describe a room with closed doors or a storeroom (Lk 12:3, 24). Jesus instructs his listeners to go into that room and close the door. They are to pray as they are to give to the poor, "in secret."

Not only are our prayers to be secret, between us and the Father alone, they are also to be simple. The unseen Father does not listen more closely to long-winded prayers.[19] In fact, our prayers should be shortened by the confidence that the Father knows what we are going to ask for even before we ask.

Jesus follows his advice on prayer with a concrete example. He had advised simplicity in prayer, and his prayer is a perfect jewel of simplicity. Different parts of the Lord's Prayer are echoed in other known prayers of the synagogue, most notably the Qaddish:

> Magnified and sanctified be his great name in the world which he hath created according to his will.
>   May he establish his kingdom during your life and during your days, and during the life of all the house of Israel,
>   even speedily and at a near time, and say ye, Amen.
>   Let his name be blessed forever and to all eternity.[20]

Referring to God as Father, asking that his kingdom would quickly appear, asking for the promise of daily bread, like the manna of Exodus 16—these are all found in other prayers. What is striking is the brevity, the simplicity and the childlike confidence displayed in the prayer of Jesus.

Fasting, the final pillar of observance, is taken up in the same structured way. The hypocrites fast "to be seen." In fact, they exaggerate the appearance of their faces to let everyone know they are fasting. Like those who give and pray only to be seen, they too have already received all the reward they might have expected to receive. As he did with giving and praying, Jesus tells his listeners they must fast in secret.

Although the Old Testament mandated only one fast per year, on the Day of Atonement (Lev 23:27), the Pharisees were known for fasting twice a week (Lk 18:12). Jesus lays down no rules as to how often we should fast. His only rule is that of secrecy. The command to secrecy is designed to help his listeners maintain pure hearts in their giving and praying and fasting. These things are to be done to God alone, who sees in secret and rewards openly.

TRUE TREASURE

[19]*"Don't collect for yourselves treasures on earth, where moth and rust destroy and where thieves break in and steal.* [20]*But collect for yourselves treasures in heaven, where neither moth nor rust destroys, and where thieves don't break in and steal.* [21]*For where your treasure is, there your heart will be also.*

[22]*"The eye is the lamp of the body. If your eye is good, your whole body will be full of light.* [23]*But if your eye is bad, your whole body will be full of darkness. So if the light within you is darkness—how deep is that darkness!*

[24]*"No one can be a slave of two masters, since either he will hate one and love the other, or be devoted to one and despise the other. You cannot be slaves of God and of money."*

*W*ith each word on praying, giving and fasting, Jesus promised a reward from the Father (Mt 6:5, 6, 18). In verses 19-24, he explores further the idea of true treasure. Earthly treasures can be consumed by moths (such as costly clothing) or can succumb to rust (probably a reference to coins). Thieves can dig through the walls of a house and steal. In other words, earthly treasure will always be vulnerable to loss. Heavenly treasure, on the other hand, is incorruptible. In heaven there are no moths or thieves or any rust.

With the final two blocks of chapter 6, the tone seems to shift. It begins to remind me of a collection of the *logia*, the sayings that Papias said were originally collected by Matthew.

The first reference to the eye as the lamp of the body does not appear to connect in the same structured way that all the previous statements were connected. It is almost as if the statement should stand alone. Likewise, the admonition that no one can serve two masters appears only loosely connected to the above statements on treasure. Taken together, Matthew 6:22-24 admonishes single-mindedness, focus on the light and dedication solely to God.

HOW TO BE WORRY FREE

[25]"This is why I tell you: Don't worry about your life, what you will eat or what you will drink; or about your body, what you will wear. Isn't life more than food and the body more than clothing? [26]Look at the birds of the sky: They don't sow or reap or gather into barns, yet your heavenly Father feeds them. Aren't you worth more than they? [27]Can any of you add a single cubit to his height by worrying? [28]And why do you worry about clothes? Learn how the wildflowers of the field grow: they don't labor or spin thread. [29]Yet I tell you that not even Solomon in all his splendor was adorned like one of these! [30]If that's how God clothes the grass of the field, which is here today and thrown into the furnace tomorrow, won't He do much more for you— you of little faith? [31]So don't worry, saying, 'What will we eat?' or 'What will we drink?' or 'What will we wear?' [32]For the idolaters eagerly seek all these things, and your heavenly Father knows that you need them. [33]But seek first the kingdom of God and His righteousness, and all these things will be provided for you. [34]Therefore don't worry about tomorrow, because tomorrow will worry about itself. Each day has enough trouble of its own."

The final section of Matthew 6 returns to a series of structured statements based on the phrase "do not worry." Jesus admonishes his hearers not to worry about food, clothes or the future. His appeal in each case is disarmingly simple, almost childlike. First he points to the birds, who though they do not work for food, are fed by the Father. Likewise, clothes should not be a cause for concern. As the birds are fed, so the flowers are clothed by the Father and yet are more beautiful even than Solomon himself (see 1 Kings 10:1-29; 2 Chron 9:1-28).

The evidence is all around you, Jesus says. It is as obvious as the well-fed birds and the beautiful flowers. God cares for his creation, of which you are the most valued part. Three times the phrase "don't worry" is repeated (Mt 6:25, 31, 34).

Jesus concludes this section by returning to the original topic of Matthew 5:3: the kingdom. The kingdom is of supreme importance, not food or clothing or the future. The nine benedictions promised the kingdom (Mt 5:3, 10). Those who keep Jesus' commandments are promised the kingdom (Mt 5:19). His exemplary prayer echoes the promise of the kingdom (6:10). Every aspect of their engagement with the kingdom will provide the basis of their new and radical identity.

MATTHEW 7

DO NOT JUDGE

[1]*"Do not judge, so that you won't be judged. [2]For with the judgment you use, you will be judged, and with the measure you use, it will be measured to you. [3]Why do you look at the speck in your brother's eye but don't notice the log in your own eye? [4]Or how can you say to your brother, 'Let me take the speck out of your eye,' and look, there's a log in your eye? [5]Hypocrite! First take the log out of your eye, and then you will see clearly to take the speck out of your brother's eye. [6]Don't give what is holy to dogs or toss your pearls before pigs, or they will trample them with their feet, turn, and tear you to pieces."*

*I*n Matthew 7, Jesus provides four blocks of concluding remarks. He encourages his listeners to stop judging others, to be persistent in prayer, to be watchful as the end approaches and to understand his words as the foundation of their very lives. The next large block of teaching will not occur until chapter 10.

In a cultural and religious context that was constantly demanding that one judge one's own standing with God as well as everyone in close proximity, Jesus counters with the liberating command not to judge. In fact, he says, our refusal to judge others will liberate us, freeing us from judgment. A judgmental attitude inevitably leads to a harshness of spirit that renders a person unable to receive forgiveness. (In Luke 7:36-50, the story of Simon the Pharisee and the sinful woman provides the perfect illustration.)

In Matthew 7:3-5, Jesus presents an unforgettable illustration that drives home his point. (It has been pointed out earlier that he rarely uses imagery in his parables that specifically involves carpentry so, chances are, he was probably a builder rather than a simple carpenter.) The person with a massive plank in Jesus' parable is not blind to the tiny speck in his brother's eye. Rather he is blind to his own blindness. Jesus calls him a hypocrite—that is, a person who wears a mask, or in this case a plank!

His statement in verse 6 seems disconnected from the previous teaching. Owing to the fact that it is a statement that is unique to Matthew, there is a chance that it was one of Matthew's *logia*. Jesus' image is based on a popular story of a man who throws his seed pearls to some pigs who were attacking him. In the story the ruse does not work and the pigs turn on him and attack. The connection between pigs and dogs is that both were considered unclean and both are scavengers, sometimes even devouring corpses.

DO NOT GIVE UP ASKING

7"Keep asking, and it will be given to you. Keep searching, and you will find. Keep knocking, and the door will be opened to you. ⁸For everyone who asks receives, and the one who searches finds, and to the one who knocks, the door will be opened. ⁹What man among you, if his son asks him for bread, will give him a stone? ¹⁰Or if he asks for a fish, will give him a snake? ¹¹If you then, who are evil, know how to give good gifts to your children, how much more will your Father in heaven give good things to those who ask Him! ¹²Therefore, whatever you want others to do for you, do also the same for them—this is the Law and the Prophets.

¹³"Enter through the narrow gate. For the gate is wide and the road is broad that leads to destruction, and there are many who go through it. ¹⁴How narrow is the gate and difficult the road that leads to life, and few find it."

*T*he next block of teaching (Mt 7:7-21) contains Jesus' summary in regard to prayer (see Mt 6:5-15). It is manifestly simple, even childlike, like his early exemplary prayer. If you ask, it will be given; if you knock, the door will open.

Just as he followed up his statement on judging with the example of the plank and the speck, here he illustrates his encouragement to confidence in prayer with another vivid word picture. A good parent would not give a stone to a child who is hungry for bread. Even worse, he would not give a detestable snake to a child who is hungry for a fish. It is a given that his listeners are evil; perhaps some of them even recognize that they are. Yet they still possess a rudimentary idea of how to give good gifts. How much more, says Jesus in rabbinic fashion, will their heavenly Father give them good things if they will but ask. Our confidence in prayer is not rooted in our ability to pray but in the manifestly loving nature of our Father. The simplicity of his exemplary prayer in Matthew 6 reflects this childlike confidence that his Father is the one who gives good gifts to those who confidently and persistently knock.

Matthew 7:12 seems disconnected from the previous teaching on prayer. We have come to know it as the Golden Rule. Yet, if we look closely and do our homework, we will see that there is a fascinating connection between verses 11 and 12. It is a human connection, and the human's name was Hillel the Elder. He was one of the greatest teachers of his day, and he still commands a measure of respect in Judaism. He died in approximately A.D. 10, which means there is a remote chance that he might have been among the teachers Jesus engaged with in the temple as a boy (Lk 2:42-52).

Hillel developed seven rules of interpretation known as the Middoth. The first rule was known as the *qal wahōmer*. It is an argument from lesser to greater—that is, if something is true in a lesser case, then "how much more" will it be true in the larger case. When Jesus reasons that his evil human parents know how to give good gifts then "how much more" will the Father in heaven know how to give good gifts, he is appealing to Hillel's first principle.

What follows in verse 12 is yet another reference to Hillel. When he was once asked to sum up the Law and the Prophets, Hillel responded, "What is hateful to you do not do to your neighbor. That is the whole Torah. The rest is commentary."[21] The fact that the author of Matthew recognized such a sophisticated connection between the sayings of Jesus and Hillel points to his scribal expertise.

SERMON SUMMARY

[15]*"Beware of false prophets who come to you in sheep's clothing but inwardly are ravaging wolves.* [16]*You'll recognize them by their fruit. Are grapes gathered from thornbushes or figs from thistles?* [17]*In the same way, every good tree produces good fruit, but a bad tree produces bad fruit.* [18]*A good tree can't produce bad fruit; neither can a bad tree produce good fruit.* [19]*Every tree*

that doesn't produce good fruit is cut down and thrown into the fire. ²⁰*So you'll recognize them by their fruit.*

²¹*"Not everyone who says to Me, 'Lord, Lord!' will enter the kingdom of heaven, but only the one who does the will of My Father in heaven.* ²²*On that day many will say to Me, 'Lord, Lord, didn't we prophesy in Your name, drive out demons in Your name, and do many miracles in Your name?'* ²³*Then I will announce to them, 'I never knew you! Depart from Me, you lawbreakers!'*

²⁴*"Therefore, everyone who hears these words of Mine and acts on them will be like a sensible man who built his house on the rock.* ²⁵*The rain fell, the rivers rose, and the winds blew and pounded that house. Yet it didn't collapse, because its foundation was on the rock.* ²⁶*But everyone who hears these words of Mine and doesn't act on them will be like a foolish man who built his house on the sand.* ²⁷*The rain fell, the rivers rose, the winds blew and pounded that house, and it collapsed. And its collapse was great!"*

²⁸*When Jesus had finished this sermon, the crowds were astonished at His teaching,* ²⁹*because He was teaching them like one who had authority, and not like their scribes.*

*M*atthew 7:15-27 contains a summary of Jesus' first sermon in the Gospel of Matthew. The penultimate charge is to enter the narrow gate, to follow the narrow road. When we remember that Matthew's first listeners were being pressured by the majority—those of the wide gate and the broad path—to conform to their majority point of view, Jesus' words become all the more focused.

Part of keeping to the narrow road means keeping an eye out for false prophets. They have the appearance of the sheep outwardly but inwardly they are ferocious as wolves. The secret, according to Jesus, is to be mindful of their fruits. Good trees cannot bear bad fruit nor can bad trees produce good fruit. As we keep our feet to the narrow path, we must understand that it is not the outward appearance that matters but rather the fruit produced.

Next Jesus projects his listeners into the future, to the Day of Judgment. Here he makes evident the fate of those whose outward appearance says one thing while their hearts another. The theme of confusion at the last day captivates Jesus' imagination (see Mt 25:13, 41). As he looks into the future, he sees the appalling moment when men and women who call him "Lord" and who even perform miracles in his name will be revealed as false prophets, as those who have hidden themselves in sheep's clothing all along.

In his final image, Jesus shifts from the picture of disguised wolves to one of foolish builders. It is his final warning in a sermon to those who might listen but not embrace his words completely. His listeners are relegated to two images: a wise builder and a foolish builder.

The wise builder is one who constructs his house on the sure foundation of the rock of Jesus' words. Though all the forces of nature come against that house, because of its solid foundation, it does not fall (see Prov 24:3). On the other hand, some of his listeners, though they hear his words, will not integrate them fully into the way they understand the world. As a result, they will be foundation-less. Perhaps speaking as a builder himself, Jesus posits the supremely foolish notion of building a house on top of sand. Not only will that house succumb to the extremes of nature, when it does fall, it will be with a great crash.

The conclusions of Jesus great sermon found in Matthew 7 relate to the new identity of Matthew's first audience. Who are they?

- They are the ones who do not judge in a world that is founded on judging.

- They are the ones who pray with childlike confidence, in simplicity trusting the nature of their Father.

- They are the ones who follow the narrow path of the minority.

- Ultimately, they are the ones who make Jesus' words the ultimate foundation of their lives.

The first great block closes with a formula, "when Jesus had finished this sermon" (Mt 7:28), which will be repeated in the closings of each one of the five blocks (see Mt 11:1; 13:53; 19:1; 26:1). Matthew wants us to know his listeners were amazed, and why: because Jesus taught with a sense of authority that other teachers lacked. The closing reference to "their" teachers reminds us of those first believers, sitting in the synagogue from which they will soon be asked to leave by these teachers, who misuse what small authority they have to persecute the first followers of Jesus.

MATTHEW 8

THE DISOBEDIENT LEPER

8:1–4

THE CONFIDENT CENTURION

8:5–13

THE ONE WHO CARRIES OUR ILLNESS

8:14–17

THE HOMELESS SON OF MAN

8:18–22

TWO DEMONIC CONFRONTATIONS

8:23–34

THE DISOBEDIENT LEPER

¹When He came down from the mountain, large crowds followed Him. ²Right away a man with a serious skin disease came up and knelt before Him, saying, "Lord, if You are willing, You can make me clean."

³Reaching out His hand He touched him, saying, "I am willing; be made clean." Immediately his disease was healed. ⁴Then Jesus told him, "See that you don't tell anyone; but go, show yourself to the priest, and offer the gift that Moses prescribed, as a testimony to them."

*T*he ministry is established. Jesus has provided his manifesto of the new kingdom. Now he will come down from the mountain and begin his work in earnest. Matthew 8 begins the second major section of Matthew's Gospel. It will come to a conclusion in the opening verses of chapter 10 when Jesus will call and commission the Twelve. This second section will be preoccupied with the question "Who is Jesus?" and will open with two "trios" of miracles:

1. The cleansing of a leper
2. The healing of the centurion's servant
3. The healing of Peter's mother-in-law

1. The calming of the demonic storm
2. The exorcising of two demoniacs
3. The healing of the paralytic

Not until Matthew 8 does Jesus perform his first miracle. It is no coincidence that he opens this phase of the ministry by healing a leper. The Greek word for "leper," *lepros*, reflects an entire range of diseases of the skin. The Talmud states, "cleansing a leper is akin to raising the dead."[22] (Note that Mark's Gospel begins Jesus' ministry as well with the healing of a leper in Mark 1.)

Leprosy was looked upon as a living parable of sin (Lev 13:36). The testimony of a healed leper would have been a powerful witness to the whole ministry of Jesus (see 2 Kings 5:13-15).

In the most strict sense, both Jesus and the leper are violating the law. The leper should not be approaching Jesus, and Jesus most certainly should not be touching the leper (Lev 13:45-46). There seems to be no doubt in the nameless leper's heart and mind that Jesus possesses the power to heal him. The question is only whether he has the desire to do so. Perhaps this reflects the self-image of someone who has been shunned for years.

As with almost every one of his miracles, Jesus performs it in an unmiraculous way. There are no histrionics, no waving of hands in the air. With absolute compassion and authority he says, "Be clean," and the cure is immediate and total.

When Matthew draws from Mark's narrative (the entire Gospel of Mark is contained in Matthew except for forty-four verses), he always shortens the story, and this example is no exception. Here Mark, who is so interested in what scholars have misleadingly labeled the "messianic secret," tells us that despite Jesus' warning not to tell, the leper spreads the news. The result in Mark's Gospel is that Jesus must retreat to the wilderness in a constant effort to get away from the large crowds who are interested only in Jesus' gifts and not his message. Matthew is not interested in that particular aspect of the story. For him the significance of the healing of the leper is enough. The power of the story is found in the testimony it offers to the priest who must examine the leper and pronounce the healing genuine on the basis of the law, which Jesus has come to perfect and fulfill.

To Matthew's first audience, the account of the healing of the leper would provide a significant piece of the puzzle of Jesus' identity. He is the one with absolute authority. His power to cleanse a leper, the first of his miracles, would hint at his more significant power to forgive sin. It is highly significant that the priest who received the leper's offerings (Lev 14:4-32; Deut 24:8) would have been the first witness from the old orthodoxy of Jesus' power. Who knows if perhaps this very priest might have been the first of his group to become a follower of Jesus (Acts 6:7).

THE CONFIDENT CENTURION

5When He entered Capernaum, a centurion came to Him, pleading with Him, 6"Lord, my servant is lying at home paralyzed, in terrible agony!"

[7]"I will come and heal him," He told him.

[8]"Lord," the centurion replied, "I am not worthy to have You come under my roof. But only say the word, and my servant will be cured. [9]For I too am a man under authority, having soldiers under my command. I say to this one, 'Go!' and he goes; and to another, 'Come!' and he comes; and to my slave, 'Do this!' and he does it."

[10]Hearing this, Jesus was amazed and said to those following Him, "I assure you: I have not found anyone in Israel with so great a faith! [11]I tell you that many will come from east and west, and recline at the table with Abraham, Isaac, and Jacob in the kingdom of heaven. [12]But the sons of the kingdom will be thrown into the outer darkness. In that place there will be weeping and gnashing of teeth." [13]Then Jesus told the centurion, "Go. As you have believed, let it be done for you." And his servant was cured that very moment.

*T*he second miracle of the first trio concerns the healing of the slave of a nameless centurion. Once more Matthew tells the story but streamlines the narrative. He is a selective minimalist. Only Matthew and Luke tell the story of the healing of the centurion's slave; Mark does not see fit to weave it into his narrative. In Luke, the story opens with a group of synagogue elders coming to Jesus on behalf of the soldier (Lk 7:3-4). They seek to motivate Jesus by mentioning that the Roman soldier has made the extravagant donation of the town synagogue. (The basalt foundation that lays beneith the existing third-century synagogue is believed to be the remainder of his gift to the people of Capernaum.) Perhaps Matthew omits this connection to the synagogue for the sake of his first readers, who are experiencing persecution enough without this Gentile connection to their new movement.

In the past, I have taken for granted that the centurion was retired from the military. This explains his wealth, since he would have received the equivalent of twenty years' pay as a bonus upon retiring. But recent excavations to the east of Capernaum have uncovered a Roman military outpost, complete with a Roman-style bathhouse.[23] So the status of the centurion must remain an open question. Tacitus tells us that of the twenty-five legions that existed in Jesus' day, four were stationed in the area around Syria and Palestine.[24]

When Jesus hears of his predicament, he offers a shocking proposal. He is willing to actually go to the soldier's home to heal the slave, though Jews were forbidden from entering Gentile homes (Acts 10:28). For the second time since Matthew 8 began, Jesus is willing to violate a Jewish tradition for the sake of showing *ḥesed*.

The soldier, acquainted with Jewish law, counters that he is undeserving to have Jesus come under his roof. This indicates his posture toward Jesus specifically and to the Jewish community in general. He is almost certainly a "God-fearer," a Gentile who observes the basic tenets of Judaism but has not become a full convert. This would also explain Luke's detail that he had donated the synagogue building to the town of Capernaum (Lk 7:5; see also Acts 10:22; 17:4).

What follows is an amazing exposé inside the mind of this remarkable man. As the leader of a Roman century (sixty to eighty soldiers), he understands authority. He is under the absolute authority of his superior, and his men are in absolute subjection to him. When he issues an order, disobedience is not an option. This would include even the command for a soldier to fall on his sword and commit suicide if the legion received the order of decimation.

This is the only time in Matthew's Gospel that Jesus is said to be amazed or astonished. In Luke's account, Jesus' response is a brief fourteen words. In Matthew, Jesus uses the occasion to prophesy that at the great messianic feast (see Is 25:6-9; 56:3-8) many outsiders from the east and the west will sit alongside the great patriarchs in the kingdom, but many who were originally invited to be the subjects of that kingdom (that is, the Jews) will be thrown outside in despair. Matthew sees the story in light of the kingdom and its unexpected and unsettling nature.

The healing of the slave is almost an afterthought. It is clearly not the primary focus of the story. So often the miracle in any given account is not really the miracle. There is often a "miracle behind the miracle," and this story is no exception. Jesus merely says, "Go . . . let it be done for you" (Mt 8:13). In absentia, Jesus' absolute power is made manifest, and the slave is healed offstage.[25] The true miracle, miraculous enough to amaze even Jesus himself, is the faith of the Roman soldier.

THE ONE WHO CARRIES OUR ILLNESS

¹⁴When Jesus went into Peter's house, He saw his mother-in-law lying in bed with a fever. ¹⁵So He touched her hand, and the fever left her. Then she got up and began to serve Him. ¹⁶When evening came, they brought to Him many who were demon-possessed. He drove out the spirits with a word and healed all who were sick, ¹⁷so that what was spoken through the prophet Isaiah might be fulfilled:

> *He Himself took our weaknesses*
> *and carried our diseases.*

*O*nce again, Matthew shortens Mark's already brief account of the healing of Peter's mother-in-law. When they enter Peter's house, which is just eighty feet down a narrow alleyway from the Capernaum synagogue, they find Peter's mother-in-law in bed with what Luke the doctor informs us is a "high fever" (Lk 4:38). Around the Sea of Galilee, this malady was sometimes referred to as "lake fever." Some have proposed that she was suffering from malaria. Whatever the source of the sickness, to suffer from a high fever in the first century was extremely serious.

Matthew tells us that Jesus simply touched her and the fever "left." Her immediate response was to get up and serve Jesus and his companions. I wonder if Peter's description of his ideal woman (1 Pet 3:3-6) is reflective of qualities he witnessed in this remarkable woman.

The response of the town to the healing of the slave and Peter's mother-in-law? Many who are sick and demon possessed gather around Peter's house and find deliverance and healing. This story helps us understand why Peter's house, excavated in 1968, became a church as well as a place followers of Jesus later regarded as a holy spot. Graffiti on the walls of the house, written on the white plastered walls, for centuries to come continued to ask for healing.

Whereas Mark uses the story as an occasion to present yet another strong warning of secrecy (Mk 3:12), only Matthew understands it as a fulfillment of the prophecy of Isaiah 53:4. As a critical part of his unfolding exposé dealing with the question "Who is Jesus?" Matthew answers: Jesus is the one who "took our weaknesses and carried our diseases" (Mt 8:17).

Remembering that our identity is always linked to Jesus' identity, what does this passage say about us? That we are the ones who have had our diseases taken up and our illnesses carried away in him.

THE HOMELESS SON OF MAN

[18] When Jesus saw large crowds around Him, He gave the order to go to the other side of the sea. [19] A scribe approached Him and said, "Teacher, I will follow You wherever You go!"

[20] Jesus told him, "Foxes have dens and birds of the sky have nests, but the Son of Man has no place to lay His head."

[21] "Lord," another of His disciples said, "first let me go bury my father."

[22] But Jesus told him, "Follow Me, and let the dead bury their own dead."

*T*his passage opens with a hint that Jesus is trying to get away from the crowd by crisscrossing the lake once more. The opening verse sets the tone for the two brief interactions that follow.

First we meet a scribe (*grammateus*). The role of the scribe began as a simple administrative position (1 Chron 27:32; Ezra 4:8-23; 7:6). Ezra is described as a "scribe" in Nehemiah 8. Initially scribes were utilized for their ability to write as copyists and as composers of official documents. As time went on, the office of scribe became an institution in Israel, and by Jesus' time scribes were teachers, scholars, lecturers and copiers all rolled into one.[26]

In general Matthew takes the more generous approach to the scribes, whereas Mark reveals them as one of Jesus' principal enemies. Only Matthew tells us the story of this scribe who wanted to follow Jesus. The scribe addresses Jesus as "teacher," which is probably what he is looking for in someone to follow. He presents himself as a volunteer who is willing to follow Jesus anywhere—but Jesus does not accept volunteers. He calls his disciples.

Jesus' response is a reminder of the cost of being one of his disciples, whose identities are always rooted in his. He, the Son of Man, has no place to lay his head. Even now it appears that Jesus has moved in with

Simon Peter. After he left Nazareth on his mission, Jesus never had a home of his own.

The next person is described as one of Jesus' disciples (*mathētōn*). Occasionally Matthew uses this word to describe an uncommitted follower, as in this passage (Mt 5:1; 9:37; 12:49; 17:16). He addresses Jesus not as "teacher," but rather as "Lord" (*kyrios*), though his use of the term does not necessarily mean he is fully committed to Jesus as his "master." Luke tells us that Jesus had issued the call to this man, "follow me" (Lk 9:59). Matthew, the selective minimalist, does not seem to think we need this detail. What matters to him is the man's reluctance to follow immediately, something Matthew himself will do (Mt 9:9). The man's excuse is the most valid of all excuses in Judaism: he needs to go and bury his father.

Some commentaries soften the story by suggesting that perhaps the father is sick and has not yet died. Others, pointing to the two-stage burial customs of Jesus' day, explain that though the father has died and is in the tomb, the man is requesting a year's delay to accomplish stage two of the burial and reentomb the bones of his father.

While interesting, these explanations seem to miss the point. What matters is not the man's sincerity or lack thereof, but rather Jesus' radical command. The theme of faith before family is clear in Jesus teaching, nowhere more than in Matthew's Gospel (see Mt 10:35-37; 12:46-50). The Talmud states, "He who is confronted by the death of a relative is freed from reciting the Shema, from the 18 benedictions, and from all the commandments stated in the Torah."[27] In Judaism family is given priority over faith. In light of Jesus' identity of absolute lordship, nothing, absolutely nothing, comes before him. All of our old obligations vanish when we take up his cross (Mt 10:38).

TWO DEMONIC CONFRONTATIONS

23 As He got into the boat, His disciples followed Him. 24 Suddenly, a violent storm arose on the sea, so that the boat was being swamped by the waves. But He was sleeping. 25 So the disciples came and woke Him up, saying, "Lord, save us! We're going to die!"

26 But He said to them, "Why are you fearful, you of little faith?" Then He got up and rebuked the winds and the sea. And there was a great calm.

²⁷The men were amazed and asked, "What kind of man is this?—even the winds and the sea obey Him!"

²⁸When He had come to the other side, to the region of the Gadarenes, two demon-possessed men met Him as they came out of the tombs. They were so violent that no one could pass that way. ²⁹Suddenly they shouted, "What do You have to do with us, Son of God? Have You come here to torment us before the time?"

³⁰Now a long way off from them, a large herd of pigs was feeding. ³¹"If You drive us out," the demons begged Him, "send us into the herd of pigs."

³²"Go!" He told them. So when they had come out, they entered the pigs. And suddenly the whole herd rushed down the steep bank into the sea and perished in the water. ³³Then the men who tended them fled. They went into the city and reported everything—especially what had happened to those who were demon-possessed. ³⁴At that, the whole town went out to meet Jesus. When they saw Him, they begged Him to leave their region.

*T*he more closely we integrate the stories of the storm on the Sea of Galilee and the confrontation with the Gadarene demoniacs, the clearer they both become. Each narrative feeds the other.

Once again Jesus and his disciples crisscross the lake, when suddenly, out of nowhere a furious storm descends on them. Here many commentaries expound on the weather patterns around the Sea of Galilee and how they are known to breed sudden storms. These explanations miss the point. The nature of the storm is described by Matthew with the Greek word *seismos*, the word from which we get our *seismograph*. Literally the storm is described as a "violent shaking." Several of the disciples had grown up around this lake, and while they have seen the sudden storms to which the commentaries refer, they have never seen a storm like this. The waves are literally washing over the boat. Their deaths are imminent. Those sudden storms may be normal, but this storm is anything *but* normal.

The only thing more abnormal than the shaking of the storm is Jesus asleep in the midst of the danger. His deep sleep is no doubt a result of exhaustion. He has been pouring himself out for some time without a break. Centuries earlier the psalmist witnessed this event through his prophetic imagination:

> Others went to sea in ships, conducting trade on the vast waters.
> They saw the Lord's works, His wonderful works in the deep.
> He spoke and raised a tempest that stirred up the waves of the sea.
> Rising up to the sky, sinking down to the depths, their courage melting away in anguish,
> They reeled and staggered like drunken men, and all their skill was useless.
> Then they cried out to the Lord in their trouble, and He brought them out of their distress.
> He stilled the storm to a murmur, and the waves of the sea were hushed. They rejoiced when the waves grew quiet.
> Then He guided them to the harbor they longed for. (Ps 107:23-30)

Abruptly awakened, Jesus wipes the sleep from his eyes and finds the disciples beside themselves with fear. He seems surprised—disappointed that their lives should still be dominated by fear, even though they are in such a precarious situation. In the same way Jesus rebukes the demon possessed, he speaks to the deadly storm, which dies down as if exhausted.[28]

The disciples who are still wrestling with the question of Jesus' identity are amazed. "What kind of man is this?" they breathlessly mutter to themselves. Another storm is waiting for them, recorded in Matthew 14. On the occasion of that contrary windstorm, the identity of Jesus will be settled, and they will worship him for the first time (Mt 14:33).

The storm has blown them to the other side of the lake, to the eastern shore. This region, known as the Decapolis, or Ten Cities, was founded by the Roman general Pompey the Great to be a thorn in the side of the Jews in the area around the Sea of Galilee. Again it is important to maintain the intimate connection between the story of the demonically possessed men and the demonic storm.

Matthew tends to double his witnesses (see Mt 20:30; 26:60). Perhaps this reflects the Old Testament notion of everything needing to be established in the mouths of two witnesses (Deut 17:6; 19:15). While the other Gospels speak of only one person, Matthew tells us there were two. This should not be seen as a contradiction but merely as an additional detail.

Scholars disagree as to the exact location. The location is almost certainly Gadara and not the nearby Gergesa. Because Gadara is six miles from the lake, many argue against it being the location of the miracle. But in 1985, at a time when the water level of the Sea of Galilee was exceptionally low, a massive harbor was discovered near the city of Gadara. It was the largest harbor on the eastern shore of the lake, with a breakwater over 250 feet long. The harbor was so large that a mock naval battle was once put on there by the Romans for the residents of Gadara. The event was commemorated on a second-century coin minted in the area. So the image of Jesus' boat being dragged up onto the beach is probably not accurate. Most likely they piloted the boat through the breakwater and tied up along the six-hundred-foot pier.[29]

The two men, we are told, live in the cemetery beside the lake.[30] They address Jesus as "Son of God" (see Jas 2:19). The evil spirits who possess these men are frightened by Jesus' sudden appearance on the pier. Perhaps they had assumed that the furious demonic storm should have taken all their lives. Knowing that a time has been appointed for their destruction, they are terrified by the authority of Jesus' presence. Are they afraid because they think Jesus has come to pay them back for their trying to murder him and his disciples in the storm?

Knowing Jesus' intention is to cast them out of the two men, they plead to be sent into a nearby herd of pigs. The presence of the swine is another indication that we are in Gentile country. With one simple word Jesus gives the command: "Go!"[31]

The pigs, panicked by the demons coming into them, rush into the lake and drown. There are two effects of demonic possession: first to mar the image of God in a person, which the demons had been doing to the two men for who knows how long; and second to destroy life. What happens to the pigs in the story is what would have eventually happened to the two men. The bodies of the dead animals floating on the lake reveal the original intention of the storm. What happened to the pigs is what Satan had intended for Jesus and his disciples.

The nearby townspeople, having heard of the frightening incident, come out and see the aftermath of the demonic confrontation. We are tempted to judge them for their fear and for asking Jesus to leave. "How could they be so blind?" we ask ourselves. But perhaps this is to super-impose our comfortable understanding of Jesus onto the story too quickly. Perhaps their response was the only reasonable one for the moment. After all, what is the appropriate response to the sudden appearance of the disturbing power of this Jewish stranger who has apparently destroyed a large portion of the wealth of the area? Perhaps fear is an appropriate response to a man who must continually tell those close to him, "don't be afraid" (see Mt 14:27; 17:7; 28:10).

MATTHEW 9

WINNING PRAISE FOR GOD

¹So He got into a boat, crossed over, and came to His own town. ²Just then some men brought to Him a paralytic lying on a mat. Seeing their faith, Jesus told the paralytic, "Have courage, son, your sins are forgiven."

³At this, some of the scribes said among themselves, "He's blaspheming!"

⁴But perceiving their thoughts, Jesus said, "Why are you thinking evil things in your hearts? ⁵For which is easier: to say, 'Your sins are forgiven,' or to say, 'Get up and walk'? ⁶But so you may know that the Son of Man has authority on earth to forgive sins"—then He told the paralytic, "Get up, pick up your mat, and go home." ⁷And he got up and went home. ⁸When the crowds saw this, they were awestruck and gave glory to God who had given such authority to men.

*I*n response to their fearful request that he leave their region, Jesus and his disciples get back into their boat and, cutting across the northeastern corner of the lake, return to Capernaum. In Matthew 4:13 we learned that Jesus had relocated there as his preaching ministry was just beginning.

The other Synoptic Gospels also tell us the story of the healing of the paralytic. Matthew's version is half the length of Mark's or Luke's. He omits the fact that the paralytic's friends tore a hole in the roof and lowered him into the room where Jesus was teaching, probably in Peter's house. All three versions refer to the fact that Jesus was impressed when he saw their faith, not of the man on the mat, but of his friends. Often it becomes our responsibility as a friend of those who are ill to carry them (in prayer) to the presence of Jesus for healing.

Significantly, Jesus heals the man's paralysis by pronouncing that his sins are forgiven. To be healed and to be forgiven represent two sides of the same coin. In fact, one Greek word is used for both healing and being forgiven. Sin represents the worst kind of paralysis. However, not all sickness is the result of personal sin.

The ever-present scribes are offended at hearing Jesus exercise this kind of authority. To them it clearly only belongs to God. They whisper to themselves (usually a bad sign in the Gospels) that Jesus is committing blasphemy. He is infringing on the power and the name of God (see Lev 24:16). Jesus responds, once again, to the educated scribes with a formal rabbinic interpretive technique —"*how much more.*" It was formulated almost a generation earlier by the great Hillel and is known as the first of seven of his Middoth. It is an argument from lesser to greater. "Which is easier," Jesus asks, "to say, 'your sins are forgiven,' or to say, 'get up and walk'?" If the lesser case is true, to simply pronounce that sins are forgiven, then the greater case is true as well. At first Jesus had pronounced the man forgiven; now to demonstrate his authority he commands the paralyzed man to "get up."

When Jesus says, "Get up," apparently there is nothing else to do but get up (see Jn 5:8). The Son of Man, the Supreme "Human One" has absolute authority over disease, the demonic and, as we will see later in this chapter, even over death itself. Don't read too quickly over the concluding statement about the Capernaum crowd who witnessed the miracle. Would it not be natural to celebrate Jesus, who just performed a miracle? But that is not what the crowd does. In fact, the crowd never praises Jesus for any of his miracles. Matthew tells us they praise God for having given this degree of authority to man. Simply put, Jesus always wins praise for his Father by everything he does.

THE CALLING OF MATTHEW

⁹*As Jesus went on from there, He saw a man named Matthew sitting at the tax office, and He said to him, "Follow Me!" So he got up and followed Him.*

¹⁰*While He was reclining at the table in the house, many tax collectors and sinners came as guests to eat with Jesus and His disciples.* ¹¹*When the Pharisees saw this, they asked His disciples, "Why does your Teacher eat with tax collectors and sinners?"*

¹²*But when He heard this, He said, "Those who are well don't need a doctor, but the sick do.* ¹³*Go and learn what this means: I desire mercy and not sacrifice. For I didn't come to call the righteous, but sinners."*

*I*n a chapter filled with miracles, the author of Matthew's Gospel records an event that was in his own mind a miracle in and of itself.

Mark and Luke both refer to the fact that Jesus went out of town, somewhere beside the lake. There he encountered Matthew sitting at his tax table (Mk 2:13-14; Lk 5:27). He is working under the authority of Herod Antipas, collecting taxes for Rome. Josephus records that Herod collected two hundred talents (roughly five million dollars) every year from Galilee and Perea.[32] Part of that enormous burden rested on Matthew's shoulders. In the other Gospels he is referred to by his given name, Levi. "Matthew," which means "gift of God" (*maththaios*), may very well be a nickname given to him by Jesus. If it was, it would become the core of his new identity.

We are not told if this is their first meeting. Since Jesus had been ministering in the area of Capernaum for a time, there's a good chance that Matthew had had a chance to hear and see Jesus before now. Like the centurion (Mt 8:5-13), Matthew has lived and worked under the weighty authority of Rome. Like the soldier, he recognized in Jesus a different, absolute sense of authority that he gladly now places himself under. We are left to assume that someone else, another tax collector, took up Matthew's contract with Herod, as he left everything to follow Jesus.

Matthew, the minimalist, tells us in verse 10 that Jesus went to Matthew's house for dinner. However, Luke lets us know that this was a "grand banquet" (Lk 5:29). It stands to reason that Matthew's fellow tax collectors and his other acquaintances (that is, sinners) would have come to the party as well. Given the significance of the intimacy of meal fellowship in first-century Judaism, the Pharisees are understandably upset that Jesus appears to be approving of the crowd by freely associating with them. When they try to extract an answer from Jesus' own disciples, he overhears. He is the healer, the doctor, and he has come for those who are sick. The Pharisees are sick as well, but they are blind to their sickness. This is what places them outside Jesus ability to heal them for the present.

Only Matthew records the words of Jesus that follow. He opens with a very rabbinic-sounding phrase, "go and learn what this means." Jesus quotes Hosea: "I desire mercy and not sacrifice" (Hos 6:6). The Old Testament word for "mercy" is the Hebrew word *ḥesed*. This word describes the very heart of God and is used over 250 times in the Old

Testament. It is an untranslatable word, like *love*. It can properly be understood only by being incarnated. And this is what Jesus has come to do. The creators of the King James Version had to invent a new word to attempt to translate the untranslatable *ḥesed*. They came up with the compound word *lovingkindness*. The best translation I know requires an entire sentence: "when the person from whom I have a right to expect nothing gives me everything."

If *ḥesed* is a word God himself uses to define his heart, it must define Jesus' heart as well. Though Matthew—or you or me—has a right to expect nothing from God because of his stubborn disobedience, God nonetheless has come to give us everything. As long as the righteous Pharisees believe they can expect to receive from God because of their sacrifices, they are placing themselves outside the scope of Jesus' *ḥesed*. They rely on their sacrifices. Matthew has realized that all he has is Jesus' mercy. It is the supreme reason for throwing a party.

It would be a mistake to assume that the rabbis as a whole did not understand this important word, *ḥesed*. In fact, Yohanan ben Zakkai, who was responsible for the reformation of Judaism after the destruction of the temple in A.D. 70, took the words of Hosea 6:6 as his personal motto. Like Jesus himself, Yohanan was from Galilee.[33]

OLD ORTHODOXY, NEW REALITY

[14] *Then John's disciples came to Him, saying, "Why do we and the Pharisees fast often, but Your disciples do not fast?"*

[15] *Jesus said to them, "Can the wedding guests be sad while the groom is with them? The time will come when the groom will be taken away from them, and then they will fast.* [16] *No one patches an old garment with unshrunk cloth, because the patch pulls away from the garment and makes the tear worse.* [17] *And no one puts new wine into old wineskins. Otherwise, the skins burst, the wine spills out, and the skins are ruined. But they put new wine into fresh wineskins, and both are preserved."*

*N*ext we move from the concept of sacrifice to fasting. The disciples of John the Baptist come to Jesus with a question. Interestingly, they group themselves along with the Pharisees, who fasted twice a week (see Lk 18:12). The Old Testament required only one fast a year, on the Day of Atonement (Lev 23:28). As with sacrifice, they believed that fasting would win them favor with God.

Jesus responds with a parable. His disciples are the guests, and he is the bridegroom. If they are still at Matthew's grand banquet, the image would be even more profound. When the bridegroom is present, fasting is irrelevant.

Jesus' concept of fasting is connected to mourning, to lamenting our sin in order to regain a closeness to the God who freely forgives sin because of his *ḥesed*. In this sense, fasting becomes a way of regaining our sense of immediacy with God's presence. When the bridegroom, Jesus, is present, what purpose could fasting possibly serve?

Ominously Jesus' tone shifts, and he notes that the time is rapidly approaching when he, the bridegroom, will be taken from them. Then fasting will have a purpose for his followers as they try to regain the original immediacy they had with him.

In rapid succession, Jesus responds with yet another two-part parable. A new patch does not work on an old garment. Old wineskins do not work at holding new wine. The old garment is torn, and the old wineskins burst. They cannot contain the new. The old orthodoxy, represented by the Pharisees and even the disciples of John, cannot contain the new reality of the kingdom. The old orthodoxy is inadequate at expressing the new identity of the kingdom. Late in the first century, Rabbi Meir may have very well been quoting Jesus when he said, "Look not at the flask, but what it contains: there may be a new flask full of old wine, and an old flask which has not even new wine in it."[34]

POWER OVER DISEASE AND DEATH

[18]As He was telling them these things, suddenly one of the leaders came and knelt down before Him, saying, "My daughter is near death, but come and lay Your hand on her, and she will live." [19]So Jesus and His disciples got up and followed him.

[20]Just then, a woman who had suffered from bleeding for 12 years ap-

proached from behind and touched the tassel on His robe, [21]*for she said to herself, "If I can just touch His robe, I'll be made well!"*

[22]*But Jesus turned and saw her. "Have courage, daughter," He said. "Your faith has made you well." And the woman was made well from that moment.*

[23]*When Jesus came to the leader's house, He saw the flute players and a crowd lamenting loudly.* [24]*"Leave," He said, "because the girl isn't dead, but sleeping." And they started laughing at Him.* [25]*But when the crowd had been put outside, He went in and took her by the hand, and the girl got up.* [26]*And this news spread throughout that whole area.*

Once more Matthew presents a book-ended narration that is also contained in Mark. Again he virtually cuts the length of the narrative in half. Following Jesus' discussion of the old orthodoxy, a representative of that old system, a leader of the synagogue community, comes to Jesus with a desperate request. Matthew simply refers to him as a "leader." Both Mark and Luke tell us he was from the synagogue. Both Mark and Luke also know his name, Jarius.

He is frantic. His young daughter is dying, and there is nothing in his old orthodoxy to do except hire the professional mourners for her imminent funeral. He intuits, however, that something more can be done for his daughter and that only Jesus can do it. Jesus gets up (perhaps from Matthew's banquet) and follows, his disciples in tow.

Along the way a victim of the old orthodoxy, a woman who has suffered from vaginal bleeding for twelve years, comes up behind Jesus in the crowd. She touches the blue-and-white tassels of his prayer shawl, known as the zizith (see Num 15:37-41). She has heard about Jesus and has come to the magical conclusion that if she simply touches the fringe, she will be healed (Mt 14:36). In her mind, the power is in the cloak that is touching Jesus.

In the other Gospels, she is instantly healed and quickly tries to vanish in the crowd, but Jesus looks for and finds her (see Mk 5:29-34). Matthew omits this detail. He streamlines the narrative and simply has Jesus turn around and discover the woman behind him. Pointing away from himself, as he always does, he tells the woman it was her faith that healed her. In his humility he does not mention it was her faith—in him.

When the nameless woman's body is healed, her entire life is healed as well. Her continual bleeding would have rendered her perpetually unclean, cut off from every other Jewish person according to the old orthodoxy. According to the same ancient system, she would have rendered Jesus unclean by touching him (see Lev 15). But Jesus has come to fulfill the old orthodoxy and to perfect it as well. What matters most is not who did the touching but who it was she touched. Uncleanness no longer radiated from her to Jesus. Healing now came from him to her.

Matthew omits the news that the little girl has died while Jesus and his disciples were on their way to the house. In his version, Jesus simply arrives at the house to find the flute players and professional mourners doing their business, noisily acting out the prescribed mourning of the old orthodoxy.

Jesus' new reality understands that the little girl is not dead, only asleep. His coming has redefined death for us all. It is now merely a sleep from which he will someday awaken us. But the old wineskins can't contain the new wine, even as the mourners can't comprehend what Jesus' words could possibly mean. They erupt in laughter.

With Matthean abruptness, Jesus enters, takes her by the hand and "wakes her up." There is no word of the Three accompanying him and no reference *"Talitha koum."* Only the fact of a dead girl alive and the news of Jesus' power spreading all over Galilee.

ONE REQUEST HE WILL NEVER DENY

²⁷As Jesus went on from there, two blind men followed Him, shouting, "Have mercy on us, Son of David!" ²⁸When He entered the house, the blind men approached Him, and Jesus said to them, "Do you believe that I can do this?" "Yes, Lord," they answered Him. ²⁹Then He touched their eyes, saying, "Let it be done for you according to your faith!" ³⁰And their eyes were opened. Then Jesus warned them sternly, "Be sure that no one finds out!" ³¹But they went out and spread the news about Him throughout that whole area.

³²Just as they were going out, a demon-possessed man who was unable to speak was brought to Him. ³³When the demon had been driven out, the man spoke. And the crowds were amazed, saying, "Nothing like this has ever been seen in Israel!" [34]*But the Pharisees said, "He drives out demons by the ruler of the demons!"*

$\mathcal{T}$he healing of the two blind men is a story unique to Matthew's Gospel. Having healed the bleeding woman and raised the dead girl, Jesus encounters two blind men on the road who are asking for something he never fails to give: mercy (*ḥesed*). It is the perfect prayer of the new kingdom: "Have mercy!"

Jesus takes the two men from the presence of the crowd—perhaps into Peter's own home in Capernaum. Privately he asks them if they believe he can heal them. They respond, "Yes, Lord."

As with the bleeding woman Jesus healed earlier, he attributes the miracle of their healing to their belief in him. Some have said that Jesus was unable to heal those who did not believe in him. Yet even in this chapter he raised a young girl who never expressed faith in him as well as the paralytic whose friends were the ones whose faith made the difference. Is there a connection between faith in Jesus and the outcome of a prayer for healing? Most certainly there is; otherwise we would not be encouraged to be persistent in our prayers. However, is Jesus' power and authority somehow bound by a lack of faith? Absolutely not. There are no rules when it comes to these things. His lordship is absolute.

Next we see a rare Matthean example of what is falsely called the "messianic secret." This is the false notion that because Jesus occasionally warned people to keep silent concerning a miracle that he was somehow keeping his Messiah-ship a secret. It occurs three more times in Matthew's Gospel (Mt 12:16; 16:20; 17:9). Mark, who is preoccupied with this facet of Jesus' ministry, makes it clear in chapter 1 of his Gospel that Jesus' commands of secrecy were connected to an attempt to control the mob, which Jesus was ultimately not able to do. Most often when he commanded secrecy, the person healed disobeyed anyway, resulting in Jesus' ministry being hampered by miracle seekers (see Mk 1:35-38, 43; 2:2). Matthew's minimalist approach does not include an unpacking of the rationale behind Jesus' command of secrecy. His focus on the new identity of the kingdom and Jesus as the fulfillment of the Old Testament remains razor sharp.

In one last healing account, Matthew tells the story of the healing of a man who could not speak as the result of demonic possession. He provides not a single detail of the healing, only that when Jesus cast out the demon, the man could speak once more. Matthew will provide a similar account beginning in 12:22. While the crowd responds in amazement, the Pharisees, those representatives of the old orthodoxy, falsely conclude that Jesus' power to cast out demons must have come from demons. The new wine of his mercy cannot be contained in the old wineskins of their orthodoxy. Despite the clear and miraculous proofs that Jesus is the Messiah and that he has come to fulfill and perfect the old orthodoxy, they are simply blind, like the two men earlier in the chapter.

FINAL SYNAGOGUE TOUR

35 Then Jesus went to all the towns and villages, teaching in their synagogues, preaching the good news of the kingdom, and healing every disease and every sickness. 36 When He saw the crowds, He felt compassion for them, because they were weary and worn out, like sheep without a shepherd. 37 Then He said to His disciples, "The harvest is abundant, but the workers are few. 38 Therefore, pray to the Lord of the harvest to send out workers into His harvest."

*M*atthew 9:35-38 provides a concluding statement concerning all that has gone before, as well as a final verse that provides a bridge into the next chapter. Make note, Jesus is still focusing his ministry on the local synagogues. His message is the good news of the kingdom (Mt 4:17). The word of Jesus is validated by his miraculous works: casting out demons and healing. Matthew echoes a sentiment from the Old Testament book of Numbers that Jesus' compassion for the crowd was because they were like sheep without a shepherd (Num 27:17).[35]

The final verse prepares us for the lengthy discussion of chapter 10, the second of the five great teaching blocks in Matthew's Gospel. Jesus encourages his disciples to ask the "Lord of the harvest," to provide workers to move out into the field, which is ripe for harvesting. In Mat-

thew 10 Jesus will choose the Twelve and give them all the instructions
they need to do just that.

It is interesting that a late-first-century rabbi, Tarfon, made a strikingly similar statement. In the Mishnah, Abot 2:15, he said, "The day
is short and the task is great and the laborers are idle and the wage is
abundant and that Master of the house is urgent." The similarity between his statement and that of Jesus leaves open the question that he
might have actually been quoting the rabbi from Galilee.[36]

MATTHEW 10

APPOINTING THE TWELVE

10:1–4

INSTRUCTIONS TO THE TWELVE

10:5–42

APPOINTING THE TWELVE

¹Summoning His 12 disciples, He gave them authority over unclean spirits, to drive them out and to heal every disease and sickness. ²These are the names of the 12 apostles:

> *First, Simon, who is called Peter,*
> *and Andrew his brother;*
> *James the son of Zebedee,*
> *and John his brother;*
> *³Philip and Bartholomew;*
> *Thomas and Matthew the tax collector;*
> *James the son of Alphaeus, and Thaddaeus;*
> *⁴Simon the Zealot, and Judas Iscariot,*
> *who also betrayed Him.*

*M*atthew 10 provides a good illustration of what is fundamentally different about this gospel as compared to the others. When Jesus sends the twelve apostles out on their first mission, Mark devotes only two verses to Jesus' instructions to them (Mk 6:10-11). Luke provides only three verses (Lk 9:3-5). Matthew devotes an entire chapter of forty-two verses. While Matthew may be a selective minimalist in regard to the detail of the story, he is the extreme opposite when it comes to the words of Jesus. Remember in Mark we have only twenty-two minutes of "face time" with Jesus. In Luke we have fifty-three minutes with Jesus speaking directly to us. In John we have only forty-four. But in Matthew, Jesus speaks to us for more than an hour (one hour and twelve minutes).

Having just warned them that the "workers are few" (Mt 9:37), Jesus calls the Twelve from the larger group of his followers. When the Gospels say he gave them his "authority," a concept from the Old Testament world comes to the surface. It was known as the *šālîach*. The *šālîach* was the "authoritative representative." Often his task was to legally represent the one who sent him. In these cases, his word was legally binding for the one he represented. Speaking to the *šālîach* was legally the same as speaking to his master.[37]

The number of those sent ones is significant. Twelve reflects the connection of Jesus ministry to the history and fate of Israel. In Matthew 19:28 Jesus will promise the disciples that they will sit on twelve thrones, judging the twelve tribes of Israel. The term "apostle" is the Greek equivalent of the Hebrew *shaliakh*. The Twelve are Jesus' "sent ones." They are clothed with his authority. They will bear his concealed dignity.

The Twelve are

- Simon Peter—the first to be called and at the head of every list of the Twelve. In time the Twelve will develop a corporate identity in Simon Peter.

- Andrew—Simon's brother, an original follower of John the Baptist.

- James and John—the sons of Zebedee. They are hotheaded. Jesus nicknames them *Boanērges*—"Sons of Thunder" (Mk 3:17). James will be the first of the disciples to die. John will be the last.

- Philip—from Bethsaida, like Peter and Andrew. In John 1:43, Jesus sought out and found Philip and called him to be his disciple. He had also been a disciple of John the Baptist.

- Bartholomew—we know virtually nothing about this disciple, not even his name. Bar-Tolmai means the son of Tolmai. He is most likely the Nathanael of John 1:43-51.

- Thomas—Jesus had given him the nickname Didymus, "the Twin." Tradition says it was because the two looked so much alike. He has unfortunately been labeled the doubter, because he questioned the reality of the resurrection (Jn 20:25). Yet if you look closely at the passage, he is not condemned by Jesus for his doubt. Doubt is necessary for true faith to be born.

- Matthew—the source of the sayings (*logia*) contained in the five blocks of teaching in the Gospel that bears his name. His name is also a possible nickname from Jesus. "Gift of God" was a sobriquet he would have cherished, never having felt like anyone's gift before in his life. Levi is his Hebrew name.

- James, the son of Alphaeus—He may have been Matthew's brother, since in Mark 2:14 Matthew is also called the son of Alphaeus.

- Thaddeus—this may also be a nickname. It means "big hearted." Luke refers to him as "Judas" (Lk 6:16).

- Simon the zealot—The term "zealot" is based on the Hebrew *qināh* for "zeal." Scholars agree that the political party known as the Zealots did not come together until much later. If this is correct, then perhaps "the zealous one" might be yet another nickname.

- Judas Iscariot—His name appears last in every list and always with the tag "the one who betrayed him." Two explanations of his second name *Iskariōth* have been suggested by scholars. First, perhaps it means "the man (*îš*) from the village of Kerioth." The second suggested possibility is "man of the knife" (*sicarius*). There was a radical political movement known as the Sicarii, founded in Galilee in A.D. 6 by another person named Judas. But perhaps there is a third possibility and the name *Iskariōth* is yet another nickname, "knife man." During his days in the Nixon administration, before he found faith in Christ, Chuck Colson was sometimes known as the "hatchet man." Could it be that Judas had some aspect of his personality that Jesus described with this nickname? And could all the possible nicknames be connected to Jesus' mission to redefine all their identities?

INSTRUCTIONS TO THE TWELVE

⁵*Jesus sent out these 12 after giving them instructions: "Don't take the road leading to other nations, and don't enter any Samaritan town. ⁶Instead, go to the lost sheep of the house of Israel. ⁷As you go, announce this: 'The kingdom of heaven has come near.' ⁸Heal the sick, raise the dead, cleanse those with skin diseases, drive out demons. You have received free of charge; give free of charge. ⁹Don't take along gold, silver, or copper for your money-belts. ¹⁰Don't take a traveling bag for the road, or an extra shirt, sandals, or a walking stick, for the worker is worthy of his food.*

¹¹*"When you enter any town or village, find out who is worthy, and stay there until you leave. ¹²Greet a household when you enter it, ¹³and if the household is worthy, let your peace be on it. But if it is unworthy, let your*

peace return to you. ¹⁴If anyone will not welcome you or listen to your words, shake the dust off your feet when you leave that house or town. ¹⁵I assure you: It will be more tolerable on the day of judgment for the land of Sodom and Gomorrah than for that town.

¹⁶"Look, I'm sending you out like sheep among wolves. Therefore be as shrewd as serpents and as harmless as doves. ¹⁷Because people will hand you over to sanhedrins and flog you in their synagogues, beware of them. ¹⁸You will even be brought before governors and kings because of Me, to bear witness to them and to the nations. ¹⁹But when they hand you over, don't worry about how or what you should speak. For you will be given what to say at that hour, ²⁰because you are not speaking, but the Spirit of your Father is speaking through you.

²¹"Brother will betray brother to death, and a father his child. Children will even rise up against their parents and have them put to death. ²²You will be hated by everyone because of My name. But the one who endures to the end will be delivered. ²³When they persecute you in one town, escape to another. For I assure you: You will not have covered the towns of Israel before the Son of Man comes. ²⁴A disciple is not above his teacher, or a slave above his master. ²⁵It is enough for a disciple to become like his teacher and a slave like his master. If they called the head of the house 'Beelzebul,' how much more the members of his household!

²⁶"Therefore, don't be afraid of them, since there is nothing covered that won't be uncovered and nothing hidden that won't be made known. ²⁷What I tell you in the dark, speak in the light. What you hear in a whisper, proclaim on the housetops. ²⁸Don't fear those who kill the body but are not able to kill the soul; rather, fear Him who is able to destroy both soul and body in hell. ²⁹Aren't two sparrows sold for a penny? Yet not one of them falls to the ground without your Father's consent. ³⁰But even the hairs of your head have all been counted. ³¹So don't be afraid therefore; you are worth more than many sparrows.

³²"Therefore, everyone who will acknowledge Me before men, I will also acknowledge him before My Father in heaven. ³³But whoever denies Me before men, I will also deny him before My Father in heaven. ³⁴Don't assume that I came to bring peace on the earth. I did not come to bring peace, but a sword. ³⁵For I came to turn

> *a man against his father,*
> *a daughter against her mother,*
> *a daughter-in-law against her mother-in-law;*
> *36 and a man's enemies will be*
> *the members of his household.*

37 The person who loves father or mother more than Me is not worthy of Me; the person who loves son or daughter more than Me is not worthy of Me. 38 And whoever doesn't take up his cross and follow Me is not worthy of Me. 39 Anyone finding his life will lose it, and anyone losing his life because of Me will find it.

40 "The one who welcomes you welcomes Me, and the one who welcomes Me welcomes Him who sent Me. 41 Anyone who welcomes a prophet because he is a prophet will receive a prophet's reward. And anyone who welcomes a righteous person because he's righteous will receive a righteous person's reward. 42 And whoever gives just a cup of cold water to one of these little ones because he is a disciple—I assure you: He will never lose his reward!"

$\mathcal{M}$atthew clearly sets apart the verses that follow as "instructions." First, and only in Matthew, comes the command to avoid Gentile and Samaritan areas.

- Their first mission will be focused on the "lost sheep of Israel" (see Lk 24:47; Acts 13:46; Rom 1:16).

- Next Jesus repeats the core message, which we heard for the first time from John the Baptist (Mt 3:2), then from Jesus himself (Mt 4:17). These are the *words* of Jesus.

- Jesus provides that they should perform healing, exorcism and even raising the dead. These are the *works* of Jesus.

- Next he commands that they travel without provisions. This is because they will be totally dependent on Jewish hospitality (Mt 10:11; compare the seemingly contradictory instructions of Lk 22:35-36). The difference here is that on their second mission the disciples will be reaching out to the Gentiles as well and will not be able to depend on Jewish hospitality.

- In each town they visit, they are to search out someone who will reliably welcome and assist them. They are to stay in that house until they leave and not go from door to door like beggars. They are to pronounce their shalom (peace) on the house. If it is not received, they are to leave. Their only retaliation is to simply shake the dust off their feet (see Acts 13:51). They are to leave that place to the judgment of God, who will punish more severely than he did Sodom and Gomorrah (see Mt 11:21).

All of the above instructions were succinct and direct. Matthew 10:16-20 appears to be Jesus' final challenge. They are to combine innocence and shrewdness as they go; to guard against the wolves they will often find themselves in the midst of.

Verse 17 would resonate not only with the Twelve but also with Matthew's original synagogue audience, who are experiencing growing suspicion and persecution. They will be handed over to be flogged in the synagogues (Deut 25:1-3; see appendix D). They will find themselves standing condemned before governors and even kings. Every detail of Jesus' warning was experienced by his followers. This is not an antiquated word; today more Christians are murdered for the faith than at any time in the history of the world.

Jesus' final direct word to them was not to worry about what they might say during those extreme moments before the synagogue rulers and Gentile governors and kings. They will find the right words because the Father will be speaking through them. What more profoundly encouraging words could the Twelve or those sitting in the synagogue in Galilee listening to Matthew's Gospel for the first time hope to hear?

In verse 21 the tone seems to shift. While these are also words of instruction and may very well be a part of the original block of Jesus' teaching to the Twelve, they may also be read as part of the original *logia* of Matthew, no less authoritative. They are still the original words of Jesus.

Jesus predicts the dissolution of families because of him. Brothers, children, parents—they will all betray one another. In fact, they will be hated because of their allegiance to Jesus. In the face of persecution, they are to flee. It is said that when the Jewish Christians in Jerusalem heard that the Romans were coming to attack the city, they fled to the nearby city of Pella. Many survived because they had listened to these words of warning from Jesus.

The next statement reaches back to Matthew 9:34 and ahead to 12:24-27. Jesus had been accused of being in league with the demonic, of deriving his power to exorcise and heal from Beelzebub. If he has had such accusations leveled against him, his disciples will as well.

What follows (Mt 10:26-31) is a collection of sayings that could come under the heading "What Not to Fear." His listeners are not to be afraid of those who accuse them of being allied with Jesus. They are not to fear those who might even kill them. In yet another example of Hillel's *qal wahōmer*, Jesus assures them that if the Father cares for the penny-a-piece sparrows who die, "how much more" will he care for them.

Sounding somewhat disjointed—as if these are separate sayings—Jesus promises to acknowledge before the Father those who would acknowledge him. At the same time he warns those who would disown him that he will disown them as well.

Verses 34-36 are a wake-up call for those who have not yet realized the extreme, radical nature of Jesus' coming. In contradistinction to John the Baptist, who came to reunite families (Lk 1:17), Jesus has come with a sword to divide them (Lk 12:49). Jesus substantiates the severity of his calling by quoting the prophet Micah 7:6 (see Mt 4:22; 8:21-23; 16:24).

Jesus goes on in verses 37-39 to say that love for him must supersede love for family, even the love we might have for our own lives. This level of commitment to faith over family was reflected in Deuteronomy 33:9-10, where the Levites are commanded to put regard for the word of God before their legitimate commitment to parents and family. Paradoxically, this is the only way to find true life, according to Jesus. We must embrace the foolishness of the cross to be wise, let go our possessions to become wealthy and become slaves to be free. This is the radical reversal, the upside-down nature of the kingdom and the source of our new identities in him.

In the closing verses of the chapter, Jesus returns to the notion of the *šālîach* in his one-to-one identification with his "sent ones." When someone receives the follower of Jesus, it is Jesus they have truly received. Moreover, they have received the Father who sent Jesus.

MATTHEW 11

JESUS' FAILURE TO MEET EXPECTATIONS

11:1-19

CAPERNAUM AND SODOM

11:20-24

THE PAINFUL JOY OF JESUS

11:25-30

JESUS' FAILURE TO MEET EXPECTATIONS

¹When Jesus had finished giving orders to His 12 disciples, He moved on from there to teach and preach in their towns. ²When John heard in prison what the Messiah was doing, he sent a message by his disciples ³and asked Him, "Are You the One who is to come, or should we expect someone else?"

⁴Jesus replied to them, "Go and report to John what you hear and see: ⁵the blind see, the lame walk, those with skin diseases are healed, the deaf hear, the dead are raised, and the poor are told the good news. ⁶And if anyone is not offended because of Me, he is blessed."

⁷As these men went away, Jesus began to speak to the crowds about John: "What did you go out into the wilderness to see? A reed swaying in the wind? ⁸What then did you go out to see? A man dressed in soft clothes? Look, those who wear soft clothes are in kings' palaces. ⁹But what did you go out to see? A prophet? Yes, I tell you, and far more than a prophet. ¹⁰This is the one it is written about:

> *Look, I am sending My messenger ahead of You;*
> *he will prepare Your way before You.*

¹¹"I assure you: Among those born of women no one greater than John the Baptist has appeared, but the least in the kingdom of heaven is greater than he. ¹²From the days of John the Baptist until now, the kingdom of heaven has been suffering violence, and the violent have been seizing it by force. ¹³For all the prophets and the Law prophesied until John; ¹⁴if you're willing to accept it, he is the Elijah who is to come. ¹⁵Anyone who has ears should listen!

¹⁶"To what should I compare this generation? It's like children sitting in the marketplaces who call out to each other:

> *¹⁷We played the flute for you,*
> *but you didn't dance;*
> *we sang a lament,*
> *but you didn't mourn!*

¹⁸For John did not come eating or drinking, and they say, 'He has a demon!' ¹⁹The Son of Man came eating and drinking, and they say, 'Look, a glutton and a drunkard, a friend of tax collectors and sinners!' Yet wisdom is vindicated by her deeds."

$\mathcal{M}$atthew 11 opens with a closing formula that marks the end of the second great block of Jesus' teaching in Matthew's Gospel (Mt 7:28; 13:53; 19:1; 26:1). Note that the emphasis remains on Galilee and the Galilean ministry, although the synagogue is not mentioned here (Mt 9:35; 12:9). Also notice that Matthew omits any reference to the Twelve returning from their mission and reporting back to Jesus (see Mk 6:30).

In Matthew 4:12, we learned of John's arrest. Now John sends a group of his disciples with what must be the most remarkable question in all of the New Testament. Only Matthew records it, perhaps because it is a question of identity. When we remember that John knew in utero that Jesus was sent by God (Lk 1:41), that John was the first to proclaim Jesus as the Lamb of God (Jn 1:29) and that he had heard God's own voice declaring the unique sonship of Jesus (Mt 3:17), this question is all the more remarkable: Is Jesus the One, or should they be expecting someone else? Clearly John has stumbled. Jesus has failed to meet his expectations—yes, even John's expectations! And if Jesus failed to meet John's expectations, certainly he is likely to fail to meet ours. There is nothing wrong with Jesus; it is our expectations that are patently wrong.

Perhaps John remembers that Jesus had come to set the captives free (Lk 4:18). Yet he remains confined in the Machaerus, one of Herod's grim fortresses. We know this detail only because of the account of Josephus (see appendix D).

The message Jesus sends back has two parts. First, he points to the signs of the coming of the Messiah from Isaiah 35:5 and 61:1. The blind see, the lame walk, the lepers are cured—then comes a *birkot*, a blessing: Blessed is he who is not offended because of me. Jesus promises a blessing for someone who has not stumbled, because certainly John is offended. He had never expected to end his life in prison for preaching the truth, his head cut off and given to a dancing girl.

The word used for "offend" is *skandalizo*. We get our word *scandal* from it. It has to do with causing someone to stumble unexpectedly (see Mt 13:57). Even in what appears to be failure, Jesus is fulfilling prophecy. This time it is Isaiah 8:14-15:

> He will be a stone to stumble over
> and a rock to trip over,
> and a trap and a snare to the inhabitants
> of Jerusalem.
> Many will stumble over those;
> they will fall and be broken;
> they will be snared and captured.

In Romans 9:32-33, Paul, also referring to a passage in Isaiah (28:16), will say,

> They stumbled over the stumbling stone.
> As it is written: Look! I am putting a stone in Zion
> to stumble over and a rock to trip over. (See 1 Pet 2:7-8.)

Even though the prophets had seen it long ago, Jesus sends a blessing to his cousin, whose days are numbered.

Though John expressed his doubts in regard to Jesus, Jesus has nothing but affirming things to say about John. Though he may not have been what people went out in the wilderness to see, not a fragile ascetic or a person dressed like a king, indeed he was a prophet and far more. He was the immediate precursor to the Messiah. Malachi had seen it (Mal 3:1).

Even as he talks about John, Jesus cannot keep his mind off the kingdom. As great a person as John was, whoever is least in the kingdom is greater even than John. Though all the evidence might seem to the contrary, the kingdom is advancing powerfully. John, the Elijah who was to come, had testified to it when he was standing in the middle of the Jordan.

"Anyone who has ears should listen!" is Jesus' way of saying, "If you refuse to engage and really listen with all your heart and mind, you are not going to get this."

The phrase in the opening of Matthew 11:16 is rabbinic in tone; "to what should I compare?" was a typical formula used to introduce a rabbinic parable. Jesus' parable has to do with the familiar image of children playing games. He quotes a little rhyme:[38] In their make-believe games, the children played the flute yet you did not dance. Later they made a game of singing a dirge, yet you would not play along and mourn. Neither John nor Jesus was willing to play the games of the world. They would not dance to the world's tune. John was an ascetic, eating only locusts and honey, yet the "children" called him demon possessed. Jesus, on the other hand, enjoyed eating and drinking, yet those same "children" accused him of being a glutton and a drunkard, a capital offense in Judaism (Deut 21:20-21).

CAPERNAUM AND SODOM

[20] Then He proceeded to denounce the towns where most of His miracles were done, because they did not repent: [21] "Woe to you, Chorazin! Woe to you, Bethsaida! For if the miracles that were done in you had been done in Tyre and Sidon, they would have repented in sackcloth and ashes long ago! [22] But I tell you, it will be more tolerable for Tyre and Sidon on the day of judgment than for you. [23] And you, Capernaum, will you be exalted to heaven? You will go down to Hades. For if the miracles that were done in you had been done in Sodom, it would have remained until today. [24] But I tell you, it will be more tolerable for the land of Sodom on the day of judgment than for you."

*I*f you listen closely to the text, you can imagine Jesus' anger rising. The thought of the Pharisees' game-playing irritates him. Next, thinking of the Galilean cities in which he performed his miracles and yet remained largely faithless, he pronounces prophetic "woes." Verse 21 is the only reference to Chorazin, a city on a hillside overlooking the Sea of Galilee about two miles from Capernaum. Archaeologists have excavated the remains of a large third-century synagogue there. It was almost certainly built over an earlier one in which Jesus would have preached. Bethsaida is less than a mile on the other side of Capernaum. It was the hometown of Peter, Andrew and Philip. Yet it was apparently unresponsive to the ministry of Jesus.

Finally Capernaum, of all cities, Jesus' adopted hometown, where Peter lived—even Capernaum is denounced by Jesus. Take note: these are all Galilean cities, yet they rejected Jesus and the kingdom he offered. Tyre, Sidon and even Sodom—those most pagan of cities, Gentile cities—would have repented had they known the privilege of hearing Jesus' words and having him come to them.

It is difficult to imagine the emotional impact these words must have had on the crowd and even on the Twelve.

THE PAINFUL JOY OF JESUS

[25]At that time Jesus said, "I praise You, Father, Lord of heaven and earth, because You have hidden these things from the wise and learned and revealed them to infants. [26]Yes, Father, because this was Your good pleasure. [27]All things have been entrusted to Me by My Father. No one knows the Son except the Father, and no one knows the Father except the Son and anyone to whom the Son desires to reveal Him.

[28]"Come to Me, all of you who are weary and burdened, and I will give you rest. [29]All of you, take up My yoke and learn from Me, because I am gentle and humble in heart, and you will find rest for yourselves. [30]For My yoke is easy and My burden is light."

*I*n a moment, Jesus' mood seems to change. In verse 25, he is praising the Father, who works in such mysterious ways for his good pleasure. In Luke 10:21, a more complete version of this story is provided. We are told that Jesus was "full of joy through the Holy Spirit" (NIV) at the thought of it.

I imagine Jesus speaking verse 27 to himself as much as to his disciples. It is almost as if he is assuring himself; yes, the Father has committed all things to him. Yes, he uniquely knows the Father and can reveal him to whomever he chooses (Jn 1:18). After the emotional roller coaster of the past several verses, Jesus is tired as he speaks the final comforting words of Matthew 11. He invites everyone who is weary, as he is weary at the moment, to come to him to find rest. He speaks as the rabbi once more as he makes reference to the yoke. To every Jewish person the word *yoke* meant one thing: the law.

The Mishnah says:

> *He that takes upon himself the yoke of the law,*
> *from him shall be taken away the yoke of the kingdom*

> *and the yoke of worldly care;*
> *but he that throws off the yoke of the law,*
> *upon him shall be laid the yoke of the kingdom*
> *and the yoke of worldly care.*[39]

(The reference to the "kingdom" has to do with repressive empires, like Rome, and not Jesus' kingdom.)

Jesus' invitation to take up his easy yoke and to learn from him—that is, to make him your only rabbi—is the most certain promise of rest. Why? Because he is manifestly gentle and humble. Unlike the 613 burdensome commands of the old orthodoxy, Jesus promises rest for the soul. The Pharisees have transformed the promise of Sabbath rest into a day of niggling observance. Jesus, who has come to fulfill the law, will reestablish the true rest that is the perfection of the law.

MATTHEW 12

THE IDENTITY OF JESUS: LORD OF THE SABBATH

¹At that time Jesus passed through the grainfields on the Sabbath. His disciples were hungry and began to pick and eat some heads of grain. ²But when the Pharisees saw it, they said to Him, "Look, Your disciples are doing what is not lawful to do on the Sabbath!"

³He said to them, "Haven't you read what David did when he and those who were with him were hungry—⁴how he entered the house of God, and they ate the sacred bread, which is not lawful for him or for those with him to eat, but only for the priests? ⁵Or haven't you read in the Law that on Sabbath days the priests in the temple violate the Sabbath and are innocent? ⁶But I tell you that something greater than the temple is here! ⁷If you had known what this means: I desire mercy and not sacrifice, you would not have condemned the innocent. ⁸For the Son of Man is Lord of the Sabbath."

*T*he closing verses of Matthew 11 prepared us for the opening story of chapter 12. Jesus had been reaching out, inviting his listeners to find rest (Sabbath) in him, to exchange the burdensome yoke of the Pharisees' old orthodoxy for the restful yoke of learning from him. As chapter 12 opens, it is the Sabbath, and Jesus' hungry disciples are picking and eating raw grain. They are perfectly within their rights to do so according to Deuteronomy 23:25, which allows a person to pick the grain from a neighbor's field with their bare hands. They are not allowed to use a sickle, since that would be considered harvesting.

The Pharisees do not see a group of starving men, tired from ministry. They only see a broken law: Exodus 20:8-11, the fourth commandment to honor the Sabbath by refraining from work. In their attempt to build a fence around the law, the Pharisees had expanded the definition of work (see appendix E).

Our temptation is often to roll our eyes at the legal exactitude of the Pharisees. We might better understand them and the New Testament world in general if we took seriously the fact that those who believe their relationship with God is dependent on their precise observance of the law are often operating out of genuine motives. We should remember that the Pharisees we encounter in the New Testament represent an extremely small cross section; those who tag along behind the crowds following Jesus were looking for violations while the vast majority of their group were at home working for the genuine spiritual welfare of their family and friends. It would be like someone, two thousand years from now, judging the entire Christian community based on a few hours of video from an offbeat splinter group.

Notice Jesus responds to the Pharisees with the words "haven't you read?" In Matthew 5, when speaking to the crowd, Jesus repeatedly said, "You have heard." But these are a group of highly educated and extremely well-read individuals. He refers to a passage in 1 Samuel (21:1-6) when David, who was fleeing from Saul, ate consecrated bread that was meant only for the priests to eat. Now Jesus, the Son of David, is on a different sort of mission, and his men are hungry too. Jesus parries once again, this time reminding them that even the priests do work by offering sacrifices on the Sabbath in the temple (Ex 29:38; Num 28:9).

The next three verses (Mt 12:6-8) tucked within the narration, at first might not appear to be the bombshell they truly are. However their effect is clearly seen in verse 14, when the Pharisees, for the first time, decide they are going to have to kill Jesus. First, Jesus says that he is greater than the temple. In the opening days of his ministry, when he tore up the temple market for the first time (Jn 2:13-19), in his anger he challenged the Jewish leaders that if they tore down this temple (referring to his body), he would raise it in three days. Even such a passing metaphorical allusion to the temple created a charge that would be used against his followers decades later (see Acts 6:14). Now Jesus openly states that he is greater than their most cherished institution—the temple—which, had it been built earlier in history, would have been considered one of the Seven Wonders of the World.

For the second time (see also Mt 9:13), Jesus quotes Hosea 6:6. If only the Pharisees understood that God desired *ḥesed* more than sacrifice, they would not have condemned the hungry disciples for plucking a few kernels of wheat. If they understood the loving kindness of God, they would have seen hungry human beings in need and not a violation of a law.

Finally, Jesus appropriates to himself that other most valued institution of the Pharisees: the Sabbath. It was not incendiary enough to say
that he was greater than the temple. Now Jesus declares that his lordship extends even over the Sabbath itself. This is an expression of what
true lordship simply means. *Lord* means *Lord*. In our own world, we
must determine what our most treasured point of orthodoxy is and then
realize that Jesus is even Lord over that.

THE FEARLESS HEALER

*⁹Moving on from there, He entered their synagogue. ¹⁰There He saw a
man who had a paralyzed hand. And in order to accuse Him they asked Him,
"Is it lawful to heal on the Sabbath?"*

*¹¹But He said to them, "What man among you, if he had a sheep that fell
into a pit on the Sabbath, wouldn't take hold of it and lift it out? ¹²A man is
worth far more than a sheep, so it is lawful to do what is good on the Sabbath."*

*¹³Then He told the man, "Stretch out your hand." So he stretched it out,
and it was restored, as good as the other. ¹⁴But the Pharisees went out and
plotted against Him, how they might destroy Him.*

*J*esus moves on, apparently with the Pharisees still in tow, and enters
the synagogue. It is still the Sabbath, and the Pharisees have begun to
look for reasons to accuse Jesus, who is only too happy to oblige them.

A man is there whose hand has atrophied (shriveled), probably due
to some sort of nerve damage. Jesus goes straight to the point, asking
the Pharisees if healing on the Sabbath is a violation of the law or not.
Mark tells us that at this moment Jesus was both extremely angry and
sorrowful because of the state of the Pharisees' hearts (Mk 3:5).

It is Jesus the rabbi who next appeals to them in their own language,
once more employing Hillel's *qal waḥōmer* ("how much more") argument. If an animal falls into a pit, you will pull him out on the Sabbath.
"How much more" a man. "Therefore it is lawful to do good on the
Sabbath," Jesus concludes.⁴⁰

What follows is one of Jesus' unmiraculous miracles. He makes no
pronouncement of healing, only the command to stretch out the with-

ered hand, which is immediately restored. In Matthew's Gospel this is where the plot begins. The Pharisees cannot silence or out-reason Jesus. The only thing left to do is to kill him (see Mk 14:1; Jn 5:18; 7:1; 11:53).

GOD'S GENTLE SERVANT

¹⁵*When Jesus became aware of this, He withdrew from there. Huge crowds followed Him, and He healed them all.* ¹⁶*He warned them not to make Him known,* ¹⁷*so that what was spoken through the prophet Isaiah might be fulfilled:*

> ¹⁸*Here is My Servant whom I have chosen,*
> *My beloved in whom My soul delights;*
> *I will put My Spirit on Him,*
> *and He will proclaim justice to the nations.*
> ¹⁹*He will not argue or shout,*
> *and no one will hear His voice in the streets.*
> ²⁰*He will not break a bruised reed,*
> *and He will not put out a smoldering wick,*
> *until He has led justice to victory.*
> ²¹*The nations will put their hope in His name.*

*I*n response to the plot to take his life, Jesus retreats, yet the crowds still follow him. Throughout the Gospels, whenever he tries to evade the presence of the crowd, he is always and eventually found out (see Mk 1:45; 7:24). Matthew lets us know that despite the fact that exercising his power to heal is working against Jesus' ministry, he still cannot resist the compassionate desire to heal them all, though he does warn them again not to tell anyone. This story provides an intimate look at Jesus' heart. He is the one who cannot help himself when it comes to the deep needs of the lost sheep around him. As we have come to expect from Matthew, he substantiates even this small character sketch of Jesus with a passage from the Old Testament. This time it is Isaiah 42:1-4. The image is of the gentle, young servant (the Greek word *pais* means either slave or boy). He is deeply loved by the Father (Mt 3:17).

And by the power of his Spirit, the gentle servant will accomplish what all the wars in history have not been able to provide: justice.

Matthew 12:19-21 completes the prophetic character sketch of Jesus, the gentle servant. He does not argue or raise his voice. He is manifestly gentle. A fragile reed that has been bent, he cannot bring himself to break. A guttering wick that is about to die, he will not blow out. This is his identity, his personality, and Isaiah saw it six hundred years before. Jesus will accomplish justice by the unlikely means of gentleness.

THE SON OF DAVID

22 Then a demon-possessed man who was blind and unable to speak was brought to Him. He healed him, so that the man could both speak and see. 23 And all the crowds were astounded and said, "Perhaps this is the Son of David!"

24 When the Pharisees heard this, they said, "The man drives out demons only by Beelzebul, the ruler of the demons."

25 Knowing their thoughts, He told them: "Every kingdom divided against itself is headed for destruction, and no city or house divided against itself will stand. 26 If Satan drives out Satan, he is divided against himself. How then will his kingdom stand? 27 And if I drive out demons by Beelzebul, who is it your sons drive them out by? For this reason they will be your judges. 28 If I drive out demons by the Spirit of God, then the kingdom of God has come to you. 29 How can someone enter a strong man's house and steal his possessions unless he first ties up the strong man? Then he can rob his house. 30 Anyone who is not with Me is against Me, and anyone who does not gather with Me scatters. 31 Because of this, I tell you, people will be forgiven every sin and blasphemy, but the blasphemy against the Spirit will not be forgiven. 32 Whoever speaks a word against the Son of Man, it will be forgiven him. But whoever speaks against the Holy Spirit, it will not be forgiven him, either in this age or in the one to come.

33 "Either make the tree good and its fruit good, or make the tree bad and its fruit bad; for a tree is known by its fruit. 34 Brood of vipers! How can you speak good things when you are evil? For the mouth speaks from the overflow of the heart. 35 A good man produces good things from his storeroom of good, and an evil man produces evil things from his storeroom of evil. 36 I tell you *that on the day of judgment people will have to account for every careless word they speak. ³⁷For by your words you will be acquitted, and by your words you will be condemned."*

$\mathcal{T}$he healing that takes place in Matthew 12:22 almost certainly takes place within the context of verse 15, when Jesus had withdrawn to a more secluded place and was warning people not to tell who he was. Matthew is not interested in the details of the healing of the blind and mute man who is possessed by a demon. The central issue is simply Jesus' power over the demonic. This power astonishes the people, who arrive at a conclusion that at first might not seem as obvious to you and me. They ask if, in light of the exorcism, Jesus might indeed be the Son of David. The piece of the puzzle you and I are missing is the fact that only David in all of the Old Testament was able to exorcise a demon (1 Sam 16:23). Now someone has come on the scene manifesting the same power, without even using a harp!

The Pharisees respond in language reminiscent of Matthew 9:34. Jesus' power over demons, they say, comes from the master of demons, Beelzebub (see 2 Kings 1:2). Jesus responds with two appeals to common sense: If Satan is driving out Satan, his house is divided against itself and will eventually fall. It just doesn't make sense. Similarly, you cannot rob a strong man's house unless you first tie him up. Satan simply wouldn't allow Jesus to rob his house. Again it simply does not make any sense.

In verse 27 Jesus acknowledges that some of the Pharisees have been successful in casting out demons. Does the illogic they are applying to Jesus apply to them as well? No, there is only one commonsense conclusion in the midst of all of this. Jesus cast out demons by the Spirit of God. The inescapable conclusion? The kingdom of God has come.

If it is true that the kingdom has come, empowered by the Spirit of God, then verses 30-32 follow as an inevitable conclusion. Jesus' challenge to the Pharisees rises or falls based on this conclusion. If the kingdom is here, those who are not with Jesus are working against him. Even as you cannot possibly serve Satan by driving out his demons, you cannot work against the kingdom of God and claim to be a part of that kingdom at the same time. Likewise, you cannot speak against the Spirit that empowers the kingdom. You might speak blasphemy against the representative of the kingdom, the Son of Man, and possibly be forgiven. But you cannot speak against the Spirit that empowers the kingdom without effectively and eternally being expelled from the kingdom. You cannot be pardoned when you deny the only possible means of forgiveness—that is, the Spirit.

GREATER THAN JONAH AND SOLOMON

38 Then some of the scribes and Pharisees said to Him, "Teacher, we want to see a sign from You."

39 But He answered them, "An evil and adulterous generation demands a sign, but no sign will be given to it except the sign of the prophet Jonah. 40 For as Jonah was in the belly of the huge fish three days and three nights, so the Son of Man will be in the heart of the earth three days and three nights. 41 The men of Nineveh will stand up at the judgment with this generation and condemn it, because they repented at Jonah's proclamation; and look—something greater than Jonah is here! 42 The queen of the south will rise up at the judgment with this generation and condemn it, because she came from the ends of the earth to hear the wisdom of Solomon; and look—something greater than Solomon is here!

43 "When an unclean spirit comes out of a man, it roams through waterless places looking for rest but doesn't find any. 44 Then it says, 'I'll go back to my house that I came from.' And returning, it finds the house vacant, swept, and put in order. 45 Then off it goes and brings with it seven other spirits more evil than itself, and they enter and settle down there. As a result, that man's last condition is worse than the first. That's how it will also be with this evil generation."

Could this group of Pharisees and scribes perhaps represent a different crowd? Or are they trying to change the subject, hoping to deflect the intensity of Jesus? A sign—they want to see a sign, when Jesus has just delivered a blind man from demonic possession. Whoever they are and whatever their motive, it doesn't seem to work. Jesus remains focused and intense. Asking for a sign reveals a precondition of the heart not to believe. It is an indication of wickedness. Even as Jesus will not dance to their tune (Mt 11:19), so now he will not yield to their disbelieving demands. People who ask for signs never believe them when they come.

"But, I take that back," Jesus might have said. A sign will be given—the sign of the prophet Jonah (who was also from Galilee). Jonah was in the fish's belly for three days (Jon 1:17), and the Son of Man will be in the heart of the earth for three days as well. The pagans responded when Jonah preached. Now someone greater than Jonah is here, and those same pagans will condemn the stubborn and disbelieving Pharisees on the Day of Judgment. The Queen of the South came all the way from Africa to listen to Solomon. Now someone greater than Solomon is here, and yet they refuse to listen.

This evil generation, which disbelievingly asks for signs, may indeed be delivered of their demons. But all they do with their empty house is sweep it clean. The Pharisees may have put their house in order, but they have not allowed it to be filled by the Spirit of the kingdom of God, the Spirit they have blasphemed. So what happens to their empty house? According to Jesus, it is reinhabited by seven other demons who are more evil still. The self-reformation of getting your house in order is worthless, according to Jesus. Your life must be filled by the kingdom's Spirit. Someone far greater than Jonah or Solomon, the gentle servant, the Son of David, the Lord of the Sabbath has spoken.

A NEW FAMILY OF FAITH

⁴⁶He was still speaking to the crowds when suddenly His mother and brothers were standing outside wanting to speak to Him. ⁴⁷Someone told Him, "Look, Your mother and Your brothers are standing outside, wanting to speak to You."

⁴⁸But He replied to the one who told Him, "Who is My mother and who are My brothers?" ⁴⁹And stretching out His hand toward His disciples, He said, "Here are My mother and My brothers! ⁵⁰For whoever does the will of My Father in heaven, that person is My brother and sister and mother."

We can use Mark's version of this story (Mk 3:21) to clarify this story. They are in Capernaum, probably in Peter's house.

The picture is one of Jesus being inundated by the crowd. His mother and brothers cannot even get into the house, it is so filled with people. They must send Jesus a message that they are waiting outside to see him. Once again, Matthew has stripped the story of detail. Only Mark tells us they have come to take Jesus away from the crowd. Jesus has been so covered up with ministry, he has ceased eating, and they are understandably worried. In fact, they have concluded that he is out of his mind (Mk 3:21).

But Matthew wants to focus on the heart of the story, not the details. He is interested in the demand of Jesus in regard to faith before family. Certainly Jesus is not violating the law concerning family (Ex 20:12). He will express his opinion on this clearly (Mt 15:4).

This is a moment that would have resonated with Matthew's original audience. Many of their families have determined that they are out of their minds as well. But for Matthew, that is not the point. Identity is the real issue. And he has good news for his first hearers, many of whom are about to lose their families. The good news: they have become the brothers and sisters of Jesus himself. They are now a part of his family, even as he chose, years ago in Capernaum, to make himself a part of their family.

MATTHEW 13

THE PARABLE OF THE SOILS

¹On that day Jesus went out of the house and was sitting by the sea. ²Such large crowds gathered around Him that He got into a boat and sat down, while the whole crowd stood on the shore.

³Then He told them many things in parables, saying: "Consider the sower who went out to sow. ⁴As he was sowing, some seed fell along the path, and the birds came and ate them up. ⁵Others fell on rocky ground, where there wasn't much soil, and they sprang up quickly since the soil wasn't deep. ⁶But when the sun came up they were scorched, and since they had no root, they withered. ⁷Others fell among thorns, and the thorns came up and choked them. ⁸Still others fell on good ground and produced a crop: some 100, some 60, and some 30 times what was sown. ⁹Anyone who has ears should listen!"

¹⁰Then the disciples came up and asked Him, "Why do You speak to them in parables?"

¹¹He answered them, "Because the secrets of the kingdom of heaven have been given for you to know, but it has not been given to them. ¹²For whoever has, more will be given to him, and he will have more than enough. But whoever does not have, even what he has will be taken away from him. ¹³For this reason I speak to them in parables, because looking they do not see, and hearing they do not listen or understand. ¹⁴Isaiah's prophecy is fulfilled in them, which says:

> You will listen and listen,
> yet never understand;
> and you will look and look,
> yet never perceive.
> ¹⁵For this people's heart has grown callous;
> their ears are hard of hearing,
> and they have shut their eyes;
> otherwise they might see with their eyes
> and hear with their ears,
> understand with their hearts
> and turn back—
> and I would cure them.

¹⁶"But your eyes are blessed because they do see, and your ears because they

do hear! [17]*For I assure you: Many prophets and righteous people longed to see the things you see yet didn't see them; to hear the things you hear yet didn't hear them.*

[18]*"You, then, listen to the parable of the sower:* [19]*When anyone hears the word about the kingdom and doesn't understand it, the evil one comes and snatches away what was sown in his heart. This is the one sown along the path.* [20]*And the one sown on rocky ground—this is one who hears the word and immediately receives it with joy.* [21]*Yet he has no root in himself, but is short-lived. When pressure or persecution comes because of the word, immediately he stumbles.* [22]*Now the one sown among the thorns—this is one who hears the word, but the worries of this age and the seduction of wealth choke the word, and it becomes unfruitful.* [23]*But the one sown on the good ground—this is one who hears and understands the word, who does bear fruit and yields: some 100, some 60, some 30 times what was sown."*

$\mathcal{M}$atthew 13 contains the third large block of Jesus' teaching (see appendix A). It is a collection of parables, each of which describes a different aspect of the kingdom with which Jesus has been so preoccupied. This scene is set in a particularly detailed way. We are told it was the same day, so we can imagine the emotional aftermath of the confrontation with Jesus' family. Also we see Jesus leaving the house, probably Peter's house, and sitting by the lake. The shore of the Sea of Galilee is exceedingly rocky, so this needs to be woven into our imaginative picture. The large crowd begins to collect around the once solitary Jesus to the point that he must move into a boat and push a little way from the shore.

Though Jesus has told small parabolic stories before in Matthew's Gospel, this is the first time the word "parable" (*parabolē*) is actually used. Though a few more parables will be sprinkled throughout the rest of the Gospel, this is the only block of parables. Two of the core parables in this collection are explained. The others don't really call for an unpacking. These parables are different in nature from the interactive parables of Jesus that call for identification with one or more characters in the story (for example, the prodigal son and the good Samaritan).

The parables of the kingdom are purely illustrative.

First is the parable of the soils (Mt 13:3-8). The farmer goes out to sow the seed. It is important to note that, in the ancient world, first the seed was sown and then the soil was turned over with the plow. This means the farmer in the parable is not carelessly scattering the seed. It is not immediately apparent what the true nature of the soil is before it is turned over by the plow.

First, wild birds swoop down and devour the seed when it has barely touched the ground. Next, some of the seed falls on rocky soil, which could not sustain the plants for very long. Other seed falls on soil that is already choked with thorns. Finally, some of the seed falls on good soil and produces a truly amazing harvest. Jesus concludes the first parable with his challenge to listen and hear. It is as if he is saying, "If you don't really listen with all of your heart and mind, you will not understand any of this." If you do not engage with your imagination, you might as well be unproductive soil.

In an aside, the disciples ask Jesus why he uses parables in his teaching. He responds that the mysteries of the kingdom are being given to them. Parables are a way of giving even more understanding to those who already have understanding. They also function in such a way as to take away from those who stubbornly refuse to understand, to hear or see.

Verse 13 is sometimes mistakenly interpreted to say that Jesus uses parables to blind and deafen people, that he is purposely trying to be obscure. The key is that the passage from Isaiah 6:9-13, which he quotes, should be understood in the light of fulfillment, a major theme in Matthew's Gospel. Even though they see (the miracles), they do not really see them. Even though they hear (the teaching), they do not understand. The purpose of all this is to fulfill Isaiah's prophecy. The people do not see or hear because of their own stubborn disbelief, their "callous" hearts (Mt 13:15). The Father's intention is not that they remain blind and deaf. In fact, if they would turn, he longs to heal them. Understanding the context of the words of Isaiah is the key, and the context was the continual and stubborn disbelief of the people.

Jesus' tone changes from frustration to thanksgiving in verse 16. He turns and pronounces a blessing on the disciples, because they do have the hearts to see and hear. In verses 18-23, Jesus explains the different soils to his disciples. The evil one is represented by the wild birds, which snatches up the seed. The rocky soil is the person who at first hears the word joyfully but is distracted by trouble and persecution, and so the seed is unfruitful. The thorny soil represents the person who receives the seed of the word but is choked by worries and wealth. Finally, the good soil is the person who hears and understands and produces a crop for the kingdom.

THE PARABLE OF THE WEEDS

²⁴He presented another parable to them: "The kingdom of heaven may be compared to a man who sowed good seed in his field. ²⁵But while people were sleeping, his enemy came, sowed weeds among the wheat, and left. ²⁶When the plants sprouted and produced grain, then the weeds also appeared. ²⁷The landowner's slaves came to him and said, 'Master, didn't you sow good seed in your field? Then where did the weeds come from?'

²⁸ "'An enemy did this!' he told them.

"'So, do you want us to go and gather them up?' the slaves asked him.

²⁹"'No,' he said. 'When you gather up the weeds, you might also uproot the wheat with them. ³⁰Let both grow together until the harvest. At harvest time I'll tell the reapers: Gather the weeds first and tie them in bundles to burn them, but store the wheat in my barn.'"

While the other Gospels contain the parable of the soils, the parable of the weeds is unique to Matthew's Gospel. Perhaps it relates directly to the life situation of his first hearers. Their small community might contain informers, spies who have been sown amidst their congregation. In this second kingdom parable, good seed is sown in a field. At night an enemy sows weeds among the wheat. The word for "weed" (*zizanion*) describes a weedy rye, which initially looks just like wheat, yet has poisonous seeds, which is evident in verse 26. It does not become apparent to the slaves (*douloi*) until the wheat matures. They double-check with the owner of the field, who assures them he planted good seed in the beginning. He concludes an enemy has tried to sabotage the crop. When the servants suggest they pull up the weeds, the owner directs them to let the two plants grow together, lest they accidentally pull up some of the wheat in the process. When the harvest comes, he says they will collect the weeds for burning and then gather the wheat into the barn.

Let's jump ahead to verses 36-43 for Jesus' explanation of this parable. Inside Peter's house, the disciples ask for a private explanation. Jesus identifies himself as the sower—that is, the Son of Man. The good seeds are the sons and daughters of the kingdom, and the weeds are those who belong to the evil one. The harvest is the end of the age, the Day of Judgment. The angels are the harvesters (Rev 14:15). The rest of the story unfolds predictably. The weeds are pulled up and thrown into the fire. The righteous ones shine like the sun, for they are the produce of the good seed planted by the Son of Man. Once more, Jesus concludes with the challenge to truly hear.

THE PARABLE OF THE MUSTARD SEED AND THE YEAST

31 He presented another parable to them: "The kingdom of heaven is like a mustard seed that a man took and sowed in his field. 32 It's the smallest of all the seeds, but when grown, it's taller than the vegetables and becomes a tree, so that the birds of the sky come and nest in its branches."

33 He told them another parable: "The kingdom of heaven is like yeast that a woman took and mixed into 50 pounds of flour until it spread through all of it."

34 Jesus told the crowds all these things in parables, and He would not speak anything to them without a parable, 35 so that what was spoken through the prophet might be fulfilled:

> *I will open My mouth in parables;*
> *I will declare things kept secret*
> *from the foundation of the world.*

36 Then He dismissed the crowds and went into the house. His disciples approached Him and said, "Explain the parable of the weeds in the field to us."

37 He replied: "The One who sows the good seed is the Son of Man; 38 the field is the world; and the good seed—these are the sons of the kingdom. The weeds are the sons of the evil one, ^{39}*and the enemy who sowed them is the Devil. The harvest is the end of the age, and the harvesters are angels.* ^{40}*Therefore, just as the weeds are gathered and burned in the fire, so it will be at the end of the age.* ^{41}*The Son of Man will send out His angels, and they will gather from His kingdom everything that causes sin and those guilty of lawlessness.* ^{42}*They will throw them into the blazing furnace where there will be weeping and gnashing of teeth.* ^{43}*Then the righteous will shine like the sun in their Father's kingdom. Anyone who has ears should listen!"*

*B*etween the parable of the weeds and Jesus' explanation lies a two-part parable, a section telling the same truth. The first part of the parable has to do with a mustard seed. In Jesus' day, it is the smallest seed anyone could imagine, yet it is capable of growing an enormous plant. The kingdom is like that, Jesus says.

In the second half of the parable, Jesus makes the same point with yet another image. This time he uses the picture of yeast, usually a negative metaphor in the Bible (see Mt 16:6-11). Like the tiny mustard seed, a small amount of yeast will leaven a large amount of dough. In both parables, what starts out as something small yields impressive results in the end. It is inherent in the nature of the mustard seed and the yeast. The kingdom is like that: though it starts out small, the promise is a remarkable harvest.

Matthew concludes this dual parable by stating that Jesus used parables whenever he talked to the crowd. For Matthew, even the way Jesus taught was a matter of prophetic fulfillment. This time the prophet is Asaph, the psalmist. In Psalm 78 he looked ahead and saw someone who would utter previously hidden and dark sayings. The point being, the truths of Jesus parables were hidden before. The parables are a means of unveiling truth, not making it more obscure.

THREE PARABLES UNIQUE TO MATTHEW

^{44}*"The kingdom of heaven is like treasure, buried in a field, that a man found and reburied. Then in his joy he goes and sells everything he has and buys that field.*

⁴⁵*"Again, the kingdom of heaven is like a merchant in search of fine pearls.*
⁴⁶*When he found one priceless pearl, he went and sold everything he had, and*
bought it.

⁴⁷*"Again, the kingdom of heaven is like a large net thrown into the sea. It*
collected every kind of fish, ⁴⁸*and when it was full, they dragged it ashore, sat*
down, and gathered the good fish into containers, but threw out the worthless
ones. ⁴⁹*So it will be at the end of the age. The angels will go out, separate the*
evil people from the righteous, ⁵⁰*and throw them into the blazing furnace. In*
that place there will be weeping and gnashing of teeth.

⁵¹*"Have you understood all these things?"*

"Yes," they told Him.

⁵²*"Therefore," He said to them, "every student of Scripture instructed in*
the kingdom of heaven is like a landowner who brings out of his storeroom
what is new and what is old." ⁵³*When Jesus had finished these parables, He*
left there.

*N*ext we jump ahead to yet another dual set of parables that teach
the same lesson. It should be obvious by now that if Jesus were purposely
being obscure, he would not teach with multiple and redundant examples. These are the parables of the treasure and the pearl (Mt 13:44-46).
Again, these stories are unique to Matthew. In part 1 of this section, the
kingdom is like a hidden treasure. Haphazardly it is discovered by someone who proceeds to rebury it in the field. He then joyfully sells all his
possessions to buy the field in order to possess the treasure. The point of
the parable is that the kingdom is worth giving up everything for.

Part 2 of the parable teaches the same lesson. Now it is a pearl that
is found by a businessman. Like the man who bought the field to own
the treasure, the businessman also sells everything to possess the valuable pearl. Like the treasure and the pearl, the kingdom of God is so
unutterably valuable that we must give up everything for the sake of
possessing it, even our lives.

The final parable of Matthew 13 presents the kingdom as a net.
This story would have resonated with Peter, James, Andrew and John.
Like any typical net, the net that is the kingdom gathers many different

kinds of fish. At the end of the day, the fishermen separate the good fish from the bad. In the parable, says Jesus, the fishermen represent the angels who will separate the evil from the good on the Day of Judgment, even as the sieves earlier separated the weeds from the wheat. These are straightforward parables, not in the least obscure. Jesus asks at the end of the lesson by the lake if his listeners understood (Mt 13:51). They respond, "Yes."

The next statement is another unique echo of Matthew's synagogue community. Only in Matthew does Jesus commend the scribe (*grammateus mathēteutheis*, the "student of Scripture") who has been instructed about the kingdom. This is clearly a positive reference to a scribe who is part of the Christian community—perhaps, some have even suggested, the Christian scribe who was responsible for writing the Gospel we know as Matthew.

THE END OF THE SYNAGOGUE MINISTRY

⁵⁴He went to His hometown and began to teach them in their synagogue, so that they were astonished and said, "How did this wisdom and these miracles come to Him? ⁵⁵Isn't this the carpenter's son? Isn't His mother called Mary, and His brothers James, Joseph, Simon, and Judas? ⁵⁶And His sisters, aren't they all with us? So where does He get all these things?" ⁵⁷And they were offended by Him.

But Jesus said to them, "A prophet is not without honor except in his hometown and in his household." ⁵⁸And He did not do many miracles there because of their unbelief.

*I*t has been a satisfying evening by the lake. The parables of the kingdom have been flowing from Jesus' imagination, and it seems that for once the people, or perhaps the disciples, actually seem to understand. Beginning in verse 53, Jesus moves on from Capernaum to his original hometown of Nazareth, about fifteen miles southeast. Once more he is in the synagogue, his familiar hometown synagogue, where he probably learned to read as a boy. Matthew, always sparse on details, omits the lesson Jesus gave that day. Luke 4 tells us Jesus read from the scroll of Isaiah and concluded the service with a brief sermon about how God historically had reached out to Gentiles before Jews. It is not hard to imagine how this message was received.

In Matthew's account, the ill feelings of the Nazarenes smolder long before they come to light. While at first they marvel at Jesus' wisdom, they gradually become disillusioned with the carpenter's son, whose family they all know by name. All of a sudden, perhaps after Luke's unrecorded sermon, they are offended by Jesus.

This was par for the course in the life of a prophet, who is not honored in his own hometown. From a luminous scene beside one of the most beautiful lakes in the world to a scene of rejection from what had once been a familiar setting. What would Jesus' emotional response to such a day have been?

But this is what the small beginnings of the kingdom are like: a mustard seed and a lump of yeast. If the parables are true, Jesus has every reason to hope. If the kingdom is truly worth selling everything for, even your own life, then perhaps as he left the dismal scene in Nazareth Jesus had reason to hope. After all, there are different kinds of soil; though this Nazareth crowd might be unproductive, there are other more fertile soils waiting to hear the word that is the seed of the kingdom of God.

MATTHEW 14

THE LUDICROUS DEATH OF JOHN

14:1–12

THE MIRACLE OF PERFECT PROVISION

14:13–21

THEIR FIRST TIME TO WORSHIP

14:22–36

THE LUDICROUS DEATH OF JOHN

¹At that time Herod the tetrarch heard the report about Jesus. ²"This is John the Baptist!" he told his servants. "He has been raised from the dead, and that's why supernatural powers are at work in him."

³For Herod had arrested John, chained him, and put him in prison on account of Herodias, his brother Philip's wife, ⁴since John had been telling him, "It's not lawful for you to have her!" ⁵Though he wanted to kill him, he feared the crowd, since they regarded him as a prophet.

⁶But when Herod's birthday celebration came, Herodias's daughter danced before them and pleased Herod. ⁷So he promised with an oath to give her whatever she might ask. ⁸And prompted by her mother, she answered, "Give me John the Baptist's head here on a platter!" ⁹Although the king regretted it, he commanded that it be granted because of his oaths and his guests. ¹⁰So he sent orders and had John beheaded in the prison. ¹¹His head was brought on a platter and given to the girl, who carried it to her mother. ¹²Then his disciples came, removed the corpse, buried it, and went and reported to Jesus.

$\mathcal{M}$atthew 14 begins a solitary section of Jesus' ministry. In verse 13 he will retreat to a secluded place, apparently to mourn for his cousin John. Nevertheless, the crowds are able to find him, and he is eventually mobbed by at least ten thousand hungry people. Again, in verse 23, he retreats into the hills for solitary prayer, but is interrupted by the disciples, who were caught in a windstorm.

In verse 1, Herod is described as a tetrarch, a term that originally meant a ruler over a fourth part of the kingdom but eventually was used to describe anyone who ruled any segment of a divided province. In Herod Antipas's case, it was the third of his father Herod the Great's original kingdom. Antipas ruled for a lengthy thirty-five years (4 B.C.– A.D. 39). His wife, Herodias, eventually undermined his rule by overstepping her bounds with the insane Caligula. Herod has somehow heard about Jesus of Nazareth and falsely concludes that he is John the Baptist risen from the dead. This bizarre conclusion is a small window into his fragmented mind. This misunderstanding becomes the occasion for Matthew's Gospel to give an account of John's murder.

Josephus tells us that John had been held in the Macherus, one of Herod the Great's grim castle-fortresses, on Antipas's orders (see appendix D). John had publicly denounced Herod's adulterous relationship with his brother Philip's wife, Herodias (see Lev 18:16; 20:21), and for that Herodias influenced her husband to have John arrested.

On a visit to Rome to see Philip, Herod had fallen in love with Herodias and seduced her. Next he divorced his own wife, the daughter of King Aretas IV. He convinced Herodias to divorce his brother and marry him. The father of his ex-wife started a border war over the incident.

Now it is Herod's birthday, and a party is being given in his honor. This, in itself, would have been looked down upon by the Jews, who viewed birthday celebrations as a Gentile custom. In the course of the evening, his stepdaughter (we know only that her name was Salome from Josephus) pleases him with a questionable dance. Perhaps in a drunken stupor, Herod promises her more than he has the authority to give. Yet, through her mother's influence, all she wants is John the Baptist's head on a platter.

To avoid being humiliated in front of his guests, Herod concedes to her demand, and the greatest prophet of all time dies a ludicrous death, his head chopped off and given to a dancing girl.

John's disciples claim the body and report the devastating news to Jesus, who retreats to a lonely place, presumably to mourn (Mt 14:13).

THE MIRACLE OF PERFECT PROVISION

13When Jesus heard about it, He withdrew from there by boat to a remote place to be alone. When the crowds heard this, they followed Him on foot from the towns. 14As He stepped ashore, He saw a huge crowd, felt compassion for them, and healed their sick.

15When evening came, the disciples approached Him and said, "This place is a wilderness, and it is already late. Send the crowds away so they can go into the villages and buy food for themselves."

16"They don't need to go away," Jesus told them. "You give them something to eat."

[17] "But we only have five loaves and two fish here," they said to Him.

[18] "Bring them here to Me," He said. [19] Then He commanded the crowds to sit down on the grass. He took the five loaves and the two fish, and looking up to heaven, He blessed them. He broke the loaves and gave them to the disciples, and the disciples gave them to the crowds. [20] Everyone ate and was filled. Then they picked up 12 baskets full of leftover pieces! [21] Now those who ate were about 5,000 men, besides women and children.

*J*esus fails in his attempt to find solitude. He turns around and five thousand men, possibly a total crowd of ten thousand or more, are standing behind him. His response? His heart goes out to them in compassion.

They must have spent the majority of the day together, with Jesus teaching and healing. The disciples understandably become worried about providing for the mob. They need to go into town and buy food.

Perhaps with a twinkle in his eye, Jesus responds, "You give them something." It was Jesus' habit, then as now, to give impossible tasks to his disciples, not that they should be defeated but that they would learn to depend on his perfect provision.

The disciples round up five loaves of bread and two small fish. John tells us they took them from a little boy. It is a hopeless situation.

It is yet another of Jesus' unmiraculous miracles. Look closely at the text; there is not a word of miraculous language. There is no pronouncement, no waving of hands in the air. In fact, many scholars have concluded that in fact no miracle took place. But this is to misunderstand the way Jesus performed most of his miracles.

He simply pronounces the *bĕrākāh*, or blessing.[41] Then he hands the food to the disciples, who distribute it to the hungry people. Even the crowd seems unaware that a miracle has occurred.

After the miraculous feeding comes the real miracle, in my opinion. Jesus commands the disciples to pick up the leftovers (Jn 6:12). They scour the hillside and gather twelve small baskets of crumbs. The word used for "basket" is *kophinos*, a lunch-pail-sized basket. If you don't engage with your imagination, you will miss the real miracle, which was not one of abundance. The miracle of the feeding of the five thousand was one of perfect provision. The twelve disciples collected twelve small baskets of crumbs so that they too might be fed. All this is by the power of the one who had taught them to pray only for their daily bread and who apparently never uses that power to feed himself.

THEIR FIRST TIME TO WORSHIP

²²Immediately He made the disciples get into the boat and go ahead of Him to the other side, while He dismissed the crowds. ²³After dismissing the crowds, He went up on the mountain by Himself to pray. When evening came, He was there alone. ²⁴But the boat was already over a mile from land, battered by the waves, because the wind was against them. ²⁵Around three in the morning, He came toward them walking on the sea. ²⁶When the disciples saw Him walking on the sea, they were terrified. "It's a ghost!" they said, and cried out in fear.

²⁷Immediately Jesus spoke to them. "Have courage! It is I. Don't be afraid."

²⁸"Lord, if it's You," Peter answered Him, "command me to come to You on the water. ²⁹"Come!" He said.

And climbing out of the boat, Peter started walking on the water and came toward Jesus. ³⁰But when he saw the strength of the wind, he was afraid. And beginning to sink he cried out, "Lord, save me!"

³¹Immediately Jesus reached out His hand, caught hold of him, and said to him, "You of little faith, why did you doubt?" ³²When they got into the boat, the wind ceased. ³³Then those in the boat worshiped Him and said, "Truly You are the Son of God!"

³⁴Once they crossed over, they came to land at Gennesaret. ³⁵When the men of that place recognized Him, they alerted the whole vicinity and brought to Him all who were sick. ³⁶They were begging Him that they might only touch the tassel on His robe. And as many as touched it were made perfectly well.

*A*fter the enormous corporate meal, there is an apparent urgency in Jesus to send the disciples away and dismiss the crowd. John provides the missing key. He tells us the crowd was contemplating making Jesus a king by force (Jn 6:15). Jesus sends them all away as quickly as possible and renews his attempt at solitude.

When you stand on top of any of the hills surrounding the Sea of Galilee, you can always see a boat anywhere on the lake. As Jesus goes to prayer, he looks down and sees the disciples rowing against a contrary wind. This is not the same kind of storm we saw earlier in Matthew 8.

Between three and six in the morning, the exhausted disciples see a figure coming toward them, moving across the water. Only one thing floats above the water in their minds, a ghost (*phantasma*). Above the noise of the wind and their own screaming, they hear a familiar voice. He shouts, "It is I," or literally "I AM." This is the unutterable name of God from Exodus 3:14, the name whose pronunciation is now lost; we can only approximate it as Yahweh.

Only Matthew provides the detail of Peter walking on the water in his account. Peter is not the buffoon he is often portrayed as being. His words to Jesus here are complicated. First he says, "If it's You." It remains a very real possibility that Peter thinks this is a ghost or a delusion, perhaps the aftereffects of a piece of undigested fish. His next statement is even more interesting. "Command me to come to You," Peter cries out. He seems to understand that if he is to come to Jesus, to walk on the water, the impetus must begin with Jesus. Only his command and not Peter's intentions can make a miracle come true. It is no simpleton who makes the request. This is the first such miracle performed by a disciple.

Jesus simply responds, "Come!"

That Peter must "climb" out of the boat is an indication of the size of the ship. Rembrandt, in one of his sketches of this incident, shows Peter hanging from the gunwales. Then, it occurs. Peter walks on the water confidently, believingly. At some point the wind and the waves, perhaps even his own common sense, begin to work against the miracle and Peter begins to sink. And this is when the real miracle occurs.

"Lord, save me!" he cries.

The miracle? The "if" of verse 28 has disappeared completely. The deeper truth of this story is that often sinking is more important than walking, more life-changing, more transformational.

Immediately Jesus is there to help, reaching out his hand and catching his confused and frightened friend. And then comes another miracle we often overlook. When the two climb back up into the boat, for the very first time in all their months together, the disciples "worship" Jesus. "You are the Son of God," they confess in the stillness that had settled around them.

The time for solitude is over. As they land on the other side of the lake, close to the Plain of Gennesaret, on the northwest shore of the Sea of Galilee, they are surrounded once more.[42] The rumor has reached here that by touching the fringe of Jesus' prayer shawl someone can be healed (see Mt 9:20). The Pharisees are waiting as well, with more vexing questions. If you have ever desperately sought out solitude for yourself and were unable to find it, know that you cannot experience any frustration that Jesus has not first experienced.

MATTHEW 15

JESUS ATTACKS THE ORAL LAW

15:1–20

BREAD FOR THE PUPPIES

15:21–28

A MIRACLE OF ABUNDANCE

15:29–39

JESUS ATTACKS THE ORAL LAW

[1]*Then Pharisees and scribes came from Jerusalem to Jesus and asked,* [2]*"Why do Your disciples break the tradition of the elders? For they don't wash their hands when they eat!"*

[3]*He answered them, "And why do you break God's commandment because of your tradition?* [4]*For God said:*

> *Honor your father and your mother; and,*
> *The one who speaks evil of father or mother*
> *must be put to death.*

[5]*But you say, 'Whoever tells his father or mother, "Whatever benefit you might have received from me is a gift committed to the temple"—* [6]*he does not have to honor his father.' In this way, you have revoked God's word because of your tradition.* [7]*Hypocrites! Isaiah prophesied correctly about you when he said:*

> [8]*These people honor Me with their lips,*
> *but their heart is far from Me.*
> [9]*They worship Me in vain,*
> *teaching as doctrines the commands of men."*

[10]*Summoning the crowd, He told them, "Listen and understand:* [11]*It's not what goes into the mouth that defiles a man, but what comes out of the mouth, this defiles a man."*

[12]*Then the disciples came up and told Him, "Do You know that the Pharisees took offense when they heard this statement?"*

[13]*He replied, "Every plant that My heavenly Father didn't plant will be uprooted.* [14]*Leave them alone! They are blind guides. And if the blind guide the blind, both will fall into a pit."*

[15]*Then Peter replied to Him, "Explain this parable to us."*

[16]*"Are even you still lacking in understanding?" He asked.* [17]*"Don't you realize that whatever goes into the mouth passes into the stomach and is eliminated?* [18]*But what comes out of the mouth comes from the heart, and this defiles a man.* [19]*For from the heart come evil thoughts, murders, adulteries, sexual immoralities, thefts, false testimonies, blasphemies.* [20]*These are the things that defile a man, but eating with unwashed hands does not defile a man."*

*T*he confrontation with the Pharisees and the scribes who have come all the way from Jerusalem represents a ratcheting up of the pressure on Jesus to conform. Jesus' disciples appear to be lax in many areas of legal observance, especially in regard to the Sabbath and their willingness to associate freely with sinners. According to the Pharisees, neither are they observing the tradition of the elders involving the washing of hands before they eat.

The battle lines will be drawn between the command of God, which Jesus champions, and the traditions of the elders or the oral law, embraced by the Pharisees. When Moses came down from Mount Sinai with the Ten Commandments, he entrusted them to the priests. What was Moses doing during the other forty days and nights on the mountain? The Pharisees reasoned God was entrusting to Moses the oral law, which eventually were handed down to the 120 elders of the Great Synagogue during the time of Ezra. The Pharisees considered themselves the descendents of these elders. According to the rabbinical Pirke Aboth ("Sayings of the Fathers"), "Moses received the (Oral) Law from Sinai and committed it to Joshua, and Joshua to the elders, and the elders to the Prophets; and the Prophets committed it to the men of the Great Synagogue."[43] The Pharisees therefore claimed their authority came directly from Moses by way of the elders of Israel.

Jesus counters their question with a much more inflammatory one: "Why do you break God's command because of your traditions?" Referring to the fifth commandment (Ex 20:12), Jesus says the Pharisees have violated it as well as the law that says anyone who dishonors a parent must be put to death (Ex 21:17). In Jesus' mind, their violation is centered on a tradition known as *korban*. This was a scheme to avoid parental responsibility. An older child could declare anything *korban* or "committed to the temple." This did not mean that it would immediately be turned over to the temple treasury, only that it was dedicated to be given eventually. Grown children were devoting to the temple money that was supposed to be used to provide for their aging parents. Jesus attacks this tradition as a violation of the fifth commandment.

He quotes Isaiah, who refers to such traditions as "rules taught by men" (Is 29:13 NIV 1984). Since 90 percent of the oral law involves rules of clean and unclean, Jesus redefines in strictly spiritual terms what causes uncleanness (Mt 15:11). What goes into a person's mouth does not render one unclean, but what comes out of the mouth. What goes into the mouth eventually passes through the body, says Jesus (Mt 15:17). But what comes out of the mouth has its source in the heart. It is not dirty hands that render a person unclean but an unclean heart.

BREAD FOR THE PUPPIES

²¹When Jesus left there, He withdrew to the area of Tyre and Sidon. ²²Just then a Canaanite woman from that region came and kept crying out, "Have mercy on me, Lord, Son of David! My daughter is cruelly tormented by a demon."

²³Yet He did not say a word to her. So His disciples approached Him and urged Him, "Send her away because she cries out after us."

²⁴He replied, "I was sent only to the lost sheep of the house of Israel."

²⁵But she came, knelt before Him, and said, "Lord, help me!"

²⁶He answered, "It isn't right to take the children's bread and throw it to their dogs."

²⁷"Yes, Lord," she said, "yet even the dogs eat the crumbs that fall from their masters' table!"

²⁸Then Jesus replied to her, "Woman, your faith is great. Let it be done for you as you want." And from that moment her daughter was cured.

*J*esus and his disciples move on once more, all the way up to the coast of the Mediterranean, some forty miles away. This is now the third time he seems to be trying to get away from the crowd. Mark will specifically say Jesus was trying to keep his presence there a secret (Mk 7:24).

Here he encounters a desperate woman whose daughter is possessed by a demon. She is described as a Canaanite, traditionally Israel's worst enemies in Old Testament times (Jezebel had been from the town of Sidon; 1 Kings 16:31). Three times she will address Jesus as "Lord." She initially comes crying out to him, "Son of David!" Most significantly she comes asking for something she knows she does not deserve:

mercy. No one who asks Jesus for mercy will ever be turned away.

It is difficult to guess just why Jesus initially ignores the woman. Is he testing her? Finally the frustrated disciples ask him to send the woman away. In verse 24, it is almost as if Jesus is talking to himself. Like the first time he sent out the disciples (Mt 10:5-6), he says he is sent only to the lost sheep of Israel. Again she cries out, "Lord, help me!"

Jesus' initial response is frequently misunderstood to mean he is calling the woman a "dog," an animal that was unclean in Judaism. However, the term he uses in every account is the diminutive *puppy*. It is an image from her world, for Gentiles were known to keep dogs as pets. Jesus is still gently pushing her away. For the third time she calls Jesus "Lord." He evidently finds her response engaging, if not charming. Even puppies get crumbs from the table. She is not asking to violate his program that for the moment is focused on the Jews. She is only asking for their leftover crumbs, just as the disciples had eaten the leftover crumbs at the first miraculous feeding.

The term *woman* is also less abrupt than it sounds to our ears. Jesus refers to his own mother with this word in John 2:4. It actually has the force of a loving "my dear."

The healing of the daughter happens offstage, almost as an afterthought, because the miracle is not the point of the story. The point, the real miracle if you will, is the persistent faith of the Gentile woman, who asks for what she knows she does not deserve.

A MIRACLE OF ABUNDANCE

[29]*Moving on from there, Jesus passed along the Sea of Galilee. He went up on a mountain and sat there,* [30]*and large crowds came to Him, having with them the lame, the blind, the deformed, those unable to speak, and many others. They put them at His feet, and He healed them.* [31]*So the crowd was amazed when they saw those unable to speak talking, the deformed restored, the lame walking, and the blind seeing. And they gave glory to the God of Israel.*

[32]*Now Jesus summoned His disciples and said, "I have compassion on the crowd, because they've already stayed with Me three days and have nothing to eat. I don't want to send them away hungry; otherwise they might collapse on the way."*

33The disciples said to Him, "Where could we get enough bread in this desolate place to fill such a crowd?"

34"How many loaves do you have?" Jesus asked them.

"Seven," they said, "and a few small fish."

35After commanding the crowd to sit down on the ground, 36He took the seven loaves and the fish, and He gave thanks, broke them, and kept on giving them to the disciples, and the disciples gave them to the crowds. 37They all ate and were filled. Then they collected the leftover pieces—seven large baskets full. 38Now those who ate were 4,000 men, besides women and children. 39After dismissing the crowds, He got into the boat and went to the region of Magadan.

Once more they return to Galilee, the focus of so much of Matthew's Gospel and the calm lake from which Jesus appears to draw some measure of peace. Mark's Gospel gives more detail in regard to the route, which seems to avoid Capernaum, skirting the lakeshore and heading back into the area of the Decapolis, a thoroughly Gentile region (Mk 7:31). Earlier Jesus had healed two demoniacs in this region, sending them home with the instructions to tell how much the Lord had done for them (Mk 5:19). Apparently they had obeyed Jesus, for now when he returns to the area, large crowds are waiting to meet him.

Having just come from the Gentile area of Tyre and Sidon, and now in yet another Gentile area, he exercises his gifts and heals the lame, blind, crippled, dumb and many others. Listen closely to the amazed response of the Gentile crowd. Matthew tells us they gave "glory to the God of Israel." Once again, Jesus is never praised when he performs miracles. He always wins praise for the Father.

Jesus has been in the area for three days when he finally tells the disciples the people need to be fed lest they "collapse on the way." Having so soon forgotten the feeding of the five thousand, the disciples wonder aloud foolishly where they might get so much bread.

When Jesus asks them how many loaves they have, they respond, "Seven . . . and a few small fish." The pattern is repeated once again. The people are made to sit down. Jesus offers a simple blessing. The disciples hand out the food, and everyone is filled. Again, there is no miracle language, no sign that anyone even noticed a miracle had occurred. What is different, apart from the size of the crowd, is that when the disciples pick up the leftovers, they come up with seven basketfuls.

In all the accounts of this feeding of the four thousand, a unique word is used for "basket." The Greek term is *spyris*, which denotes a man-sized basket like the one used to lower Paul through an opening in the wall in Acts 9:25.

Earlier at the feeding of the five thousand, the miracle was the perfect provision of twelve small baskets for the Twelve. At the feeding of the four thousand, the miracle is abundance, as seven man-sized baskets of leftovers are collected. In Matthew 16:9-10 Jesus will recap the two miracles for the disciples and be careful to use the two different words for "basket." The key to understanding the two miracles is found in the small detail of the different types of baskets.

Now that Jesus' concern for the crowd's welfare is satisfied, they get into the boat once more and go directly across the lake to the area of Magadan (probably a variant of Magdala). Once more the Pharisees will be waiting, but this time Jesus and his disciples will be joined by a new group of adversaries.

MATTHEW 16

ENGAGING THE PHARISEES

16:1–4

THE YEAST OF THE PHARISEES

16:5–12

PETER'S CONFESSION AND BLESSING

16:13–20

PETER'S REBUKE AND CURSING

16:21–28

ENGAGING THE PHARISEES

¹The Pharisees and Sadducees approached, and as a test, asked Him to show them a sign from heaven.

²He answered them: "When evening comes you say, 'It will be good weather because the sky is red.' ³And in the morning, 'Today will be stormy because the sky is red and threatening.' You know how to read the appearance of the sky, but you can't read the signs of the times. ⁴An evil and adulterous generation demands a sign, but no sign will be given to it except the sign of Jonah." Then He left them and went away.

$\mathcal{T}$he Pharisees and Sadducees were normally at odds with each other.[44] The Sadducees did not believe in the resurrection and held only the books of Moses as authoritative. The Pharisees accepted the Law as well as the Prophets and believed in the reality of the resurrection. Beyond their theological disagreements, they were also actively engaged in a struggle for the hearts and minds of the people. The Pharisees represented a "back to the Bible" movement. The Sadducees were committed to wealth and political power. Something bigger than all their differences has brought them together: their mutual hatred of Jesus.

They are waiting on the shoreline to test Jesus by asking him to perform a "sign from heaven," which is to say, a sign from God. Jesus responds by pointing to signs from heaven, to red evening skies that are a sign of a clear day to come and to red morning skies that are a sign of storms. What's more, they have been given the signs of the time, all of which clearly point to the coming of the kingdom. The deaf hear, the blind see and the dead are raised to life (Mt 11:5). No sign will be given them, says Jesus, but the sign of Jonah (see comments on Mt 12:38).

THE YEAST OF THE PHARISEES

⁵The disciples reached the other shore, and they had forgotten to take bread.

⁶Then Jesus told them, "Watch out and beware of the yeast of the Pharisees and Sadducees."

⁷And they discussed among themselves, "We didn't bring any bread."

[8]Aware of this, Jesus said, "You of little faith! Why are you discussing among yourselves that you do not have bread? [9]Don't you understand yet? Don't you remember the five loaves for the 5,000 and how many baskets you collected? [10]Or the seven loaves for the 4,000 and how many large baskets you collected? [11]Why is it you don't understand that when I told you, 'Beware of the yeast of the Pharisees and Sadducees,' it wasn't about bread?" [12]Then they understood that He did not tell them to beware of the yeast in bread, but of the teaching of the Pharisees and Sadducees.

Once again Jesus and his disciples board their little ship and cross the lake. Perhaps it was because of their sudden departure that the disciples forgot to bring bread. Fresh from his conflict with these two influential groups, Jesus warns the disciples against the teaching of the Pharisees and Sadducees, using the metaphor of yeast. Here he returns to the Old Testament symbol of yeast as sin (Ex 12:8, 15-20). Once more his language is obscure to them.

Overhearing their whispered conversation, Jesus confronts the disciples. His response is filled with frustration, a frustration that will continue to grow with the disciples, coming to a peak in Matthew 17:17 when Jesus finally laments, "How much longer must I put up with you?"

Bread. Why are they discussing having no bread? Have they already forgotten the twelve *spyres*, the sign of perfect provision? And the seven *kophinoi*. Was that enough bread for them? Jesus' frustration seems to jar the disciples to awareness. Under this emotional pressure they realize that he was talking about the false teaching of the Pharisees and the Sadducees.

PETER'S CONFESSION AND BLESSING

[13]When Jesus came to the region of Caesarea Philippi, He asked His disciples, "Who do people say that the Son of Man is?"

[14]And they said, "Some say John the Baptist; others, Elijah; still others, Jeremiah or one of the prophets."

[15]"But you," He asked them, "who do you say that I am?"

[16]Simon Peter answered, "You are the Messiah, the Son of the living God!"

[17]And Jesus responded, "Simon son of Jonah, you are blessed because flesh and blood did not reveal this to you, but My Father in heaven. [18]And I also say to you that you are Peter, and on this rock I will build My church, and the forces of Hades will not overpower it. [19]I will give you the keys of the kingdom of heaven, and whatever you bind on earth is already bound in heaven, and whatever you loose on earth is already loosed in heaven."

[20]And He gave the disciples orders to tell no one that He was the Messiah.

Given the emotional strain due to Jesus' frustration with the disciples, I wonder what was the tone of their conversation during the twenty-five-mile hike up to Caesarea Philippi, a thoroughly pagan city filled with temples to Pan, to dancing goats and even to Caesar himself. What was Jesus' purpose in bringing them so far into such a place to ask this important question? It is a two-part question; the first prepares for the second.

First, "Who do people say that the Son of Man is?" The disciples respond with a list of prophets, from John the Baptist to Elijah to Jeremiah, the weeping prophet. The second question is more direct, more pointed, and calls for a more costly answer: "Who do you say that I am?"

Peter, in whom the Twelve already possess a corporate identity, answers Jesus' second question, though not exactly as it was asked—that is, he does not begin his answer, "We say you are . . ." Peter speaks with a confidence that comes from outside himself. "You are," he responds, "the Messiah, the Son of the living God!"

Jesus' frustration vanishes for the moment. His face brightens, and he pronounces a *bĕrākāh* on Simon, who is speaking words that were revealed to him by the Father. Jesus had predicted he would be called Peter (Jn 1:42). Now the moment has come, and his confession has actualized that name. "You are Peter," Jesus responds. In a Gospel based on identity, this is a supreme moment. The two friends are defining each other. You are the Christ. You are Peter, the rock. And on that rock, Jesus will found his own synagogue, his own congregation. (The Greek word usually translated here as "church" should almost certainly be translated "congregation"; see Heb 2:12.)

The congregation founded on the rock will be unstoppable; the gates of Hades will not come against it. "I will give you [*you* is plural here, referring to all the disciples] the keys of the kingdom." The disciples will ultimately be about what the congregation is all about: binding the influences of the evil one and loosing or setting free those who have been held captive. This is a light and luminous moment between Jesus and his disciples. Yet on the way down the mountain, he warns them to keep it all a secret. The reason for the command to secrecy will be revealed in the next section.

PETER'S REBUKE AND CURSING

21From then on Jesus began to point out to His disciples that He must go to Jerusalem and suffer many things from the elders, chief priests, and scribes, be killed, and be raised the third day. 22Then Peter took Him aside and began to rebuke Him, "Oh no, Lord! This will never happen to You!"

23But He turned and told Peter, "Get behind Me, Satan! You are an offense to Me because you're not thinking about God's concerns, but man's."

24Then Jesus said to His disciples, "If anyone wants to come with Me, he must deny himself, take up his cross, and follow Me. 25For whoever wants to save his life will lose it, but whoever loses his life because of Me will find it. 26What will it benefit a man if he gains the whole world yet loses his life? Or what will a man give in exchange for his life? 27For the Son of Man is going to come with His angels in the glory of His Father, and then He will reward each according to what he has done. 28I assure you: There are some standing here who will not taste death until they see the Son of Man coming in His kingdom."

*N*ow that the word *Christ* has been spoken with faith, Jesus must begin the process of undeceiving the disciples. The picture or image of the Messiah they have inherited from the Judaism of the day (most particularly from the Pharisees) is that of a glorious king who will conquer the Romans, establishing his throne in Jerusalem. It is an image they will cling to all the way to the cross.

Jesus begins to explain that, starting at this moment, they are leaving for Jerusalem, where he will suffer and be killed. When the disciples hear the word *killed* or *cross*, they always stop listening. This is why they never seem to hear Jesus' words about being raised from the dead. They are simply too stunned when they hear him say he is going to die, especially in such a grotesque way.

When Peter takes Jesus aside and rebukes him for saying he must suffer, he is betraying the fact that he is still invested in the old definition of the triumphant Messiah king. He echoes the teaching of the Pharisees when he says, "It will never happen to you." But more than that, he understands that his identity is forever rooted in Jesus' identity. When he confessed a moment before that Jesus was the Christ, that confession had clear implications for Peter as well.

In verse 23, Jesus turns the blessing of verse 17 into a curse. Peter is no longer speaking the words of God, but the words of man. He has become Jesus' adversary. The rock is now a stumbling stone.

Jesus concludes by cementing his identity and fate with theirs. If they follow him, they too must take up a cross. Jesus defines them. If they want to save their lives or souls, they must lose them. Nothing is more precious than the life or the soul. But they are not to be fooled. The Son of Man will come someday in glory with his angels. In fact, three of them will be entrusted in just six days with a precursory vision of that glory.

MATTHEW 17

THE TRANSFIGURATION

17:1–13

"HAVE MERCY"

17:14–23

AN UNMIRACULOUS MIRACLE

17:24–27

THE TRANSFIGURATION

¹After six days Jesus took Peter, James, and his brother John and led them up on a high mountain by themselves. ²He was transformed in front of them, and His face shone like the sun. Even His clothes became as white as the light. ³Suddenly, Moses and Elijah appeared to them, talking with Him.

⁴Then Peter said to Jesus, "Lord, it's good for us to be here! If You want, I will make three tabernacles here: one for You, one for Moses, and one for Elijah."

⁵While he was still speaking, suddenly a bright cloud covered them, and a voice from the cloud said:

> *This is My beloved Son.*
> *I take delight in Him.*
> *Listen to Him!*

⁶When the disciples heard it, they fell facedown and were terrified.

⁷Then Jesus came up, touched them, and said, "Get up; don't be afraid." ⁸When they looked up they saw no one except Him—Jesus alone. ⁹As they were coming down from the mountain, Jesus commanded them, "Don't tell anyone about the vision until the Son of Man is raised from the dead."

¹⁰So the disciples questioned Him, "Why then do the scribes say that Elijah must come first?"

¹¹"Elijah is coming and will restore everything," He replied. ¹²"But I tell you: Elijah has already come, and they didn't recognize him. On the contrary, they did whatever they pleased to him. In the same way the Son of Man is going to suffer at their hands." ¹³Then the disciples understood that He spoke to them about John the Baptist.

*T*he transfiguration can occur only after Peter's confession. The transfiguration is not proof. First the confession must be made in faith. Then the revelation of Jesus' glory can occur on the mountaintop. The location is lost, and scholars are still debating. Some say it happened on Mount Hermon, which lies close to Caesarea Philippi. Others point to a mountain in Galilee called Tabor. Apparently the author of Matthew's Gospel does not think we need to know.

Jesus takes with him the Three: Peter, James and John. He had created three concentric circles of friends. The largest group was known as the Seventy. They are mentioned only in Luke's Gospel (Lk 10:17) and are patterned after the seventy elders of Israel (Ex 24:1, 9; Num 11:16, 24). The next circle is the Twelve, clearly a reflection of the twelve tribes of Israel (Mt 19:28).

The background of the innermost circle, the Three, is less obvious. In 2 Samuel 23:13, just after David sings his final song, a brief account of the exploits of some of his finest warriors is given. Of these leading warriors, three are singled out. They are remembered for fearlessly defying the Philistines, who were guarding Bethlehem. David, who is dying of thirst, longs for a drink from the well of his birthplace. The three bravely fight their way through the Philistines and bring David back the water he was thirsty for, though he would not drink. Abishai was their leader. He had once killed three hundred men with his spear. The names of the other two warriors are not given.

Perhaps Peter, James and John are Jesus' (the Son of David) Three. This would explain the story of Peter, clearly the leader and the Abishai of the Three, jumping into the middle of the armed detachment of soldiers who had come to arrest Jesus, brandishing his own sword.

There, on the nameless mountain, Jesus is transfigured. The Three are privileged to see his true, luminous nature. Appearing on either side of Jesus are Moses and Elijah, the superstars of the Old Testament and the only two men who had spoken to God on Mount Sinai (Ex 24:15-18; 1 Kings 19:8). It is the moment when Moses' request, made so many centuries before, was granted and he was able to see the glory, the face of God (Ex 33:18; see 2 Cor 4:6).

To fully understand the story, we must realize that the disciples were terrified. This emotion is the key that unlocks the narrative. Peter's first words can also be translated in the form of a question, a question based on his fear. "Is it good for us to be here?" he stammers.

There is every reason to believe that it is not good, not safe for them to be there. In the Old Testament, to be on the top of a mountain that is glowing and to witness the appearance of Moses and Elijah means only one thing: you are probably about to die. When Moses was on the top of the mountain, those at the bottom were warned not even to touch the mountain's base lest they die.

The fear also explains Peter's proposal to build three shelters or tabernacles to protect the Three from the radiance of Jesus and his two companions. But just at that moment, a cloud envelops them. There will be no need for the protection of the shelters. God has provided the shelter of a glowing cloud. From the cloud comes a voice, speaking the words every child most needs to hear (Mt 17:5; see also Mt 3:17). The trembling Three are commanded to listen to him. In terrified response, they fall to the ground. It all makes perfect sense, given the context of their fear.

The next sensation they experienced is a touch on the shoulder. It is Jesus, and he is himself again. "Get up," they hear him say, literally, "No fear." Whenever Jesus reveals himself in a new way, he must tell them not to be afraid, for apparently it can be a fearful thing to see him as he truly is (Mt 14:27; 28:10).

On the way down the mountain, once more Jesus commands their silence (see Mt 16:20). It is not that he is keeping his Messiah-ship a secret, only that he knows he must first undeceive them regarding what it means to be the Messiah. This he will try to do during their final ten-day to two-week walk back down the Jordan Valley and up to Jerusalem and the cross that is waiting for him there.

"HAVE MERCY"

[14]*When they reached the crowd, a man approached and knelt down before Him.* [15]*"Lord," he said, "have mercy on my son, because he has seizures and suffers severely. He often falls into the fire and often into the water.* [16]*I brought him to Your disciples, but they couldn't heal him."*

[17]*Jesus replied, "You unbelieving and rebellious generation! How long will I be with you? How long must I put up with you? Bring him here to Me."* [18]*Then Jesus rebuked the demon, and it came out of him, and from that moment the boy was healed.*

[19]*Then the disciples approached Jesus privately and said, "Why couldn't we drive it out?"*

[20]*"Because of your little faith," He told them. "For I assure you: If you have*

faith the size of a mustard seed, you will tell this mountain, 'Move from here to there,' and it will move. Nothing will be impossible for you. [21][However, this kind does not come out except by prayer and fasting.]"

[22]As they were meeting in Galilee, Jesus told them, "The Son of Man is about to be betrayed into the hands of men. [23]They will kill Him, and on the third day He will be raised up." And they were deeply distressed.

$\mathcal{A}$t the bottom of the mountain, a crowd is waiting. A crowd always seems to be waiting. A father is there with his son, who has been experiencing seizures because of a demon that has taken possession of him. One of the aims of demonic possession is the eventual death of the person who is possessed. This demon has been throwing the boy into fire and water, attempting to take his life. In Luke's account, the demon tries one final time to kill the boy by throwing him into a severe seizure just before Jesus delivers him (Lk 9:42). Jesus' authority is absolute. He speaks, and the boy is instantly healed.

In private the disciples ask why they had failed to do this themselves. Jesus encourages them that nothing will be impossible for them if only they will exercise their tiny mustard seed of faith. Like the mustard seed in the parable (Mt 13:31), the beginnings may be small, but even a small faith can move mountains.

The emotions are still running high. They have just received one of the severest rebukes from Jesus (Mt 17:17). Now as they gather together in Galilee, Jesus continues to hammer away at their old delusion about the Messiah of the old orthodoxy. The Christ of the new reality will be killed. The disciples are deeply distressed. It seems they never heard that he would rise on the third day.

AN UNMIRACULOUS MIRACLE

[24]When they came to Capernaum, those who collected the double-drachma tax approached Peter and said, "Doesn't your Teacher pay the double-drachma tax?"

[25]"Yes," he said.

When he went into the house, Jesus spoke to him first, "What do you think,

Simon? Who do earthly kings collect tariffs or taxes from? From their sons or from strangers?"

²⁶"From strangers," he said.

"Then the sons are free," Jesus told him. ²⁷But, so we won't offend them, go to the sea, cast in a fishhook, and take the first fish that you catch. When you open its mouth you'll find a coin. Take it and give it to them for Me and you."

Only Matthew tells the story of the coin in the fish's mouth. But we never see either the fish or the coin. It is a different group of disciples that returns to Capernaum than the ones who left days before. Notice that for once there is no crowd waiting or following along, but only two collectors of the temple tax (see Ex 30:13).

These are not tax collectors as Matthew was a tax collector. They are collecting the tax for the maintenance of the temple. When they asked Peter if Jesus pays the tax, he immediately responds, "Yes." The truth is, Peter is not sure, but he is used to responding to the kind of authority represented by these men. Teachers are supposed to be exempt from this tax. For the collectors even to ask is somewhat of an insult.

Peter steps inside his house, and Jesus asks, in essence, "Who pays taxes? Do the sons of kings pay or strangers?"

Peter actually knows the answer to this question. "Strangers," he responds.

Clearly the sons of kings are exempt, so by all rights Jesus should not pay the tax on his own Father's house. What Jesus says next is puzzling to say the least: "But so we won't offend them . . ." Peter no doubt wondered, *Since when does Jesus not want to offend these people?*

Jesus tells Peter to take his hand line (the only reference to this mode of fishing in the Gospels) and cast it into the lake. The first fish has a coin in its mouth that will cover the tax for the both of them. Here the story ends. We are left to assume that everything occurred just as Jesus said—a safe assumption.

Clearly the miracle and the story is not the point. So, what is the miracle behind the unseen miracle? Remember, these are their final days in Galilee. Soon they will leave for the final journey to Jerusalem

(Mt 19:1). This is the last time for Jesus and Peter to spend time together in private, there in his home in Capernaum. Tired from their
hike back from Caesarea Philippi, they come home to find two religious men waiting to coerce a tax from Jesus that he should not have to
pay in the first place. There should have been a confrontation. Jesus
should have sent them packing. Yet he chooses not to do so. Mysteriously, he does not want to offend them. And why? This is the miracle:
Jesus chooses to exercise his miraculous power to make a coin appear to
pay the tax so that he and his friend might spend their last few hours
together in peace.

MATTHEW 18

WHO IS THE GREATEST?

¹At that time the disciples came to Jesus and said, "Who is greatest in the kingdom of heaven?"

²Then He called a child to Him and had him stand among them. ³"I assure you," He said, "unless you are converted and become like children, you will never enter the kingdom of heaven. ⁴Therefore, whoever humbles himself like this child—this one is the greatest in the kingdom of heaven. ⁵And whoever welcomes one child like this in My name welcomes Me.

⁶"But whoever causes the downfall of one of these little ones who believe in Me—it would be better for him if a heavy millstone were hung around his neck and he were drowned in the depths of the sea! ⁷Woe to the world because of offenses. For offenses must come, but woe to that man by whom the offense comes. ⁸If your hand or your foot causes your downfall, cut it off and throw it away. It is better for you to enter life maimed or lame, than to have two hands or two feet and be thrown into the eternal fire. ⁹And if your eye causes your downfall, gouge it out and throw it away. It is better for you to enter life with one eye, rather than to have two eyes and be thrown into hellfire!"

𝓜atthew 18 is truly the calm before the storm. Jesus and the disciples will leave for Jerusalem. This is their last time to be together within the familiar confines of Capernaum.

All along the way to Jerusalem, the argument will surface again and again, "Who is the greatest?" We are tempted to roll our eyes at the disciples for their self-centeredness. But this is the first time they have ever used the term "kingdom of heaven," so perhaps we should give them credit for the fact that they are slowly moving in the right direction. It is still the wrong question, but they are at least thinking in the right categories.

If indeed they are still in Peter's house, I like to think that the child Jesus placed in their midst was one of Peter's children. From the very beginning, with his nine benedictions, Jesus presented the kingdom in radically reversed terms. His answer to the question of who is the greatest: the one who is the smallest—that is, a child. And what exactly makes children small? Humility—namely, knowing they are small.

Jesus presses home the seriousness of the image when he says that this kind of childlike humility is a make-or-break affair in terms of entering the kingdom. It is a kingdom of children. This is a central part of their new identity in a world that values importance and status. In the disciples' world, the world of Judaism, entrance into the kingdom is something that one earned by strictly maintaining personal righteousness. Children intuitively understand they have nothing to give, nothing to promote themselves. They are completely dependent on the parent who loves them.

Jesus concludes by radically identifying himself with those who become like children. It is the same language he used when he sent the disciples out on their first mission (Mt 10:40).

In Matthew 18:6, the value of childlikeness is expressed from another perspective. Because children bear a concealed dignity, if anyone causes them to sin or stumble, a horrific punishment awaits them. The image Jesus calls to mind is of a large "ass-turned" millstone being hung around the neck of an offender who is then thrown into the sea. From where they sit in Peter's house, they can hear the sounds of the waves outside. This brutal image had actually been acted out by the Romans, who threw a number of Jewish zealots into the Sea of Galilee with millstones tied around their necks. But listen closely; this suffocating image is not what is going to happen to those who cause the children to stumble but something unimaginably worse. In fact, says Jesus, it would be better to drown this way then to experience what God has in store for those who cause the little ones to sin.

Verse 7 has the disconnected tone of one of Matthew's original *logia*. The connection is the idea of the fate of those who cause others to sin. Given the fallen nature of the world, such things must come. But woe to that person through whom they come. Absolutely everything that can be done must be done to keep oneself from sin. Jesus' imagery is horrific, hyperbolic—the cutting off the hand, the gouging out of the eye.

THE LONELY LOST SHEEP

10 "See that you don't look down on one of these little ones, because I tell you that in heaven their angels continually view the face of My Father in heaven. 11[For the Son of Man has come to save the lost.] 12What do you think? If a man has 100 sheep, and one of them goes astray, won't he leave the 99 on the hillside and go and search for the stray? 13And if he finds it, I assure you: He rejoices over that sheep more than over the 99 that did not go astray. 14In the same way, it is not the will of your Father in heaven that one of these little ones perish."

$\mathcal{T}$his is the first parable since Matthew 13, if you don't count the parabolic reference to the Pharisees' teaching as yeast (Mt 16:6). It is tied to what came before by the phrase "these little ones" (Mt 18:6).

Jesus introduces the parable by reminding the disciples of the concealed dignity of the little ones. In fact, they are in the charge of angels who continually look upon the face of God in heaven. Jesus engages the disciples with the words "What do you think?" It is not a figure of speech but a genuine invitation to enter into the story at the level of their imaginations.

A man has an average-sized flock of one hundred sheep, but one wanders off. The one that is lost becomes valuable precisely because of its lostness, so he leaves the ninety-nine to go and find it. The parable is another reflection of Hillel's *qal wahōmer*. "How much more," Jesus might have said, "will the Father seek one of the little ones if they should become lost." This is Jesus' final answer to the original question of who is the greatest in the kingdom. The little ones are so valued by the Father that he is not willing that any of them should ever become lost.

THE PROCESS OF FORGIVING YOUR BROTHER

15 "If your brother sins against you, go and rebuke him in private. If he listens to you, you have won your brother. 16But if he won't listen, take one or two more with you, so that by the testimony of two or three witnesses every fact may be established. 17If he pays no attention to them, tell the church. But if he

doesn't pay attention even to the church, let him be like an unbeliever and a tax
collector to you. [18]I assure you: Whatever you bind on earth is already bound in
heaven, and whatever you loose on earth is already loosed in heaven. [19]Again,
I assure you: If two of you on earth agree about any matter that you pray for,
it will be done for you by My Father in heaven. [20]For where two or three are
gathered together in My name, I am there among them."

*J*esus has talked about the person who causes one of the little ones to
sin. Now he looks at sin from another perspective: the brother who sins
against you (Mt 18:15-26). These instructions are forward looking and
have in mind the future congregations of Jesus' followers.

The first step in dealing with brothers or sisters who sin against you
is to go to them in private and show them their fault. It was considered
a sin in Judaism for one person to publicly humiliate another. If the
person listens, the matter is settled. Remember always that the objec-
tive of all of Jesus' instructions here is the eventual restoration of the
person who has sinned and not his or her punishment.

If the one who sinned against you refuses to listen in private, the
next step is to take two or three witnesses along to try to convince and
convict that person of the wrong she or he have done. This instruction
is based on Deuteronomy 19:15.

If that does not work, the matter should be brought before the entire
congregation. The word used here *ekklēsia,* which is usually translated
"church," should almost certainly be rendered "congregation" or even
"synagogue" (see Heb 2:12). Coming before the entire congregation is
the final step in the attempt to restore the person who has sinned. If that
person refuses to listen to the congregation, he or she must be regarded
as a pagan, literally as a Gentile (*ethnikos*) or as a tax collector, who would
be looked upon in Judaism as the worst sort of hardhearted traitor.

Even exclusion from the congregation bears the hope that once outside the community the offender will see the light and return in repentance. The goal is always forgiveness and restoration. Yet stubborn
hardheartedness will always be a dark force to be reckoned with in the
community of Jesus' followers. Just as Jesus granted the keys of the

kingdom to his disciples (Mt 16:19), he reminds them that the process of binding and loosing, of convicting and setting free here on earth will have eternal consequences. When you come together, even when only two of you are there and agree in this process, the Father in heaven will act upon it. Why? Because when two or three of you are serving together in the process of binding and loosing, Jesus himself is involved in the process right alongside you.[45]

A WILLINGNESS TO FORGIVE LITTLE

[21]Then Peter came to Him and said, "Lord, how many times could my brother sin against me and I forgive him? As many as seven times?"

[22]"I tell you, not as many as seven," Jesus said to him, "but 70 times seven. [23]For this reason, the kingdom of heaven can be compared to a king who wanted to settle accounts with his slaves. [24]When he began to settle accounts, one who owed 10,000 talents was brought before him. [25]Since he had no way to pay it back, his master commanded that he, his wife, his children, and everything he had be sold to pay the debt.

[26]"At this, the slave fell facedown before him and said, 'Be patient with me, and I will pay you everything!' [27]Then the master of that slave had compassion, released him, and forgave him the loan.

[28]"But that slave went out and found one of his fellow slaves who owed him 100 denarii. He grabbed him, started choking him, and said, 'Pay what you owe!'

[29]"At this, his fellow slave fell down and began begging him, 'Be patient with me, and I will pay you back.' [30]But he wasn't willing. On the contrary, he went and threw him into prison until he could pay what was owed. [31]When the other slaves saw what had taken place, they were deeply distressed and went and reported to their master everything that had happened.

[32]"Then, after he had summoned him, his master said to him, 'You wicked slave! I forgave you all that debt because you begged me. [33]Shouldn't you also have had mercy on your fellow slave, as I had mercy on you?' [34]And his master got angry and handed him over to the jailers to be tortured until he could pay everything that was owed. [35]So My heavenly Father will also do to you if each of you does not forgive his brother from his heart."

$\mathcal{A}$ll of this talk about binding, loosing and forgiving sin has set Peter's mind turning. He asks a practical question in light of Jesus' words of restoring the brother who sins against you. How many times should a person extend forgiveness? Peter suggests to him the generous number of seven times. The Talmud mandated that a person be forgiven only three times.[46]

Jesus' response is not to be taken literally. This is a wonderful example of the way numbers can have an emotional value in Judaism as much as a numerical value. A good paraphrase of Jesus answer might be, "More times than you can possibly imagine."

This lesson is too important to be missed. So Jesus provides a parable to make his point. Again, it is set in the context of the kingdom of heaven, always the kingdom of heaven. A slave owed an impossibly large amount to his king; ten thousand talents is equal to sixty million days' wages. Again the number has an emotional value. Certainly, it would be humanly impossible for such a debt to ever be repaid. It is a bigger debt than Peter could possibly imagine.

Custom dictated that the man and his wife and children be sold into slavery to repay the debt. Note that this is a pagan example; the Jews did not look kindly on such Gentile practices. The slave begs for more time to pay off the impossible debt; imagine working for sixty million days. The master, realizing the hopelessness of the situation, goes beyond giving him more time. He cancels the entire debt. The slave is no longer bound. The king has exercised his privilege and used the keys of his authority to loose the slave.

Once he had been set free, the slave finds one of his fellow slaves who owes him a relatively small debt of one hundred days' work. He violently attacks the man and demands that he be repaid immediately. He inflicts on his fellow slave the punishment he had been threatened with and has the man thrown into prison.

One of the key concepts of mercy (hesed) is that once we are shown mercy, we become obligated to give mercy. Upon realizing that the person from whom we have a right to expect nothing has given us everything, we must reciprocate.

When Peter, who is as yet unaware of the weight of his sin—the impossible amount of his debt—offers to forgive only seven times, he has become the ungrateful slave of the parable. Jesus leaves the parable open-ended to allow Peter the freedom to make the realization for himself.

MATTHEW 19

DIVORCE AND THE LITTLE CHILDREN

19:1-15

A FLAWED QUESTION

19:16-30

DIVORCE AND THE LITTLE CHILDREN

¹*When Jesus had finished this instruction, He departed from Galilee and went to the region of Judea across the Jordan.* ²*Large crowds followed Him, and He healed them there.* ³*Some Pharisees approached Him to test Him. They asked, "Is it lawful for a man to divorce his wife on any grounds?"*

⁴*"Haven't you read," He replied, "that He who created them in the beginning made them male and female,"* ⁵*and He also said:*

> *"For this reason a man will leave*
> *his father and mother*
> *and be joined to his wife,*
> *and the two will become one flesh?*

⁶*So they are no longer two, but one flesh. Therefore, what God has joined together, man must not separate."*

⁷*"Why then," they asked Him, "did Moses command us to give divorce papers and to send her away?"*

⁸*He told them, "Moses permitted you to divorce your wives because of the hardness of your hearts. But it was not like that from the beginning.* ⁹*And I tell you, whoever divorces his wife, except for sexual immorality, and marries another, commits adultery."*

¹⁰*His disciples said to Him, "If the relationship of a man with his wife is like this, it's better not to marry!"*

¹¹*But He told them, "Not everyone can accept this saying, but only those it has been given to.* ¹²*For there are eunuchs who were born that way from their mother's womb, there are eunuchs who were made by men, and there are eunuchs who have made themselves that way because of the kingdom of heaven. Let anyone accept this who can."*

¹³*Then children were brought to Him so He might put His hands on them and pray. But the disciples rebuked them.* ¹⁴*Then Jesus said, "Leave the children alone, and don't try to keep them from coming to Me, because the kingdom of heaven is made up of people like this."* ¹⁵*After putting His hands on them, He went on from there.*

*I*n Matthew 19, Jesus begins to move in the direction of Jerusalem. The formal journey begins in 20:17. If we remain sensitive to the flow of the ministry, from this point he is on his way to the cross. The formal ministry is effectively over. There will be blocks of teaching along the way and when he arrives back in Jerusalem, but these tend to be short and presented in a hostile setting. As Jesus leaves Galilee, I wonder if he pondered that when he returned he would be resurrected from the dead and his work would finally be done. The large crowds that are following him are also making their way to Jerusalem for Passover.

Matthew wants us to know the Pharisees are "testing" Jesus—that is, they are not asking the question for themselves but rather to see if Jesus will provide the orthodox answer. The issue of divorce loomed large in the world of the Pharisees, with their desire to be scrupulously law abiding. The question requires Jesus to interpret Deuteronomy 24:1-4 and specifically what the word *indecent* (NIV) means in regard to the offending woman. There were two popular schools of thought on the subject. The stricter and more popular school of Shammai stated that *indecent* referred only to committing adultery. The gentler followers of Hillel, with whom Jesus sided most frequently, concluded that *indecent* meant anything, including the improper preparation of a meal.[47]

Jesus is not drawn into the controversy immediately. He begins by defining marriage, not divorce. "Haven't you read . . ." is the language of scribal debate. He goes all the way back to the beginning, to the first two chapters of Genesis. God's intention that man and woman be one is echoed in the harmony of their names in Hebrew: *îš* (man) and *išāh* (woman). If you condense Jesus' understanding of marriage, it comes down to oneness. The two are united, have become one flesh, are no longer two but one, are "what God has joined." All this in the space of two verses! That fundamental oneness is the issue in Jesus' mind—that and the fact that God has created that oneness.

In verse 7 the Pharisees seek to return to the topic of divorce. Why did Moses make the provision for divorce if the two are one? It is almost as if they have been drawn into the discussion and are no longer trying to test Jesus but really want to know what he thinks. Hardness of the heart is the reason for the provision of divorce, Jesus responds. His mind is stuck on the original purpose of marriage. From the beginning it was not God's intention that the oneness be violated. He hates divorce (Mal 2:16). Later in the Talmud the rabbis taught, "He who divorces his wife is hated before God."

Pushed for an answer, Jesus sides with Shammai. Marital unfaithfulness is the only valid grounds for divorce. But his statement takes the strict stance of the Shammanites even further. If someone puts away his wife apart from marital unfaithfulness and then remarries, he commits adultery. This is the logical conclusion of Jesus' earlier statement on the oneness that is marriage.

The central issue is, can man break a bond that was created by God? Jesus' conclusion: adultery is the result of remarriage, because the bond God made cannot be broken by man. A very real question remains: Is every marriage indeed based on a bond created by God? I would answer no. Because of the hardness of the human heart, people can marry outside of the will of God. But those who have spoken their vows before God must take seriously their promises to each other and to him. As Dietrich Bonhoeffer said in a marriage ceremony from a prison cell, "When God answers 'yes' to your 'yes' he creates holy matrimony."

In the centuries that followed, the rabbis eventually declared that divorce should actually be required in the case of adultery, since marital unfaithfulness essentially dissolves the marriage.

The severity of Jesus' words are not lost on his disciples. They make a logical conclusion that in light of what he has just said, it might be better for a man not to get married at all. What follows is a statement of Jesus that is unique to Matthew and so may have had a bearing on the unique life situation of his community. This teaching is not for everyone, says Jesus. He would never negate the biblical purpose and calling of marriage. Yet for the sake of the kingdom, some have, and will, renounce married life altogether.

The little vignette with the children that follows and the lengthy discussion of divorce seem to be intimately linked. After being exposed to a topic so saturated in hardheartedness, Jesus is presented with a group of small children, who are the principal victims of divorce. Yet the disciples, already having forgotten Jesus' words concerning the "little ones," hardheartedly drive the children away. Jesus must rebuke and remind them of what he said earlier, that the children are the unique possessors of the kingdom of heaven. I sometimes wonder if Jesus, on his way to Jerusalem with all that awaited him there and having renounced marriage for the kingdom of heaven, wanted to hold the children as much as they wanted to be held by him. Matthew concludes ominously, "He went on from there."

A FLAWED QUESTION

[16] Just then someone came up and asked Him, "Teacher, what good must I do to have eternal life?"

[17] "Why do you ask Me about what is good?" He said to him. "There is only One who is good. If you want to enter into life, keep the commandments."

[18] "Which ones?" he asked Him. Jesus answered:

> *Do not murder;*
> *do not commit adultery;*
> *do not steal;*
> *do not bear false witness;*
> *[19] honor your father and your mother;*
> *and love your neighbor as yourself.*

[20] "I have kept all these," the young man told Him. "What do I still lack?"

[21] "If you want to be perfect," Jesus said to him, "go, sell your belongings and give to the poor, and you will have treasure in heaven. Then come, follow Me."

[22] When the young man heard that command, he went away grieving, because he had many possessions.

[23] Then Jesus said to His disciples, "I assure you: It will be hard for a rich person to enter the kingdom of heaven! [24] Again I tell you, it is easier for a camel to go through the eye of a needle than for a rich person to enter the kingdom of God."

[25] When the disciples heard this, they were utterly astonished and asked, "Then who can be saved?"

[26] But Jesus looked at them and said, "With men this is impossible, but

with God all things are possible."

27Then Peter responded to Him, "Look, we have left everything and fol-lowed You. So what will there be for us?"

28Jesus said to them, "I assure you: In the Messianic Age, when the Son of Man sits on His glorious throne, you who have followed Me will also sit on 12 thrones, judging the 12 tribes of Israel. 29And everyone who has left houses, brothers or sisters, father or mother, children, or fields because of My name will receive 100 times more and will inherit eternal life. 30But many who are first will be last, and the last first."

*P*erhaps the next young man in the story is on his way to Passover as well and in the midst of the moving crowd comes up to Jesus with his flawed question. It is flawed because eternal life is not obtained by doing good things. You can feel the disconnect between them in Jesus' response. Why is the man asking him about what is good? The point is that only God is good, and the point will eventually be made that only God makes the gift of eternal life possible. When Jesus concludes that the young man must obey the commands, he is drawing the man out, not contradicting himself.

When asked which commandments, Jesus responds with five of the Ten Commandments and adds the injunction from Leviticus 19:18 to love neighbors.

The response of the young man has caused church congregations to gasp in disbelief for centuries. The thought of someone actually believing they have kept all the commandments seems incredulous to those who have embraced the doctrines of grace. But we should not be so quick to gasp or to dismiss this sincere young man. He is a part of the old ortho-doxy that has reduced the law to something that is actually "keepable." This was, after all, the ultimate goal of the Pharisees. This is why they build a fence around the Torah. Even Paul, in his previous life, flatly states that in regard to the law he was "blameless" (Phil 3:6). And Jesus does not rebuke or belittle the young man. That is not his style. Instead he engages the man's imagination and appeals to what is best in him.

If this is genuinely what he wants, to be perfect, then the rich man must sell everything and give it to the poor. That is the "good thing" he must do. The sincerity of Jesus' statement is demonstrated in his extension of the call to follow him, which at the moment means to follow him to Jerusalem and the cross waiting there. Jesus is literally opening the door of the kingdom to this young man.

Without a word, the man turns and sadly walks away. Mark said that when Jesus looked at him earlier, he loved him (Mk 10:21). He loved his misplaced zeal, loved his mixed motives, loved him for all his faults and foibles. The sad truth is that he had not kept all the commandments; he had broken the very first one and made money his God.

Perhaps with a sigh, Jesus comments to the disciples that it is hard for the rich to enter the kingdom. Yet remember that Jesus had at least three very wealthy followers that we know of: Joseph of Arimathea (Mt 27:57), Zacchaeus (Lk 19:2-10) and Matthew himself, who left the considerable wealth of his profession to follow him.

His language, always picturesque and over-the-top, Jesus brings to mind the biggest animal any of them knows anything about: the camel. In our time he might have used an elephant or even a whale. The impossibility of a camel going through the eye of a needle is more impossible than the impossibility of a rich person entering the kingdom of God.[48]

The disciples' world is understandably rocked. In their minds, the rich are at the head of the line to the kingdom of God. Wealthy people were wealthy because, after all, God had blessed them. "Who can be saved?" really means, "It sounds like no one can be saved."

It is impossible, Jesus responds, "with men." But saving is God's business. His business is making impossible things possible. These words are spoken by the man who is on his way to die to make entering the kingdom of heaven possible for the rich and poor alike.

Peter clears his throat and reminds Jesus of what he already knows. The disciples have left everything to follow Jesus. Peter is speaking the truth after all; he is not the buffoon he is often pictured as being. His home in Capernaum sits, even at this moment, empty of his presence.

Jesus responds, saying that at the regeneration of all things (see Is 65–66) there are thrones waiting for each one of them. And all that they have left will be multiplied a hundred times over.

MATTHEW 20

THE ECCENTRIC EMPLOYER: A PARABLE OF *ḤESED*

20:1–16

THE THIRD ANNOUNCEMENT OF SUFFERING

20:17–19

A REQUEST TO BE FIRST

20:20–28

TWO BLIND MEN

20:29–34

THE ECCENTRIC EMPLOYER: A PARABLE OF ḤESED

¹"For the kingdom of heaven is like a landowner who went out early in the morning to hire workers for his vineyard. ²After agreeing with the workers on one denarius for the day, he sent them into his vineyard. ³When he went out about nine in the morning, he saw others standing in the marketplace doing nothing. ⁴To those men he said, 'You also go to my vineyard, and I'll give you whatever is right.' So off they went. ⁵About noon and at three, he went out again and did the same thing. ⁶Then about five he went and found others standing around, and said to them, 'Why have you been standing here all day doing nothing?'

⁷"'Because no one hired us,' they said to him.

"'You also go to my vineyard,' he told them. ⁸When evening came, the owner of the vineyard told his foreman, 'Call the workers and give them their pay, starting with the last and ending with the first.'

⁹"When those who were hired about five came, they each received one denarius. ¹⁰So when the first ones came, they assumed they would get more, but they also received a denarius each. ¹¹When they received it, they began to complain to the landowner: ¹²'These last men put in one hour, and you made them equal to us who bore the burden of the day and the burning heat!'

¹³"He replied to one of them, 'Friend, I'm doing you no wrong. Didn't you agree with me on a denarius? ¹⁴Take what's yours and go. I want to give this last man the same as I gave you. ¹⁵Don't I have the right to do what I want with my business? Are you jealous because I'm generous?'

¹⁶"So the last will be first, and the first last."

𝓜atthew 19 closes with one of two statements that will provide the bookends for the opening parable: "But many who are first will be last, and the last first." The second bookend comes at the closing of this parable: "so the last will be first, and the first last" (Mt 20:16). In between these bookends lies a remarkable parable of ḥesed.

The writer of Matthew provides no introduction for the story. We are left to suppose that the crowd is perhaps mixed: Pharisees who are represented by those who work all day and "sinners" who make a day's wage for only an hour's work.

To do the math of the parable, we must understand that the ancient workday lasted roughly from six in the morning to six at night. The first laborers in the parable are hired around six to work in the vineyard.[49] At nine in the morning, more workers are hired and agreed to work for "whatever is right." Apparently they are desperate and the harvest must be going well, since it requires more workers. At noon, three and finally five, he hires more. The last group may be a bit questionable. When the landowner asks them why they are hovering around the market so late in the day, they simply respond, "Because no one hired us." They are hardly an inspiring bunch.

The Old Testament mandated that day workers be paid on a daily basis because of their tenuous existence (Deut 24:14-15). In verse 8, at the end of the day, everyone is called in, and the foreman is instructed to pay the last group first. It is all a set-up. The phrase "last first" is a sign that this really is a story about the kingdom.

Behold, the slackers receive an entire day's pay—one denarius! This gives reason for the first hired workers to expect a windfall. Perhaps, if indeed the harvest was so abundant, they had all the more reason to hope for an extraordinary payday. But, to their disappointment, they are paid according to their original agreement with the landowner in verse 2—one denarius.

As workers sometimes do, they begin to protest. After all, it isn't fair, is it? Rabbi Ben He He said in the Pirke Aboth ("Sayings of the Fathers"), "According to the labor is the reward." That was the Jewish work ethic and, I might add, the Protestant work ethic as well.

The landowner responds warmly, "Friend." He seems surprised, given their clear agreement. In verse 15 he literally says the worker's eye is evil (see Mt 6:23). Therefore, according to Jesus, he is full of darkness. Why? He hates the fact that the landowner has shown *ḥesed*.

Remember our working definition of *ḥesed*: "when the person from whom I have a right to expect nothing gives me everything." So many of Jesus' parables are really about *ḥesed*. Occasionally one of the characters is what I refer to as a "hater of *ḥesed*." Like the elder brother in the parable of the prodigal son and like these workers, they hate the fact that God is a God of *ḥesed*, or "lovingkindness." They are representatives of the old orthodoxy, like Ben He He. In fact, there is an ancient version of this parable told by the rabbis that has a completely different motto at the end:

> A King had a vineyard for which he engaged many laborers, one of who was especially apt and skillful. What did the King do? He took this labor from his work, and walk through the garden conversing with him. When the laborers came for their hire in the evening, the skillful labor also appeared among them and received a full day's wages from the King. The other laborers were angry at this and said, "We have toiled the whole day, while this man has worked but 2 hours; why does the king give him the full hire even asked us?" The king said to them, "Why are you angry? Through his skill he has done more work in 2 hours and you have all day."[50]

Only Matthew tells us the parable of the eccentric employer. As his first hearers sat huddled in the synagogue in Galilee, perhaps it struck them that they were the recipients of the extravagant wage for which they did little or nothing. The Father of Jesus, the owner of the vineyard, is the one for whom they are working. And if they are sometimes surrounded by those who hate the fact that God is a God of lovingkindness, they are to take comfort in the fact that Jesus saw it all coming long ago. In fact, he had told the story just for them. The conclusion of the second bookend might well be considered the motto of the kingdom: "The last will be first, and the first last."

THE THIRD ANNOUNCEMENT OF SUFFERING

[17]While going up to Jerusalem, Jesus took the 12 disciples aside privately and said to them on the way: [18]"Listen! We are going up to Jerusalem. The Son of Man will be handed over to the chief priests and scribes, and they will condemn Him to death. [19]Then they will hand Him over to the Gentiles to be mocked, flogged, and crucified, and He will be resurrected on the third day."

𝓜atthew 20:17 reminds us that we are still on the road with Jesus, going up to Jerusalem. Along the way he will predict his death four times. This, the third prediction, is the most graphic and detailed. He will be betrayed and passed from the Jews to the Gentiles. The mocking, flogging and crucifixion are images that make his disciples' blood run cold. I imagine them clamping their eyes shut, trying to avoid the image in their mind's eye.

They are confused and tired and now worried, so much so they never even hear Jesus say and "be resurrected on the third day."

A REQUEST TO BE FIRST

[20] Then the mother of Zebedee's sons approached Him with her sons. She knelt down to ask Him for something. [21]"What do you want?" He asked her.

"Promise," she said to Him, "that these two sons of mine may sit, one on Your right and the other on Your left, in Your kingdom."

[22] But Jesus answered, "You don't know what you're asking. Are you able to drink the cup that I am about to drink?"

"We are able," they said to Him.

[23] He told them, "You will indeed drink My cup. But to sit at My right and left is not Mine to give; instead, it belongs to those for whom it has been prepared by My Father." [24] When the 10 disciples heard this, they became indignant with the two brothers. [25] But Jesus called them over and said, "You know that the rulers of the Gentiles dominate them, and the men of high position exercise power over them. [26] It must not be like that among you. On the contrary, whoever wants to become great among you must be your servant, [27] and whoever wants to be first among you must be your slave; [28] just as the Son of Man did not come to be served, but to serve, and to give His life—a ransom for many."

She is Mary's sister, James and John's mother and Jesus' aunt. She will be at the foot of the cross and at the tomb three days later. Her name is Salome, and she wants a favor. In Matthew 19:28, Jesus had promised the disciples twelve thrones. Now, as she kneels before him, she has a request in regard to the seating arrangements. Might her sons sit on either side of him in the kingdom?

Jesus does not seem irritated by her request. There is not a word of rebuke, although when the others hear about it they are upset (Mt 20:24). No, he seems concerned for them instead. They don't know what they're asking for. To be on Jesus' right and left in a few days won't mean sitting on thrones but hanging on crosses.

"Are you able to drink the cup that I am about to drink?" he asks, referring to his suffering.

"We are able," they reply.

And the truth is, the two brothers will be the first and last of his disciples to die. James will be martyred (Acts 12:2). John will be the last to die, an old man, in the city of Ephesus.

Jesus tells them he cannot give them these places; only the Father can give them to the ones for whom they have been prepared, which also makes us realize that those other two places, the crosses on either side of Jesus, have already been assigned to two others as well.

Jesus sees the occasion as a chance to teach a lesson he's been trying to teach them all the way from Galilee. The matter will be settled only when he washes their feet (Jn 13). He appeals to their identities as Jewish men. They have been thinking like Gentiles, who relish power and position and lording it over people. That's the Roman mindset in a nutshell.

But they are to aspire to be slaves in the kingdom. In the upside-down value system on which it is based, where the last is first, being a slave puts you on the top of the ladder. As always their identities are tied to Jesus' identity. He, the Son of Man, the Supreme Human, came to serve and to give his life as a ransom (*lytron*), the technical term for the price paid to redeem slaves.

TWO BLIND MEN

29 As they were leaving Jericho, a large crowd followed Him. 30 There were two blind men sitting by the road. When they heard that Jesus was passing by, they cried out, "Lord, have mercy on us, Son of David!" 31 The crowd told them to keep quiet, but they cried out all the more, "Lord, have mercy on us, Son of David!"

32 Jesus stopped, called them, and said, "What do you want Me to do for you?"

³³"Lord," they said to Him, "open our eyes!" ³⁴Moved with compassion, Jesus touched their eyes. Immediately they could see, and they followed Him.

*J*ericho, the oldest city in the world, is the last stop before Jerusalem. It is a fifteen-mile walk straight uphill to the holy city from there. The large crowd is still there, following Jesus up the hill to Passover. The writer of Matthew doubles his witnesses again. Even as he told us there were two demon-possessed men at Gadara, here he lets us know that there were two blind men in Jericho waiting for Jesus. Mark mentions only one of them. He tells us his name is Bartimaeus, and he is the disciple for whom Jesus has been looking for three years. He (or they) play a less significant role in Matthew's Gospel.

Their cry acknowledges that Jesus is the Son of David and that they want Jesus to give them both something they do not deserve: mercy (*ḥesed*). It is a request to which Jesus will always respond, even when he is determinedly headed to Jerusalem.

Jesus' question, "What do you want Me to do for you?" seems pointless. But it is vital that the two men put into words their deepest need. It is a harder question than you might imagine. For years I have placed myself in the story, in Bartimaeus's shoes. When Jesus asks me, "What can I do for you?" to this day I have not come up with an answer.

They are asking for *ḥesed*, and Jesus, moved by compassion, touches their eyes. At his touch they can see. Then they simply get up and follow him, along with the rest of the crowd, to Jerusalem to the cross and to the rock tomb of a wealthy follower, where Jesus will forever change the world.

MATTHEW 21

THE "TRIUMPHAL" ENTRY

¹When they approached Jerusalem and came to Bethphage at the Mount of Olives, Jesus then sent two disciples, ²telling them, "Go into the village ahead of you. At once you will find a donkey tied there, and a colt with her. Untie them and bring them to Me. ³If anyone says anything to you, you should say that the Lord needs them, and immediately he will send them."

⁴This took place so that what was spoken through the prophet might be fulfilled:

> *⁵Tell Daughter Zion,*
> *"Look, your King is coming to you,*
> *gentle, and mounted on a donkey,*
> *even on a colt,*
> *the foal of a beast of burden."*

⁶The disciples went and did just as Jesus directed them. ⁷They brought the donkey and the colt; then they laid their robes on them, and He sat on them. ⁸A very large crowd spread their robes on the road; others were cutting branches from the trees and spreading them on the road. ⁹Then the crowds who went ahead of Him and those who followed kept shouting:

> *Hosanna to the Son of David!*
> *He who comes in the name*
> *of the Lord is the blessed One!*
> *Hosanna in the highest heaven!*

¹⁰When He entered Jerusalem, the whole city was shaken, saying, "Who is this?" ¹¹And the crowds kept saying, "This is the prophet Jesus from Nazareth in Galilee!"

With Matthew 21 we formally begin the Passion Week, from the Latin *passio*, which means "to suffer." It is the week that paradoxically celebrates the time of Jesus' suffering. In the Gospels, the period of time (one week) takes up roughly one third of the story. If the Gospels were simple biographies, this would be an unforgivable flaw. But they are testimonies, stories that tell us everything we need to know to place our faith in Jesus of Nazareth. They are flawed biographies, but they are perfect testimonies.

The road up from Jericho comes around the back side of the Mount of Olives to Bethany, a town known today as Azariyeh, the town of Lazarus. From here one can see across the Kidron Valley to Jerusalem and can imagine the enormous temple complex that would have been there in A.D. 33.

Jesus sends two of his disciples—perhaps Peter and John, who seem to be his errand boys for most of the week—to nearby Bethphage to fetch a colt for him to ride into the city. This incident is sometimes regarded as a clairvoyant miracle of Jesus. It is just as likely a prearranged provision. Only Matthew mentions both the donkey and her colt. Only Mark seems to know that no one has ever ridden the colt (Mk 11:2).

Only Matthew uses the fulfillment formula from Zechariah 9:9 to substantiate the event with the colt. His first hearers would have resonated with this, the first of many fulfillments of prophecy that will occur during this final week.

That Jesus enters the city "gentle and riding on a colt" is symbolic. The mount a conquering king rode upon entering a defeated city was a clear sign as to that city's fate. If he was riding a warhorse, that meant he was coming in judgment (see Rev 6:2; 19:11). If he was riding a donkey, that meant he was coming in peace (see 1 Kings 1:33). It is not likely that the king is going to do much fighting from the back of a colt. Jesus is not coming in judgment; he is coming to submit himself to suffering the penalty of the judgment of the world's sin.

Everything happens precisely according to plan. The colt is brought. Its mother probably walks alongside to calm the little animal that has never been ridden. The crowd around Jesus place their cloaks on the road (see 2 Kings 9:13) for the colt to walk on.

The crowd waves branches and shouts phrases from one of the Passover psalms (Ps 118:25-26). The term *hosanna* means "oh save!" That Jesus is addressed as the Son of David completes the image. He is entering the city as a king, without question. Earlier, beside the lake, the crowd wanted to make him king by force, and Jesus fled. Now their desire to see him crowned will serve his purpose, not to place him on a throne but on a cross.

Thirty-three years before, upon his birth, it was said the whole city was "disturbed" by Jesus' coming (Mt 2:3). Now the whole city is "shaken" by his appearing. The newborn King that Herod the Great had so feared and tried to kill has returned, appropriately enough, to die.

It is a king who is entering the city but it is also a prophet. In verse 11, Jesus is also called the "prophet . . . in Galilee." Only Matthew, with his focus on Galilee for the sake of his first Galilean hearers, gives us this detail.

A PROPHET IS IN THE TEMPLE

12Jesus went into the temple complex and drove out all those buying and selling in the temple. He overturned the money changers' tables and the chairs of those selling doves. 13And He said to them, "It is written, My house will be called a house of prayer. But you are making it a den of thieves!"

14The blind and the lame came to Him in the temple complex, and He healed them. 15When the chief priests and the scribes saw the wonders that He did and the children shouting in the temple complex, "Hosanna to the Son of David!" they were indignant 16and said to Him, "Do You hear what these children are saying?"

"Yes," Jesus told them. "Have you never read:

> *You have prepared praise*
> *from the mouths of children and nursing infants?"*

17Then He left them, went out of the city to Bethany, and spent the night there.

*J*esus' entrance was kingly. His appearance in the temple is prophetic (see Jer 19). This is the second temple cleansing. The first public act of Jesus' ministry was to clear the traders from the temple (Jn 2:13-25). Now, two years later, he is back once more. In view of the fact that the temple was protected by fierce Benjaminite guards, it was a bold act indeed. But they don't seem to have had the courage to try to stop Jesus.

Jesus is outraged for two reasons. First, the marketplace has been moved into the court of the Gentiles, impeding their freedom to pray there; hence the quote from Isaiah 56:7: "My house will be called a house of prayer for all nations." Second, it appears the sacrifices required for the poor, specifically doves, have been unfairly marked up, hence the "den of robbers" quote from Jeremiah 7:11. There is no indication that an unfair percentage was being added to the money exchange. The added percentage mandated by the temple authority covered only a slight decrease in the silver coins caused by normal wear.

After the disturbance dies down in the temple, the priests look over and see a group of the blind and lame surrounding Jesus, the priest king. He is laying his hands on them and healing them. Rightly considered, this is as stunning a moment in the story as the expulsion. The temple was no place for the blind and the lame.

The priests and scribes see these wonders and hear the children shouting, "Hosanna!" yet they become indignant. The healing and joy of the new reality cannot be contained in the old wineskins of their old orthodoxy.

A LESSON FROM THE LEAVES

[18]Early in the morning, as He was returning to the city, He was hungry. [19]Seeing a lone fig tree by the road, He went up to it and found nothing on it except leaves. And He said to it, "May no fruit ever come from you again!" At once the fig tree withered.

[20]When the disciples saw it, they were amazed and said, "How did the fig tree wither so quickly?"

[21]Jesus answered them, "I assure you: If you have faith and do not doubt, you will not only do what was done to the fig tree, but even if you tell this mountain, 'Be lifted up and thrown into the sea,' it will be done. [22]And if you believe, you will receive whatever you ask for in prayer."

*cA*fter spending the night in Bethany (Mt 21:17), Jesus and his disciples cross the Kidron Valley and reenter the city. For whatever reason (perhaps Martha had overslept), Jesus is hungry and goes to a fig tree by the road for something to eat. Even though its leaves were green, there is no fruit. In disgust, Jesus pronounces a curse on the tree. It immediately withers.

This is a disturbing story of the only destructive miracle Jesus ever performs. It only becomes clear when you realize the story has nothing to do with the fig tree. The tree is only a symbol of the temple, which outwardly appears fruitful, like the leaves on the tree. Yet Jesus' previous day in the temple had revealed how seriously barren it had become, with priests looking at wonders and seeing only broken rules. Mark goes so far as to say it wasn't even the season for figs (Mk 11:13). It's not about the tree, and it never was.

The disciples are amazed at what Jesus is able to do. He turns the moment of hidden disappointment (he never explains the tree to them) into an encouraging lesson. If they will only have faith, if they will only believe, God will respond to their every request and prayer, and they will be powered up to do amazing things.

QUESTIONS OF AUTHORITY

²³*When He entered the temple complex, the chief priests and the elders of the people came up to Him as He was teaching and said, "By what authority are You doing these things? Who gave You this authority?"*

²⁴*Jesus answered them, "I will also ask you one question, and if you answer it for Me, then I will tell you by what authority I do these things. *²⁵*Where did John's baptism come from? From heaven or from men?"*

*They began to argue among themselves, "If we say, 'From heaven,' He will say to us, 'Then why didn't you believe him?' *²⁶*But if we say, 'From men,' we're afraid of the crowd, because everyone thought John was a prophet." *²⁷*So they answered Jesus, "We don't know." And He said to them, "Neither will I tell you by what authority I do these things."*

*J*esus reenters the fruitless, barren atmosphere of the temple. Waiting there for him is the most powerful group with which he will ever be confronted. Before it has been only the Pharisees and scribes. Now it is chief priests and elders, the men who make up the great Sanhedrin, the Supreme Court of the day. Earlier I would have said they were referring to the ruckus of the expulsion from the previous day when they asked Jesus about his authority to do "these things." But now I believe they were just as upset by the presence of the lame and the blind in the temple. Note, they do not say that what Jesus did was wrong. Their only question is one of authority. Clearly he was not acting under their authority.

It is very rabbinic thing to answer a question with another, harder question. And that is exactly what Jesus does. If they want to discuss the issue of authority, how about John the Baptist? Where did his authority come from? Was it from heaven or men? It is an unanswerable question. They cannot afford to commit to either answer. Their three word answer is rarely, if ever, heard from their lips: "We don't know."

Of course the correct answer is "from heaven." It would have been the correct answer to their first question regarding Jesus' authority as well.

TWO WORKER PARABLES

28 "But what do you think? A man had two sons. He went to the first and said, 'My son, go, work in the vineyard today.'

29 "He answered, 'I don't want to!' Yet later he changed his mind and went. 30 Then the man went to the other and said the same thing.

"'I will, sir,' he answered. But he didn't go.

31 "Which of the two did his father's will?"

"The first," they said.

Jesus said to them, "I assure you: Tax collectors and prostitutes are entering the kingdom of God before you! 32 For John came to you in the way of righteousness, and you didn't believe him. Tax collectors and prostitutes did believe him, but you, when you saw it, didn't even change your minds then and believe him.

33 "Listen to another parable: There was a man, a landowner, who planted a vineyard, put a fence around it, dug a winepress in it, and built a watch-

tower. *He leased it to tenant farmers and went away.* ³⁴*When the grape harvest drew near, he sent his slaves to the farmers to collect his fruit.* ³⁵*But the farmers took his slaves, beat one, killed another, and stoned a third.* ³⁶*Again, he sent other slaves, more than the first group, and they did the same to them.* ³⁷*Finally, he sent his son to them. 'They will respect my son,' he said.*

³⁸*"But when the tenant farmers saw the son, they said among themselves, 'This is the heir. Come, let's kill him and take his inheritance!'* ³⁹*So they seized him, threw him out of the vineyard, and killed him.* ⁴⁰*Therefore, when the owner of the vineyard comes, what will he do to those farmers?"*

⁴¹*"He will completely destroy those terrible men,"* they told Him, *"and lease his vineyard to other farmers who will give him his produce at the harvest."*

⁴²*Jesus said to them, "Have you never read in the Scriptures:*

> *The stone that the builders rejected*
> *has become the cornerstone.*
> *This came from the Lord*
> *and is wonderful in our eyes?*

⁴³*Therefore I tell you, the kingdom of God will be taken away from you and given to a nation producing its fruit.* ⁴⁴*[Whoever falls on this stone will be broken to pieces; but on whoever it falls, it will grind him to powder!]"*

⁴⁵*When the chief priests and the Pharisees heard His parables, they knew He was speaking about them.* ⁴⁶*Although they were looking for a way to arrest Him, they feared the crowds, because they regarded Him as a prophet.*

*D*uring the first days of Passover week, from Sunday to around Wednesday, Jesus goes back and forth to Jerusalem teaching in the temple area, a vast thirty-five-acre complex. The next five chapters of Matthew will contain lessons from those days. Matthew 26:1 will open with the concluding formula: "when Jesus had finished saying all this." With this, his public teaching will come to an end.

The lengthy teaching begins simply and beautifully with Jesus saying, "But what do you think?" What follows are two worker parables. They both utilize Jesus' favorite plot, comparing and contrasting two people or perhaps two groups of people.

The first parable is about two sons, another familiar theme. The first son is asked by his father to work in the vineyard. He stubbornly says no to his father, a minor outrage. Later, however, he has a change of heart and goes to work. Next the father approaches his other son with the same request. "Yes, sir," he says, yet he does not go. In both of the following parables, Jesus will conclude with an engaging question. Here he asks simply, "Which of the two did his father's will?"

It is a simple question, but answering it will be costly. The parable will take the answer the people all have in their heads and move it to their hearts. Their answer is unwittingly correct. The bait has been taken.

Literally Jesus responds, "Amen," a word he reserves to preface his most profound statements. Once more we discover it is the kingdom he has had in mind all along. His response reveals who "they" really are: the priests and the elders. The sinners will enter before *you*, he says, for *you* did not believe John while the sinners did. The repentance of the tax collectors and prostitutes should have been a powerful sign to the priests of the authority of John (see Mt 21:24-27). Yet, just as with the wonders of the temple the day before—the lame and the blind being healed—they had been blind to the miracle of repentance that was a consequence of John's authority. It was their chance—perhaps their last chance—to repent and believe.

Jesus then fires off another parable, this one based on Isaiah's Song of the Vineyard (Is 5:1-7). Again, the locus is a vineyard. The owner is an absentee landlord, so prevalent in Galilee. He carefully prepares the vineyard, rents it to some farmers and leaves. When the time for harvest arrives, he sends one of his slaves to collect what is due him. One slave they beat, one they kill, another they stone. The obviously naive landlord keeps sending his faithful slaves, yet everyone is treated the same despicable way. Finally, he sends his son. In the height of naiveté, he thinks, *They will respect my son.* When the tenants see the hapless son approaching, they decide the father must be dead, and now they will kill the son and seize the vineyard for themselves.

Once more, Jesus engages the crowd with a question, "When the owner of the vineyard comes, what will he do?"

Again, they take the bait, and the head answer begins to become a heart answer. The wretches will be destroyed, they reply.

I find it fascinating that at this point Jesus "sings" an earlier verse of the song that was sung to him in verse 9. It is from one of the Hallel songs, Psalm 118:22-23. The rejected son of the parable, who was so treacherously killed, is in fact the rejected stone of the psalm. It is the same stone that will be used by the Lord himself as the chief corner-stone of the temple. This is a wonderful thing to behold. It sounds like the radical reversal we always see when the kingdom breaks through.

Once again the "you" of verse 43 is almost certainly the chief priests and the Pharisees. In verse 45 they perceive that Jesus has been talking about them all along. As an extension to the plot of Matthew 12:14, they decide to find a way to arrest Jesus.

The rejected stone is a stumbling stone, Jesus implies in verse 44. Everyone who encounters him will experience brokenness. Either you stumble over the stone and are redemptively broken or the stone falls on you and you are completely and utterly destroyed, just like the wine-skins that can't hold the new wine.

MATTHEW 22

THE WEDDING FEAST

¹Once more Jesus spoke to them in parables: ² "The kingdom of heaven may be compared to a king who gave a wedding banquet for his son. ³He sent out his slaves to summon those invited to the banquet, but they didn't want to come. ⁴Again, he sent out other slaves, and said, 'Tell those who are invited: Look, I've prepared my dinner; my oxen and fattened cattle have been slaughtered, and everything is ready. Come to the wedding banquet.'

⁵ "But they paid no attention and went away, one to his own farm, another to his business. ⁶And the others seized his slaves, treated them outrageously and killed them. ⁷The king was enraged, so he sent out his troops, destroyed those murderers, and burned down their city.

⁸ "Then he told his slaves, 'The banquet is ready, but those who were invited were not worthy. ⁹Therefore go to where the roads exit the city and invite everyone you find to the banquet.' ¹⁰So those slaves went out on the roads and gathered everyone they found, both evil and good. The wedding banquet was filled with guests. ¹¹But when the king came in to view the guests, he saw a man there who was not dressed for a wedding. ¹²So he said to him, 'Friend, how did you get in here without wedding clothes?' The man was speechless.

¹³ "Then the king told the attendants, 'Tie him up hand and foot, and throw him into the outer darkness, where there will be weeping and gnashing of teeth.'

¹⁴ "For many are invited, but few are chosen."

$\mathcal{A}$t the end of the last chapter, we discovered that the heat was now on Jesus. The religious leaders had decided to find a way to arrest him. This was after he had told two consecutive "controversy" parables. This would be the perfect time to back off. Instead Jesus chooses to tell one more challenging parable. The writer of Matthew will then balance the three parables with three stories of conflict. The parables combine with the narrative to portray the sense of tension.

There are two unfortunate chapter breaks in this narrative section. The break for chapter 22 might have made more sense at verse

14 and the break at chapter 23 interrupts Jesus' angry confrontation with the Pharisees.[51]

The parable that opens chapter 22 is yet another kingdom parable. The son of the king is getting married, and the elaborate preparations have been completed. When you realize that the wedding of the son of the king will involve the entire country, you begin to appreciate how massive the preparations would be. Integral to understanding this parable is knowing that, before the preparations were made, invitations were sent to those privileged members of the kingdom. Now that the banquet is ready, the follow-up to the invitations are sent, and those who are invited are welcome to now come.

To the dismay of the king, everyone refuses. The extraordinarily gracious monarch then sends other slaves with the congenial message: "Everything is ready. . . . Come." Remembering that the first century was a culture of feasting, the banquet of a king would have been an extravagant event that would have gone on for days. To refuse would be like turning down an invitation to the White House.

Some of the ungrateful subjects ignore the second wave of messages and return to business as usual. Others mistreat and kill the messengers, in light of the office of the *shaliakh*, the authoritative messenger; this would be like attacking and killing the king himself.

The king's rage is understandably justified. This time he sends not slaves but soldiers, destroys the ungrateful subjects, and burns their city to the ground. Some have suggested this is a reference to the A.D. 70 sack of Jerusalem.

A mound of food is waiting. It would be a great dishonor for the son to be denied his feast, so the king tells the servants to find both good and evil and gather them for the feast. And so, at last, the wedding hall is full.

Then something puzzling occurs. In the middle of the crowd, the king notices someone who is not properly attired. He cordially calls him "friend" and asks how he got in without the proper wedding clothes. To this, the man is speechless. There is simply nothing he can say in his own defense.

You and I are at a loss here if we do not understand one more point of background. A significant part of the lavish provision of such a banquet was that, on top of the generous meal, the king would have also provided fine clothes for all his guests. The appearance of the man still wearing his own inappropriate clothes is tantamount to the ungratefulness of those first guests who were invited but ignored the repeated summons of the king. The inappropriately dressed man should be considered as one of their ungrateful number. This explains the fact that he receives the same brutal punishment they received (see Zeph 1:7-8).

The story is about the kingdom insofar as those who were originally invited have ignored and even stubbornly refused the invitation: the priests, the Pharisees and the scribes. Though they are considered the first, they will be the last, if they make it to the feast at all. Meanwhile, the tax collectors and prostitutes, who were not initially invited, have been gathered. They have been clothed in the righteousness of the son, whose wedding the banquet is meant to celebrate.

THREE CONTROVERSY STORIES

[15] Then the Pharisees went and plotted how to trap Him by what He said. [16] They sent their disciples to Him, with the Herodians. "Teacher," they said, "we know that You are truthful and teach truthfully the way of God. You defer to no one, for You don't show partiality. [17] Tell us, therefore, what You think. Is it lawful to pay taxes to Caesar or not?"

[18] But perceiving their malice, Jesus said, "Why are you testing Me, hypocrites? [19] Show Me the coin used for the tax." So they brought Him a denarius. [20] "Whose image and inscription is this?" He asked them.

[21] "Caesar's," they said to Him.

Then He said to them, "Therefore give back to Caesar the things that are Caesar's, and to God the things that are God's." [22] When they heard this, they were amazed. So they left Him and went away.

[23] The same day some Sadducees, who say there is no resurrection, came up to Him and questioned Him: [24] "Teacher, Moses said, if a man dies, having no children, his brother is to marry his wife and raise up offspring for his brother. [25] Now there were seven brothers among us. The first got married and died. Having no offspring, he left his wife to his brother. [26] The same happened to the second also, and the third, and so to all seven. [27] Then last of all the woman died. [28] In the resurrection, therefore, whose wife will she be of the seven? For they all had married her."

²⁹*Jesus answered them, "You are deceived, because you don't know the Scriptures or the power of God. ³⁰For in the resurrection they neither marry nor are given in marriage but are like angels in heaven. ³¹Now concerning the resurrection of the dead, haven't you read what was spoken to you by God: ³²I am the God of Abraham and the God of Isaac and the God of Jacob? He is not the God of the dead, but of the living."*

³³*And when the crowds heard this, they were astonished at His teaching.*

³⁴*When the Pharisees heard that He had silenced the Sadducees, they came together. ³⁵And one of them, an expert in the law, asked a question to test Him: ³⁶"Teacher, which command in the law is the greatest?"*

³⁷*He said to him, "Love the Lord your God with all your heart, with all your soul, and with all your mind. ³⁸This is the greatest and most important command. ³⁹The second is like it: Love your neighbor as yourself. ⁴⁰All the Law and the Prophets depend on these two commands."*

*V*erse 14 could have made for a better chapter break, since it ends the parable section while verse 15 begins a section containing three controversy stories. No doubt this series of tricks and traps for Jesus reflects the decision the Pharisees and chief priests made in Matthew 21:46; they are looking for a way to arrest Jesus.

The first trap involves a trick question to which Jesus can't answer either yes or no without getting into serious trouble. Two unlikely groups come together: the disciples of the Pharisees and of the Herodians, a political group initially committed to Herod the Great but now supporting his son Antipas. There is a new interesting suggestion that, since Herod had initially been so supportive of the Essenes, "Herodian" may be a term for the Essenes themselves, who inexplicably and mysteriously are not referred to anywhere in the New Testament. Whichever is the case, two unlikely groups have come together under the banner of their mutual hatred of Jesus to trip and trap him.

You can cut the insincerity of their opening statement with a knife. Then comes the question "Is it lawful to pay taxes to Caesar or not?" A yes answer gets Jesus into trouble with the loyal Jews who disdain Caesar and his taxes. A no answer gets him in trouble with the Romans. It is the kind of impossible situation at which Jesus is so good. He refuses to pretend. Jesus calls them what they are, hypocrites—people who are hiding behind a mask. He asks to be shown the silver denarius, the equivalent of a day's work, a coin that was perhaps minted in Tiberius, Herod's capital on the Sea of Galilee. It is important to note that Jesus asks two specific questions: whose portrait and whose *inscription* are on the coin.

The portrait is Tiberius, the son of Augustus. The inscription is the real crux of the issue. It would have accorded divinity to Tiberius, referring to him as divine.

We often use Jesus' conclusion as a justification for paying taxes, which it certainly is not. There are other references in the New Testament that support the idea of supporting the government with our tax money (such as Rom 13:1).

When Jesus says, "Give to Caesar what is Caesar's" (NIV 1984), in light of the inscription that claims divinity, Jesus intends that nothing belongs to Caesar. The claim to divinity belongs only to God and should be given only to him. His answer is neither yes nor no, but it nonetheless amazes them all.

Matthew is careful to note that the next attack occurred on the same day (Mt 22:23). Now it is the Sadducees who appear. They are more powerful politically than the Pharisees but have less public support. Their days are numbered however; after A.D. 70, with the destruction of the temple, they will completely disappear, and the Pharisees will be virtually the only group left standing.

The Sadducees' insincerity is as thick as the opening statement of the previous attack. They're going to ask Jesus about the resurrection, *in which they do not believe*. They put forth a ludicrous story of a woman who is married to an unfortunate succession of seven brothers. According to the Old Testament law of leverate marriage, which is based on a portion of the Scripture in which they do believe (Deut 25:5), a man is obligated to marry his brother's wife if she dies childless so that his name will not die out in Israel.

Now, at the resurrection (which they don't believe in), whose wife will she be?

To the Sadducees, Jesus gives a very pharisaic answer. In the next conflict story, he will give to the Pharisees a very Sadducaic answer. This effectively pits the two groups against each other.

His opening rejoinder would have put them on the offensive immediately. They are in error, he says. These paragons of legal observance do not know the Scriptures or the power of God, which are inextricably linked. When the resurrection occurs, no one will be married. It is a non-issue. They will be like the angels who don't need to be married, since they never die and don't need to procreate. Issue settled in one breath.

Jesus proceeds to speak about the resurrection, while they look for someplace to hide. He demonstrates the reality of the resurrection from the Sadducees' own accepted Torah. And again he uses the very edgy rabbinic rejoinder "Haven't you read?" In Exodus 3:6, God refers to himself as the God of Abraham, Isaac and Jacob. Point one is established, and it is irrefutable. He is the God of the patriarchs. Next, God is not the God of the dead, but of the living. Point two is made, and it is irrefutable as well. What may be missing in our minds is the connection between Jesus' two points. His audience wordlessly comes to a conclusion that is beyond us. The conclusion is, if God is the God of the living, Abraham, Isaac and Jacob are still alive, and so the resurrection is a reality.

The first crowd was "amazed" (Mt 22:22), and now they are "astonished" (Mt 22:33).

Teams one and two are down. The final group, the Pharisees themselves, put forward one of their "legal experts" (*nomikos*, from *nomos*, "law") with the most actively debated question in their rabbinic world: What is the greatest commandment? This is not the first time Jesus has been asked this question. When you realize that the Pharisees reckoned there were 613 commandments, you realize how complicated a question like this could become. When asked a similar question, the great Hillel responded with his own version of the Golden Rule.

Jesus will respond from the Sadducees' chosen corpus. First, he quotes the central creed of Judaism, the single most frequently recited prayer: the Shema (Deut 6:5). The most important command is to love God with everything you've got. Beyond a shadow of a doubt, that is the greatest. But there is a second command, and the two are inextricably linked: "Love your neighbor" (Lev 19:18).

There is no record of the Pharisees' response. Jesus' answer to their question was the perfect response to which there was no response.

JESUS' COUP DE GRÂCE

⁴¹While the Pharisees were together, Jesus questioned them, ⁴²"What do you think about the Messiah? Whose Son is He?"

"David's," they told Him.

⁴³He asked them, "How is it then that David, inspired by the Spirit, calls Him 'Lord':

> *⁴⁴The Lord declared to my Lord,*
> *'Sit at My right hand*
> *until I put Your enemies under Your feet'?*

⁴⁵"If David calls Him 'Lord,' how then can the Messiah be his Son?" ⁴⁶No one was able to answer Him at all, and from that day no one dared to question Him anymore.

*Y*ou begin to get the feeling that Jesus has had just about enough by now. In all the Synoptics, he poses one final unanswerable question to silence all his enemies and reveal the true depth of their ignorance of who the Messiah really is. It's a put up or shut up move.

It begins with an easy question he knows they will answer. "Whose son is the Christ?"

"The Son of David," they respond. (Easy answer!)

Next question: "How is it that David refers to the Christ as Lord?"

Jesus goes on to quote from Psalm 110, where David appears to do just that. In their world, it is incomprehensible that someone like David would ever call his son "Lord."

The final question hangs in the air, unanswered and unanswerable. That just about does it for the tricks and traps in regard to Jesus.

MATTHEW 23

SEVEN WOES

23:1–36

ONE LAMENT

23:37–39

SEVEN WOES

¹Then Jesus spoke to the crowds and to His disciples: ²"The scribes and the Pharisees are seated in the chair of Moses. ³Therefore do whatever they tell you, and observe it. But don't do what they do, because they don't practice what they teach. ⁴They tie up heavy loads that are hard to carry and put them on people's shoulders, but they themselves aren't willing to lift a finger to move them. ⁵They do everything to be observed by others: They enlarge their phylacteries and lengthen their tassels. ⁶They love the place of honor at banquets, the front seats in the synagogues, ⁷greetings in the marketplaces, and to be called 'Rabbi' by people.

⁸"But as for you, do not be called 'Rabbi,' because you have one Teacher, and you are all brothers. ⁹Do not call anyone on earth your father, because you have one Father, who is in heaven. ¹⁰And do not be called masters either, because you have one Master, the Messiah. ¹¹The greatest among you will be your servant. ¹²Whoever exalts himself will be humbled, and whoever humbles himself will be exalted.

¹³"But woe to you, scribes and Pharisees, hypocrites! You lock up the kingdom of heaven from people. For you don't go in, and you don't allow those entering to go in.

¹⁴["Woe to you, scribes and Pharisees, hypocrites! You devour widows' houses and make long prayers just for show. This is why you will receive a harsher punishment.]

¹⁵"Woe to you, scribes and Pharisees, hypocrites! You travel over land and sea to make one proselyte, and when he becomes one, you make him twice as fit for hell as you are!

¹⁶"Woe to you, blind guides, who say, 'Whoever takes an oath by the sanctuary, it means nothing. But whoever takes an oath by the gold of the sanctuary is bound by his oath.' ¹⁷Blind fools! For which is greater, the gold or the sanctuary that sanctified the gold? ¹⁸Also, 'Whoever takes an oath by the altar, it means nothing. But whoever takes an oath by the gift that is on it is bound by his oath.' ¹⁹Blind people! For which is greater, the gift or the altar that sanctifies the gift? ²⁰Therefore, the one who takes an oath by the altar takes an oath by it and by everything on it. ²¹The one who takes an oath by the sanctuary takes an oath by it and by Him who dwells in it. ²²And the one who takes an oath by heaven takes an oath by God's throne and by Him who sits on it.

²³*"Woe to you, scribes and Pharisees, hypocrites! You pay a tenth of mint, dill, and cumin, yet you have neglected the more important matters of the law—justice, mercy, and faith. These things should have been done without neglecting the others.* ²⁴*Blind guides! You strain out a gnat, yet gulp down a camel!*

²⁵*"Woe to you, scribes and Pharisees, hypocrites! You clean the outside of the cup and dish, but inside they are full of greed and self-indulgence!* ²⁶*Blind Pharisee! First clean the inside of the cup, so the outside of it may also become clean.*

²⁷*"Woe to you, scribes and Pharisees, hypocrites! You are like whitewashed tombs, which appear beautiful on the outside, but inside are full of dead men's bones and every impurity.* ²⁸*In the same way, on the outside you seem righteous to people, but inside you are full of hypocrisy and lawlessness.*

²⁹*"Woe to you, scribes and Pharisees, hypocrites! You build the tombs of the prophets and decorate the monuments of the righteous,* ³⁰*and you say, 'If we had lived in the days of our fathers, we wouldn't have taken part with them in shedding the prophets' blood.'* ³¹*You, therefore, testify against yourselves that you are sons of those who murdered the prophets.* ³²*Fill up, then, the measure of your fathers' sins!*

³³*"Snakes! Brood of vipers! How can you escape being condemned to hell?* ³⁴*This is why I am sending you prophets, sages, and scribes. Some of them you will kill and crucify, and some of them you will flog in your synagogues and hound from town to town.* ³⁵*So all the righteous blood shed on the earth will be charged to you, from the blood of righteous Abel to the blood of Zechariah, son of Berechiah, whom you murdered between the sanctuary and the altar.* ³⁶*I assure you: All these things will come on this generation!"*

With the opening of Matthew 23 we enter into the final block of the five large sections of Jesus' teaching in the book of Matthew. It will extend all the way to 25:46. In chapter 23 we will see Jesus at his most emotional in Matthew's Gospel, from disgust to rage to lament. His presentation of the woes pronounced against the Pharisees is by far the longest in all the Gospels. His portrayal of both what was commendable and, far more, what was worthy of contempt helps us understand the life situation of Matthew's first hearers, who often experienced persecution at the hands of pharisaic leaders.

Jesus begins with a unique statement: his followers must actually obey the Pharisees and "do whatever they tell you to do." This is because they are in the "chair of Moses." This phrase has two possible meanings. First, it may refer to an actual chair in the synagogue, a few examples of which have been unearthed by archaeologists, the most notable of which is in the synagogue in Chorazin. It is believed the teacher actually took this seat when giving the lesson in the synagogue. Others believe the Torah scrolls might have been placed there as an act of respect. Second, the phrase may refer to a place of authority, in much the same way that we refer to a professorial chair at a university. Either way, Jesus' initial message is the same. Remarkably, he says they should listen to and obey the Pharisees. This is his eye-opening instruction to Matthew's first listeners, who are still living under the authority of the Pharisees in their synagogues in Galilee.

But this single statement comprises all he has to say that is positive about the Pharisees. For the rest of this section, all the way to verse 36, Jesus' temper and tone will rise.

Do what they say, says Jesus, but not what they do, for even the Pharisees do not do what they say. They are all about binding the heavy burden of the law on their listeners, a load of guilt and shame and self-doubt. Yet they speak not a word of encouragement and lend not a finger to lift the load.

Contrary to Jesus' command to do works in secret (Mt 6:3-18), the Pharisees do good works only when people are looking. The phylacteries—small boxes containing Scripture and bound to the right arm and the forehead in obedience to Deuteronomy 6:6-8—were held in place by leather straps. Apparently the Pharisees made the straps extra-wide to make them more visible. The tassels on the corners of their prayer shawls (Num 15:38) they likewise made extra-long in order to be seen. In short, for them it was all about being seen, about choice seats and about being greeted as "Rabbi" in the busy marketplaces.

The word *rabbi* (based on the Hebrew root *rav*, or "great one") was still a fluid term in Jesus' day. Though there were already well-known teachers, like Hillel, Shammai and Gamaliel, there was as yet no such thing as an ordained rabbi. They were both referred to as the "Elder." This would come into being after A.D. 70, when Judaism would be reformed after the destruction of the temple.

In verse 8 Jesus turns abruptly toward his disciples, saying, "But as for you . . ." His disciples should refuse the term *rabbi*, for they have only one teacher. This statement shows that Jesus understood the term *rabbi* to be synonymous with the Greek word for "teacher" (*didaskalos*). No one is to consider themselves as "great"; they are all brothers and sisters.

Likewise, they are to refuse the term *father*, which had also begun to be applied to the rabbis. Some students had even begun employing the intimate term *abba* to them. This we would imagine Jesus absolutely abhorred (see Mk 14:36). Neither are they to accept the title "teacher." Here Matthew uses not the familiar Greek word *didaskalos*, but a term found only here. It is *kathēgētēs*, which brings together the notion of teacher and leader. Only one person should be accorded this title: Jesus himself.

His consistent witness throughout his ministry has been to the upside-down nature of the kingdom, where the least are the greatest and the last are first. Now Jesus reiterates that the servant is the greatest. That, it appears, is the only title his followers should ever covet. This, of all his teachings, the disciples must hear and understand. The time is short. If they exalt themselves, like the Pharisees, they will be humbled. If they humble themselves, as they have seen Jesus consistently do for the last three years, they will be exalted (Mt 19:30; 20:26; see Phil 2:6-11).

In verse 13 Jesus turns back to the Pharisees and pronounces seven prophetic "woes." With each one, his intensity rises. Each one is a unique condemnation of their old orthodoxy and their stubborn refusal to combine what they perceive as justice with the defining characteristic of Jesus' Father—namely mercy. The woes are as follows:

1. For locking up the kingdom and not even entering in themselves. Jesus had instructed his disciples to unlock the doors of the kingdom (Mt 16:19).

2. For doggedly pursuing converts, not to Judaism but to Pharisaism, and pouring the same poison of condemnation and guilt into their new followers.

3. For formulating ridiculous oaths, when all that is required is a simple yes or no (Mt 5:37).

4. For their suffocating observance of the small matters of the law (such as tithing on their spices) and neglecting the very heart of Torah observance: justice, mercy and faithfulness.

5. For their fundamental misunderstanding of what "clean" and "unclean" signify. They wash the outside of the cup (of their lives) and leave the inside full of filthy greed and self-indulgence. (At this point Jesus' tone clearly begins to rise when at verse 26 he inserts the epitaph "blind Pharisee!")

6. For falsely whitewashing their lives, like a newly occupied tomb, but concealing inside themselves the worst kinds of rottenness and decay. (Nothing in the Jewish imagination was more unclean than the decaying body; Num. 19:11.) The custom in Jesus' day was a two-stage burial. Bodies were washed and left in the tomb to decay for a year. Once the flesh had rotted away, the bones would be washed and placed in a bone box (ossuary). Jesus' image is of the first stage, when the body putrefied in the tomb. I imagine the Pharisees becoming livid at his use of these worst of unclean images.

7. Finally, for pretending to honor the prophets by decorating their tombs when, in fact, their forefathers murdered the prophets. The Pharisees exhibited no shame for what their ancestors had done to God's messengers.

Verse 32 is the high-water mark of Jesus' emotions. The closing "woe" was about killing the prophets. I imagine that he was almost shouting at this point, "Fill up . . . the measure of your fathers' sins!" In essence he is daring them to kill him. His tone remains at a fever pitch as he calls them vipers (see Mt 3:7; 12:34). His words become prophetic, though he is not quoting any single Old Testament passage. He has become the very voice of his Father.

Jesus' prophecy of what the Pharisees will do describes at the same time what they will do to his followers, to Matthew's first hearers. Some of them will be killed, beaten, strangled and stoned under the authority of the synagogue. The Romans will crucify some. They will be flogged and doggedly pursued from town to town by men like Saul of Tarsus. No doubt out of breath and emotionally exhausted, Jesus concludes in verse 36. This is all coming in the lifespan of this generation.

ONE LAMENT

[37] *"Jerusalem, Jerusalem! She who kills the prophets and stones those who are sent to her. How often I wanted to gather your children together, as a hen gathers her chicks under her wings, yet you were not willing!* [38] *See, your house is left to you desolate.* [39] *For I tell you, you will never see Me again until you say, 'He who comes in the name of the Lord is the blessed One'!"*

The "these things" in verse 36 of Jesus' final statement refers to the climax in A.D. 70, when Titus will surround the city of Jerusalem and completely destroy it. Josephus, who was actually an eyewitness, speaks of piles of human corpses, of cannibalism in the city and of unimaginable suffering.

In Jesus' prophetic imagination, his final words transport him to that scene in A.D. 70. At this point he undoubtedly breaks down in tears as he laments over Jerusalem. It is still the voice of the prophet speaking God's words, only now he is weeping the Father's tears.

Verse 39 marks the close of Jesus' public ministry. From this point on, all his instructions will be made in private.

MATTHEW 24

TWO QUESTIONS, TWO ANSWERS

24:1-44

A PARABLE ABOUT NOT KNOWING

24:45-51

TWO QUESTIONS, TWO ANSWERS

¹As Jesus left and was going out of the temple complex, His disciples came up and called His attention to the temple buildings. ²Then He replied to them, "Don't you see all these things? I assure you: Not one stone will be left here on another that will not be thrown down!"

³While He was sitting on the Mount of Olives, the disciples approached Him privately and said, "Tell us, when will these things happen? And what is the sign of Your coming and of the end of the age?"

⁴Then Jesus replied to them: "Watch out that no one deceives you. ⁵For many will come in My name, saying, 'I am the Messiah,' and they will deceive many. ⁶You are going to hear of wars and rumors of wars. See that you are not alarmed, because these things must take place, but the end is not yet. ⁷For nation will rise up against nation, and kingdom against kingdom. There will be famines and earthquakes in various places. ⁸All these events are the beginning of birth pains.

⁹"Then they will hand you over for persecution, and they will kill you. You will be hated by all nations because of My name. ¹⁰Then many will take offense, betray one another and hate one another. ¹¹Many false prophets will rise up and deceive many. ¹²Because lawlessness will multiply, the love of many will grow cold. ¹³But the one who endures to the end will be delivered. ¹⁴This good news of the kingdom will be proclaimed in all the world as a testimony to all nations. And then the end will come.

¹⁵"So when you see the abomination that causes desolation, spoken of by the prophet Daniel, standing in the holy place" (let the reader understand), ¹⁶"then those in Judea must flee to the mountains! ¹⁷A man on the housetop must not come down to get things out of his house. ¹⁸And a man in the field must not go back to get his clothes. ¹⁹Woe to pregnant women and nursing mothers in those days! ²⁰Pray that your escape may not be in winter or on a Sabbath. ²¹For at that time there will be great tribulation, the kind that hasn't taken place from the beginning of the world until now and never will again! ²²Unless those days were limited, no one would survive. But those days will be limited because of the elect.

²³"If anyone tells you then, 'Look, here is the Messiah!' or, 'Over here!' do not believe it! ²⁴False messiahs and false prophets will arise and perform great signs and wonders to lead astray, if possible, even the elect. [25] Take note: I have told you in advance. [26] So if they tell you, 'Look, He's in the wilderness!' don't go out; 'Look, He's in the inner rooms!' do not believe it. [27] For as the lightning comes from the east and flashes as far as the west, so will be the coming of the Son of Man. [28] Wherever the carcass is, there the vultures will gather.

[29] "Immediately after the tribulation of those days:

> The sun will be darkened,
> and the moon will not shed its light;
> the stars will fall from the sky,
> and the celestial powers will be shaken.

[30] "Then the sign of the Son of Man will appear in the sky, and then all the peoples of the earth will mourn; and they will see the Son of Man coming on the clouds of heaven with power and great glory. [31] He will send out His angels with a loud trumpet, and they will gather His elect from the four winds, from one end of the sky to the other.

[32] "Now learn this parable from the fig tree: As soon as its branch becomes tender and sprouts leaves, you know that summer is near. [33] In the same way, when you see all these things, recognize that He is near—at the door! [34] I assure you: This generation will certainly not pass away until all these things take place. [35] Heaven and earth will pass away, but My words will never pass away.

[36] "Now concerning that day and hour no one knows—neither the angels in heaven, nor the Son—except the Father only. [37] As the days of Noah were, so the coming of the Son of Man will be. [38] For in those days before the flood they were eating and drinking, marrying and giving in marriage, until the day Noah boarded the ark. [39] They didn't know until the flood came and swept them all away. So this is the way the coming of the Son of Man will be: [40] Then two men will be in the field: one will be taken and one left. [41] Two women will be grinding at the mill: one will be taken and one left. [42] Therefore be alert, since you don't know what day your Lord is coming. [43] But know this: If the homeowner had known what time the thief was coming, he would have stayed alert and not let his house be broken into. [44] This is why you also must be ready, because the Son of Man is coming at an hour you do not expect."

*A*s Jesus and his disciples leave the heated conflict with the Jewish leaders in the temple, the disciples resort to small talk in an effort to distract Jesus. The writer of Matthew says they tried to call his attention to the buildings. Surely Herod's temple, which was still not quite finished, was an awe-inspiring sight. Josephus describes its gleaming white exterior.

Jesus won't be distracted. "Don't you see all these things?" His intensity still simmering, he adds, "Not one stone will be left here on another." To this day the broken pavement and a pile of massive stones from the ruined temple still litter the outside of what remains of Herod's wall in Jerusalem, silent witnesses to the stunning accuracy of Jesus' prediction.

They make their way silently across the Kidron Valley and up onto the Mount of Olives, overlooking the vast thirty-five-acre temple complex. What follows is Jesus' most lengthy discourse concerning the end times. The key to unlocking his message is to understand that the disciples asked him two distinct questions to which he provides two completely separate answers.

Verse 3 contains the two questions:

Question 1: "When will these things happen?"

Question 2: "What is the sign of Your coming and of the end of the age?"

Jesus will answer the first question in verses 4-28. The separate second answer will follow in 29-44.

The first answer is prefaced with a warning. There will be deceivers, false Christs, like Simon bar Kokhba, who was proclaimed by Rabbi Akiba to be the Messiah.[52] "You are going to hear of wars and rumors of wars." To Jesus, this represents the status quo. He instructs the Twelve not to be alarmed. These are not signs of the end; they have been happening since the beginning of time.

Persecution will become a reality, as he has promised before. They will be hated for his sake. Wickedness will increase, as the love of many grows cold (see 2 Tim 3:3). In the face of the coming persecution, Jesus instructs his disciples and Matthew's first hearers and you and me to stand firm. The ever-present kingdom will be preached to the entire world as a testimony to the Gentiles, and then the end—the event that fulfills the answer to the second question—will come.

From verse 15 to 25, Jesus prophesied the coming destruction of Jerusalem, an event he will characterize primarily as something from which a person can flee.

Daniel had prophesied the "abomination of desolation"—that is, the event that leads to the abandoning of the temple (Dan 9:27; 11:31; 12:11). That prophecy was fulfilled in his time, in December of 167 B.C., when Antiochus IV set up a statue of Zeus on the altar of burnt offerings in the temple. In the disciples' experience, the desolating sacrilege will occur when the zealots anoint a clown as high priest in A.D. 68. When the sign appears, Jesus says, it is time to flee; he is describing an historical event from which his followers can run away. Eusebius tells us this is exactly what happened when a number of Christians in Jerusalem fled to the city of Pella and were saved from the siege.[53]

Jesus proceeds to give more details regarding the difficulties of their flight. They are not to retrieve their goods from their homes or their cloaks from where they had left them in the field. The flight will be especially difficult for pregnant and nursing women. Jesus says that they should pray the flight does not happen in the extremes of winter. It is significant that he adds that he hopes their flight will not occur on the Sabbath; despite his disagreements with the Pharisees concerning the Sabbath, Jesus still cherishes the concept of the Sabbath rest and promotes it among his followers.

If you take the time to read Josephus's account of the siege of Jerusalem in books 5 and 6 of his *Jewish Wars,* you will appreciate Jesus' words in verses 21-22. In their experience, this was the most devastating event in the history of the world.

Jesus repeats his warning about false and deceiving messiahs who may even be able to perform miracles. No matter what his followers hear, they are not to listen to the lies. Jesus will not appear in the desert or in the "inner rooms." When he does return, there will be no question. It will be a cataclysmic event, like lightning moving across the sky. Jesus has told them all they need to know in regard to their first question about the destruction of the temple. History will eventually validate the fact that Jesus' followers were ready after all.

With verse 29, everything changes. The imagery is no longer earthly—in fact, it becomes apocalyptic. Jesus opens his second answer with two quotes from Isaiah (Is 13:10; 34:4). The signs are cosmic; they involve the sun, moon and stars.

In verse 30, Jesus gives the first of four simple straightforward lessons regarding the end of the world, a four-part answer to the disciples' second question:

1. When Jesus comes, everyone will know. Signs will appear in the sky. The Son of Man will come in the clouds, accompanied by angels who will gather the faithful from the four winds. In verse 32, Jesus provides another lesson from the leaves: quite simply, green leaves are a sign that summer is coming. When the disciples see the cataclysmic signs, the time has come. The entire race of humankind will see it all fulfilled.

2. No one knows the day and hour it will occur. In an unexplainable statement, Jesus confesses that even he cannot tell the precise day or hour of his return. But people have never been ready for such momentous times. In the days of the flood of Noah, no one had a clue that the world was about to come to a watery end. It was sudden and cataclysmic.

3. Jesus' return is something from which you cannot run away. Two will be in the field; one will be taken and the other left. Two will be grinding; one will be taken and the other left. This is an event from which you cannot run. It is a cosmic moment that marks the end of history.

4. Be ready by keeping watch. Given all of the above—that no one knows when—the best you can do to be ready is to keep watch. If the homeowner had known when the thief was coming, he would have kept his house safe. But since you cannot know when the thief (Jesus) is coming, the only way to be ready is to keep a continuous watch.

A PARABLE ABOUT NOT KNOWING

⁴⁵"Who then is a faithful and sensible slave, whom his master has put in charge of his household, to give them food at the proper time? ⁴⁶That slave whose master finds him working when he comes will be rewarded. ⁴⁷I assure you: He will put him in charge of all his possessions. ⁴⁸But if that wicked slave says in his heart, 'My master is delayed,' ⁴⁹and starts to beat his fellow slaves, and eats and drinks with drunkards, ⁵⁰that slave's master will come on a day he does not expect and at an hour he does not know. ⁵¹He will cut him to pieces and assign him a place with the hypocrites. In that place there will be weeping and gnashing of teeth."

*I*n an attempt to move all this information from the heads of his disciples into their hearts, Jesus tells a parable. It provides a vivid image of how the slaves of the master can be prepared for the time of his return, which is unknown and unknowable.

The task they were assigned by their master was to feed and care for the members of his household while he was away. If those were their orders, the best way to be ready for his return is to be found in faithful obedience when he shows up. They will be rewarded by having their responsibilities as slaves enlarged to extend to even more of the master's possessions. Note that the reward is not their freedom, because their slavery to the master is in fact their greatest freedom.

But what does readiness look like? The slave who disobeys his orders and abuses his charges, thinking the master's return is not imminent, is the one who is seriously unprepared. The fate of that servant is an echo of the penalties always experienced by those who do not take the coming of the kingdom or its king seriously (see Mt 8:12; 13:42; 22:13).

MATTHEW 25

THE TEN VIRGINS

25:1–13

THE TALENTS

25:14–30

THE SHEEP AND THE GOATS

25:31–46

THE TEN VIRGINS

[1]*"Then the kingdom of heaven will be like 10 virgins who took their lamps and went out to meet the groom. [2]Five of them were foolish and five were sensible. [3]When the foolish took their lamps, they didn't take olive oil with them. [4]But the sensible ones took oil in their flasks with their lamps. [5]Since the groom was delayed, they all became drowsy and fell asleep.*

[6]*"In the middle of the night there was a shout: 'Here's the groom! Come out to meet him.'*

[7]*"Then all those virgins got up and trimmed their lamps. [8]But the foolish ones said to the sensible ones, 'Give us some of your oil, because our lamps are going out.'*

[9]*"The sensible ones answered, 'No, there won't be enough for us and for you. Go instead to those who sell, and buy oil for yourselves.'*

[10]*"When they had gone to buy some, the groom arrived. Then those who were ready went in with him to the wedding banquet, and the door was shut.*

[11]*"Later the rest of the virgins also came and said, 'Master, master, open up for us!'*

[12]*"But he replied, 'I assure you: I do not know you!'*

[13]*"Therefore be alert, because you don't know either the day or the hour."*

*F*ollowing the lengthy teaching on the end times in Matthew 24, Jesus explains the concept of being ready by telling three more parables. This is his final block of teaching in Matthew's Gospel. The narrative will resume, taking us all the way to the cross and resurrection. The fact that Jesus would create three different parables on the theme of his return should cause us to realize how important our being ready for it was to him and therefore how important it should be to us. All three parables are based on a note of confusion regarding different aspects of the return of the king. It is an urgent word to us from the king himself, who is returning soon.

The opening parable of the ten virgins discusses a note of confusion about the time of the bridegroom's return. This parable is designed to expand on Jesus' earlier teaching in 24:42, where the disciples were told to keep watch because they did not know the time of the return. Now Jesus fictionalizes the truth for them. He is adamant that they understand this.

Even more than today, to be asked to be a bridesmaid was a great honor in first-century Judaism. To come unprepared would have been looked upon as a grave insult, not unlike those who carelessly avoided the wedding banquet in Matthew 22. Half of the group is prepared while half of the group is foolishly not. Notice that the essence of preparedness is the ability to wait until the time of the return of the bridegroom.

Bridesmaids were essentially called to a late-night vigil, waiting for the return of the bridegroom. They were forced to keep their lamps burning all along since, when the time came, they would not have the time to light them. They are forced to wait until midnight, when suddenly they hear the call that the bridegroom has come.[54]

The ensuing panic and confusion can be experienced today backstage of almost any wedding, when something invariably goes wrong. The foolish bridesmaids realize their mistake and plead with the five who are prepared to borrow some of their oil. But this is not a time for sharing; the occasion is too important. So the five foolish girls leave in search of someone who will sell them the oil they foolishly did not think to bring.

While they are off on their shopping mission, the groom returns, and everyone processes into the extravagant feast. First-century wedding feasts could go on for seven days, so the detail that the door is shut is more than a necessary plot element for Jesus' story. In this more primitive time, brides were still sometimes stolen before the marriage could be consummated.

No matter how hard they knock and how loudly they plead, the foolish bridesmaids will not be let in. The conclusion is simple and straightforward, an echo of 24:42: "Be alert."

THE TALENTS

[14]"For it is just like a man going on a journey. He called his own slaves and turned over his possessions to them. [15]To one he gave five talents; to another, two; and to another, one—to each according to his own ability. Then

he went on a journey. Immediately [16] *the man who had received five talents went, put them to work, and earned five more.* [17] *In the same way the man with two earned two more.* [18] *But the man who had received one talent went off, dug a hole in the ground, and hid his master's money.*

[19] *"After a long time the master of those slaves came and settled accounts with them.* [20] *The man who had received five talents approached, presented five more talents, and said, 'Master, you gave me five talents. Look, I've earned five more talents.'*

[21] *"His master said to him, 'Well done, good and faithful slave! You were faithful over a few things; I will put you in charge of many things. Share your master's joy!'*

[22] *"Then the man with two talents also approached. He said, 'Master, you gave me two talents. Look, I've earned two more talents.'*

[23] *"His master said to him, 'Well done, good and faithful slave! You were faithful over a few things; I will put you in charge of many things. Share your master's joy!'*

[24] *"Then the man who had received one talent also approached and said, 'Master, I know you. You're a difficult man, reaping where you haven't sown and gathering where you haven't scattered seed.* [25] *So I was afraid and went off and hid your talent in the ground. Look, you have what is yours.'*

[26] *"But his master replied to him, 'You evil, lazy slave! If you knew that I reap where I haven't sown and gather where I haven't scattered,* [27] *then you should have deposited my money with the bankers. And when I returned I would have received my money back with interest.*

[28] *"'So take the talent from him and give it to the one who has 10 talents.* [29] *For to everyone who has, more will be given, and he will have more than enough. But from the one who does not have, even what he has will be taken away from him.* [30] *And throw this good-for-nothing slave into the outer darkness. In that place there will be weeping and gnashing of teeth.'"*

The second parable, the story of the three servants, has to do with confusion regarding the true character of the master. It focuses on what faithfulness should, or should not, look like in the time that remains until the return. The story opens with the news that a man is leaving on a journey. Out of what could have been several slaves, he focuses attention on just three. He divides between them an enormous amount of cash—the equivalent of over two million dollars. He must have been extremely wealthy, because later he will refer to this large sum as "a few things" (Mt 25:21, 23). The master knows his servants well enough to divide the money according to their abilities. One receives five talents, another two and finally, to the last slave, one talent is entrusted. In verses 16-18, the servants reveal that the master's estimates of them had been dead-on. The first slave, who received the five, invests the money and makes five more. In the ancient world, some investments could return as much as 50 percent. Similarly, the second slave doubled his money. The third slave, in whom the master had placed the least expectation, buries his single talent in the ground. This method of dealing with money is seen again and again in archaeological excavations where hordes of coins are unearthed, apparently hidden from the invading Romans.

After a long time, the master returns from his journey and calls the three slaves to come and account for themselves. Just as he had expected, the first slave performed accordingly and doubled his money. For the first time we hear the words we all someday hope to hear: "Well done, good and faithful slave." Like the slave in 24:47, his responsibilities are increased as a reward. Freedom is not the prize; serving the master well is, as is the intimacy of sharing in his joy. In parallel form, the slave who doubled the two talents is commended and rewarded.

Finally, the third slave appears before his master. Though his owner expected the least from him, he failed to fulfill even that. The reason? He blames the severity of his master, not his own indolence. His excuse? The master is a difficult man. According to the slave, the master's expectations are impossible. He expects to reap where he has not even sown. Given the evidence of the parable, nothing could be further from the truth. The master had "sown" two million dollars among three slaves and had tempered his expectations according to their abilities. The slave's final excuse: he was afraid and so he simply hid the money.

Whatever joy the master might have experienced because of the first two slaves vanishes in the face of his disappointment with the third. If indeed he was the sort of person the slave described with his insulting description, why didn't he simply deposit the money in the bank? It seems the master would have been happy to receive even the small amount of interest that simple act would have yielded. He would have been satisfied if the slave had only put the money in the bank and then done nothing but withdraw it upon his return.

The master repeats one of the upside-down values of the kingdom in verse 29: "For to everyone who has, more will be given, and he will have more than enough. But from the one who does not have, even what he has will be taken away from him." We heard this puzzling maxim already in 13:12 in the conclusion of the parable of the soils. When Luke tells the story, he makes clear the disconnection of the statement by having the confused servants object when the first slave receives the ten talents: "But, master, he already has ten" (Lk 19:25, paraphrase).

There is confusion upon the return of the master. Some will be afraid at his coming because they never really understood his loving-kindness. Though they might try to use their confusion as an excuse for their lack of fruit, they will not be excused. But even the productive slaves will still not yet grasp how manifestly gracious and generous the master is when they witness him blessing those who are already blessed with even deeper, incalculable blessings.

THE SHEEP AND THE GOATS

[31] *"When the Son of Man comes in His glory, and all the angels with Him, then He will sit on the throne of His glory.* [32] *All the nations will be gathered before Him, and He will separate them one from another, just as a shepherd separates the sheep from the goats.* [33] *He will put the sheep on His right and the goats on the left.* [34] *Then the King will say to those on His right, 'Come, you who are blessed by My Father, inherit the kingdom prepared for you from the foundation of the world.*

> [35] *For I was hungry*
> *and you gave Me something to eat;*
> *I was thirsty*
> *and you gave Me something to drink;*
> *I was a stranger and you took Me in;*

> [36] *I was naked and you clothed Me;*
> *I was sick and you took care of Me;*
> *I was in prison and you visited Me.'*

[37] *"Then the righteous will answer Him, 'Lord, when did we see You hungry and feed You, or thirsty and give You something to drink?* [38] *When did we see You a stranger and take You in, or without clothes and clothe You?* [39] *When did we see You sick, or in prison, and visit You?'*

[40] *"And the King will answer them, 'I assure you: Whatever you did for one of the least of these brothers of Mine, you did for Me.'* [41] *Then He will also say to those on the left, 'Depart from Me, you who are cursed, into the eternal fire prepared for the Devil and his angels!*

> [42] *For I was hungry*
> *and you gave Me nothing to eat;*
> *I was thirsty*
> *and you gave Me nothing to drink;*
> [43] *I was a stranger*
> *and you didn't take Me in;*
> *I was naked*
> *and you didn't clothe Me,*
> *sick and in prison*
> *and you didn't take care of Me.'*

[44] *"Then they too will answer, 'Lord, when did we see You hungry, or thirsty, or a stranger, or without clothes, or sick, or in prison, and not help You?'*

[45] *"Then He will answer them, 'I assure you: Whatever you did not do for one of the least of these, you did not do for Me either.'*

[46] *"And they will go away into eternal punishment, but the righteous into eternal life."*

The story of the separation of the sheep and the goats is the final block of Jesus' teaching. It is based on a moment of confusion on the Day of Judgment that seems to have captivated Jesus' imagination. He already painted this picture at the very beginning of his ministry (Mt

7:22). Now as the cross looms in the very near future, he returns to the question of what divides the sons and daughters of the kingdom from those who have indeed done things for him but never really knew their master, like the third slave in the parable of the talents.

Jesus has sketched a picture of his coming as a cataclysmic event that every eye shall see. Next he pictures all that will follow. Surrounded by his angels, he will take his place on a great throne (Lk 1:32). Everyone who had witnessed his coming, like lightning from the east to the west, will be gathered before the throne. I imagine a rainbow of skin colors, the vast diversity between young and old, rich and poor. And then, he says, the separating will begin.

The shepherd in the natural world separates sheep and goats because goats need to be kept warm at night while sheep, with their wool, can remain outdoors.[55] But this dividing seems to have no connection to that.

As the untold billions stand before either side of the throne, his voice, which John described as sounding like "cascading waters" (Rev 1:15) will announce to those on his right, "Come." And to those on the left he will say, "Depart."

What captivates my imagination about this final scene is that both groups are confused. The blessed ones to the right of the throne are told by means of a lyrical poem,

> *For I was hungry*
> *and you gave Me something to eat;*
> *I was thirsty*
> *and you gave Me something to drink;*
> *I was a stranger and you took Me in;*
> *I was naked and you clothed Me;*
> *I was sick and you took care of Me;*
> *I was in prison and you visited Me. (Mt 25:35-36)*

Try to imagine the force of these words sung by a voice that sounds like a thundering waterfall. The righteous are confused by the words from the throne. They can't remember seeing or doing any of these things. They were unaware they were doing them. "Whatever you did for one of the least of these brothers of Mine, you did for Me," Jesus responds (Mt 25:40).

The theme is his radical identification. Jesus has identified with the poor, the hungry, the thirsty, the stranger, the naked, the sick and the prisoner. Without even looking for him, the righteous found him in the poor, and they didn't even know it was Jesus. I can see the multitude on the right side of the throne turning their gaze for a moment from his luminous face and looking into one another's faces, especially in the faces of the poor who are standing in the multitude. It will be a moment of stunning recognition.

Next Jesus turns to the left and sings the same song to the other crowd, except a few of the words have been changed. I imagine he must have shifted it down to a minor key. Those who will be cast out hear the same list of the poor and the prisoner. To their horror, they understand for the first time that they neglected these subjects of the minor-key song. They respond, "When did we see you . . . ?" And he responds, "Whatever you did not do for one of the least of these, you did not do for Me either."

I assume the condemned multitude on the left is the same group Jesus talked about in 7:22, who boasted of all they had done in his name. If you put the two scenes together, you must conclude that they never really knew who he was, and he will be forced to confess, "I never knew you!" (Mt 7:23).

Of all the images of the return, this is the most disturbing to me. Two multitudes beyond counting, one joyfully confused, relieved and deliriously happy that, without even knowing it, they had loved Jesus well. The other despairingly confused, horror filled, that what they must have suspected all along turned out to be true. The person they thought they were serving never existed.

MATTHEW 26

THE PLOT BEGINS

26:1-5

THE ANOINTING

26:6-13

THE DEAL IS CLOSED

26:14-16

THE LAST SUPPER

26:17-35

THE GARDEN

26:36-46

THE ARREST

26:47-56

BEFORE CAIAPHAS

26:57-68

REDEMPTIVE TEARS

26:69-75

THE PLOT BEGINS

¹When Jesus had finished saying all this, He told His disciples, ² "You know that the Passover takes place after two days, and the Son of Man will be handed over to be crucified."

³Then the chief priests and the elders of the people assembled in the palace of the high priest, who was called Caiaphas, ⁴and they conspired to arrest Jesus in a treacherous way and kill Him. ⁵ "Not during the festival," they said, "so there won't be rioting among the people."

*T*he chapter opens with the writer of Matthew's familiar statement for closing each of the five blocks of Jesus' teaching. It is the last time we will hear that formula. From this point on, the narrative will move quickly, from one scene to the next. In verses 1-2, Jesus reminds the disciples one final time of what is about to occur in just two days. Then there is a quick cut to the Jewish leaders, members of the Sanhedrin (Mt 26:3-5). They meet together in the palatial home of the high priest, Caiaphas, whose name we hear for the first time. He was the longest-reigning high priest in the first century (eighteen years). This is a time when high priests were appointed and deposed, exchanged at the whim of the Roman governor. Together, before any investigation or trial, the Sanhedrin plans to arrest Jesus. The original idea seems to have been to take him after Passover. This was their plan, but not Jesus'.

THE ANOINTING

⁶While Jesus was in Bethany at the house of Simon, a man who had a serious skin disease, ⁷a woman approached Him with an alabaster jar of very expensive fragrant oil. She poured it on His head as He was reclining at the table. ⁸When the disciples saw it, they were indignant. "Why this waste?" they asked. ⁹ "This might have been sold for a great deal and given to the poor."

¹⁰But Jesus, aware of this, said to them, "Why are you bothering this woman? She has done a noble thing for Me. ¹¹You always have the poor with you, but you do not always have Me. ¹²By pouring this fragrant oil on My body, she has prepared Me for burial. *[13]I assure you: Wherever this gospel is proclaimed in the whole world, what this woman has done will also be told in memory of her.*"

*J*esus and the disciples are staying in Bethany every night except for the last night. The mandate was that on the night of Passover, one must stay in the city of Jerusalem. This is why they are in Gethsemane on that final night. John gives us the detail that a party was given in Jesus' honor (Jn 12:2). Matthew jumps into the story.

Simon the leper is no doubt someone Jesus had healed; perhaps this is the reason for the party in his honor. I wonder if Simon is related to Lazarus somehow, perhaps his father or his brother. A nameless woman approaches Jesus, who is reclining Greek style at the three-sided table (triclinium) and pours expensive nard on his head from an alabaster container.

John lets us know her name is Mary. She is Martha's sister. Mark lets us know the perfume was worth a year's wages, approximately three hundred denarii, which is roughly twelve thousand dollars.

The disciples are understandably upset. John tells us it was primarily Judas who did the complaining (Jn 12:4-5). They have just heard the parable about the sheep and the goats, who are divided based on their sensitivity to the poor. Perhaps that is the connection.

It is difficult to imagine Jesus' tone just now or his frame of mind as he is poised on the verge of his passion. He is protective of Mary; he always speaks up for her (see Lk 10:41-42). He tells them they will always have the poor (Deut 15:11), but he will not always be among them. In verse 12 Jesus' tone becomes more detectable when he admits she has anointed him for his burial. In verse 13 he says something that is not remotely anything he has said for anyone else: he memorializes what Mary has done. He makes her story a permanent part of his story.

THE DEAL IS CLOSED

[14]Then one of the Twelve—the man called Judas Iscariot—went to the chief priests [15]and said, "What are you willing to give me if I hand Him over

to you?" So they weighed out 30 pieces of silver for him. ¹⁶ And from that time
he started looking for a good opportunity to betray Him.

*J*udas presents us with a dark mystery. Matthew sheds more light on
him than any of the other Gospels. Was it Jesus' rebuke at the leper's
house that caused him to decide to go to the priests? None of the Gospels tell us why he did what he did. The clearest indication we have is
when Judas asks the high priest, "What are you willing to give me if I
hand him over to you?" (Luke will speak of Satan entering him at the
Last Supper; Lk 22:3.)

If it was pure and simple greed, as it appears from Matthew to be,
then Judas's deal with the priests netted him around five thousand dollars. Thirty pieces of silver in the Old Testament was the price of a
slave. I sometimes wonder if this contains an element of contempt. I
imagine Judas thinking, *If he is going to act like a slave, then I'm going to*
sell him like one. Mary pours away twelve thousand dollars out of love
for Jesus. Judas makes a profit of five thousand.

THE LAST SUPPER

¹⁷ On the first day of Unleavened Bread the disciples came to Jesus and
asked, "Where do You want us to prepare the Passover so You may eat it?"

¹⁸ "Go into the city to a certain man," He said, "and tell him, 'The Teacher
says: My time is near; I am celebrating the Passover at your place with My
disciples.'" ¹⁹ So the disciples did as Jesus had directed them and prepared the
Passover. ²⁰ When evening came, He was reclining at the table with the
Twelve. ²¹ While they were eating, He said, "I assure you: One of you will
betray Me."

²² Deeply distressed, each one began to say to Him, "Surely not I, Lord?"

²³ He replied, "The one who dipped his hand with Me in the bowl—he
will betray Me. ²⁴ The Son of Man will go just as it is written about Him,
but woe to that man by whom the Son of Man is betrayed! It would have
been better for that man if he had not been born."

²⁵ Then Judas, His betrayer, replied, "Surely not I, Rabbi?"

"You have said it," He told him.

26As they were eating, Jesus took bread, blessed and broke it, gave it to the disciples, and said, "Take and eat it; this is My body." 27Then He took a cup, and after giving thanks, He gave it to them and said, "Drink from it, all of you. 28For this is My blood that establishes the covenant; it is shed for many for the forgiveness of sins. 29But I tell you, from this moment I will not drink of this fruit of the vine until that day when I drink it in a new way in My Father's kingdom with you." 30After singing psalms, they went out to the Mount of Olives.

31Then Jesus said to them, "Tonight all of you will run away because of Me, for it is written:

> *I will strike the shepherd,*
> *and the sheep of the flock will be scattered.*

32But after I have been resurrected, I will go ahead of you to Galilee."

33Peter told Him, "Even if everyone runs away because of You, I will never run away!"

34"I assure you," Jesus said to him, "tonight, before the rooster crows, you will deny Me three times!"

35"Even if I have to die with You," Peter told Him, "I will never deny You!" And all the disciples said the same thing.

O n the opening day of the feast, the disciples ask Jesus where they should go to make the elaborate preparations for the meal. Jesus seems to have made arrangements already. I wonder if it is John Mark's spacious home he sent Peter and John to. Luke tells us the two of them, like a big and little brother, prepare the meal (Lk 22:13). They follow Jesus' instructions, telling their contact in the city that the "teacher" is celebrating the Passover at his place.

As they gather around the three-sided triclinium, Jesus begins the meal with a dark prediction that one of them is going to betray him. I wonder if Judas still has the silver in his money belt. One by one they ask, "Not I, Lord?" It is the precise moment portrayed in Da Vinci's *Last Supper*.

Jesus' reply is in the past tense. It is someone who has already dipped his hand in the bowl with him, meaning it might be any one of them. If he had openly pointed out Judas, I doubt if he would have left the room alive.

The others had said, "Not I, Lord?" But Judas says, "Not I, Rabbi?" He never calls Jesus "Lord."

As the Passover meal proper begins, the somber tone set by Jesus' dark prediction must have hung like a pall in the room. The key elements of the meal Jesus redefines in light of his own upcoming sacrifice. The broken, unleavened Passover bread is his body. They must eat it. This is not a new idea. When he first spoke of it, he lost a number of his own disciples (Jn 6:53). The cup of wine is his blood. They must drink it.

Covenants in the Old Testament are often established in blood, and the new covenant is no different—but the blood will be Jesus' blood (Jer 31:31, 34). Like the Passover lamb of the Israelites' meal, whose blood marked the door posts of the houses so the angel of death would "pass over" (Ex 12), now Jesus, the Lamb of God, will mark them with his blood, so they will never see death.

The final Passover toast was, "This year in Jerusalem, next year in the kingdom." Jesus modifies that toast, saying he won't drink again until they are together in his Father's kingdom.

They sing a hymn, possibly Psalm 113, and move out into the darkness. Judas has already slipped away unnoticed; he is on his way to gather the mob. For the next to the last time, they cross the Kidron Valley and move into the sheltering trees of Gethsemane. In the shadows, Jesus speaks another dark prediction. Before the supper, he had predicted one of them would betray him. Now in the garden, he says they will all run away. Zechariah had seen it centuries before (Zech 13:7). Again the promise of the resurrection is made as well as the reassuring word that after it is all over he will be waiting for them all back home—in Galilee. But given the impact of the prediction of their desertion, they never heard a word.

Peter boldly asserts that even if everyone else runs, he never will. He means this with all of his heart. In fact, he says, he will die if he must. Someday he will indeed do just that, in Rome, hanging upside down from a cross. But that is decades away. Tonight, Jesus says, he will deny him before the rooster crows with the coming of the dawn.

THE GARDEN

³⁶Then Jesus came with them to a place called Gethsemane, and He told the disciples, "Sit here while I go over there and pray." ³⁷Taking along Peter and the two sons of Zebedee, He began to be sorrowful and deeply distressed. ³⁸Then He said to them, "My soul is swallowed up in sorrow—to the point of death. Remain here and stay awake with Me." ³⁹Going a little farther, He fell facedown and prayed, "My Father! If it is possible, let this cup pass from Me. Yet not as I will, but as You will."

⁴⁰Then He came to the disciples and found them sleeping. He asked Peter, "So, couldn't you stay awake with Me one hour? ⁴¹Stay awake and pray, so that you won't enter into temptation. The spirit is willing, but the flesh is weak."

⁴²Again, a second time, He went away and prayed, "My Father, if this cannot pass unless I drink it, Your will be done." ⁴³And He came again and found them sleeping, because they could not keep their eyes open.

⁴⁴After leaving them, He went away again and prayed a third time, saying the same thing once more. ⁴⁵Then He came to the disciples and said to them, "Are you still sleeping and resting? Look, the time is near. The Son of Man is being betrayed into the hands of sinners. ⁴⁶Get up; let's go! See, My betrayer is near."

On their two-week journey from Galilee down the Jordan Valley and up to Jerusalem, night after night Jesus watched the moon waxing. Night after night it became larger and more luminous. He knew all along the journey that on the night of Passover it would be completely full and his suffering would begin.

They arrive at Gethsemane, and Jesus leaves eight of the disciples at the entrance to serve as lookouts. He takes the Three deeper into the shadows of the garden. The weight has begun to press down on him. He needs his men to be with him. He makes as personal a confession to them as we ever hear him make. He tells them he is so full of sorrow that he is about to die. Stanley Hauerwas reminds us that the Three were also there for the luminous transfiguration just a few weeks earlier. Now they will witness another dark transfiguration.[56]

Jesus leaves them a few steps behind and falls to the ground in agony. If there is any way out, he tells his Father, he wants out. If you don't understand this moment of supreme anguish, when Jesus' will is fighting against the will of his Father, you simply don't understand what the garden of Gethsemane was all about. The battle is won when Jesus resolves, "Not as I will, but as You will." If not for this moment, the cross would have never happened.

For the first time he goes to check on the Three. He appears to be worried about them. He finds them sleeping. He asks only Peter why they have fallen asleep.

Then Jesus returns to prayer. He gives the same request but in modified language. His resolve has held firm. If it cannot be taken away, "Your will be done," he says—the very words he had taught his disciples to pray (Mt 6:10).

Once more he goes to check on the disciples, and once more they are sleeping. The excuse is they couldn't keep their eyes open. Mark tells us they didn't know what to say (Mk 14:40).

A third and final time, Jesus goes to prayer. We are told that the request was the same. The third time he returns to find them sleeping. They have failed as his friends. They have failed even as lookouts. Judas is approaching with the mob, and they never saw him coming.

The failure of his best friends must have been a crushing blow for Jesus. When he sees them asleep for the third time, he realizes that indeed he is going to have to face this all alone. No one was ever more alone than Jesus of Galilee. Eventually even his Father would forsake him.

THE ARREST

[47]*While He was still speaking, Judas, one of the Twelve, suddenly arrived. A large mob, with swords and clubs, was with him from the chief priests and elders of the people.* [48]*His betrayer had given them a sign: "The One I kiss, He's the One; arrest Him!"* [49]*So he went right up to Jesus and said, "Greetings, Rabbi!" and kissed Him.*

[50]*"Friend," Jesus asked him, "why have you come?"*

Then they came up, took hold of Jesus, and arrested Him. ⁵¹At that mo-ment one of those with Jesus reached out his hand and drew his sword. He struck the high priest's slave and cut off his ear.

⁵²Then Jesus told him, "Put your sword back in its place because all who take up a sword will perish by a sword. ⁵³Or do you think that I cannot call on My Father, and He will provide Me at once with more than 12 legions of angels? ⁵⁴How, then, would the Scriptures be fulfilled that say it must hap-pen this way?"

⁵⁵At that time Jesus said to the crowds, "Have you come out with swords and clubs, as if I were a criminal, to capture Me? Every day I used to sit, teaching in the temple complex, and you didn't arrest Me. ⁵⁶But all this has happened so that the prophetic Scriptures would be fulfilled." Then all the disciples deserted Him and ran away.

All at once, interrupting Jesus in midsentence, Judas is suddenly there. Behind him lurks an armed mob. We gather from the presence of swords and John's technical word for a detachment of soldiers (Jn 18:3) that there are Roman soldiers as well as temple guards, a formi-dable force.

The sign of the kiss is given, and once more Judas refers to Jesus as "Rabbi." The word Jesus uses in addressing Judas is not the usual word for "friend" (*philos*) but a word that describes someone who is a comrade or perhaps a table companion (*hetairos*). Jesus knows why Judas has come, yet he refuses to play games with any of them. He wants to hear it from Judas's own lips and so he asks, "Why . . . ?" At that moment, having been given the sign of the kiss, the soldiers move in and arrest Jesus. John tells us they tie Jesus up (Jn 18:12).

All of a sudden, an unnamed disciple, the one who had promised to die with Jesus (only John tells us it was Peter) attacks with his sword, convinced no doubt that he is about to die with Jesus. Jesus stops him dead in his tracks, but not before he slices an ear off one of the high priest's slaves. Only Luke the doctor tells us Jesus healed the ear, appar-ently without anyone noticing (Lk 22:51).

For each of the twelve disciples, Jesus says he has a legion of angels ready. There are six thousand soldiers in a legion; that's a total of seventy-two thousand angels. That's more than enough to deal with the mob. More than enough even to recapture Jerusalem if Jesus had wished. But he has not come to kill the Romans. He has come to die for the Romans.

Just as he had said, all of the disciples run away. He is alone.

BEFORE CAIAPHAS

⁵⁷Those who had arrested Jesus led Him away to Caiaphas the high priest, where the scribes and the elders had convened. ⁵⁸Meanwhile, Peter was following Him at a distance right to the high priest's courtyard. He went in and was sitting with the temple police to see the outcome.

⁵⁹The chief priests and the whole Sanhedrin were looking for false testimony against Jesus so they could put Him to death. ⁶⁰But they could not find any, even though many false witnesses came forward. Finally, two who came forward ⁶¹stated, "This man said, 'I can demolish God's sanctuary and rebuild it in three days.'"

⁶²The high priest then stood up and said to Him, "Don't You have an answer to what these men are testifying against You?" ⁶³But Jesus kept silent. Then the high priest said to Him, "By the living God I place You under oath: tell us if You are the Messiah, the Son of God!"

⁶⁴"You have said it," Jesus told him. "But I tell you, in the future you will see the Son of Man seated at the right hand of the Power and coming on the clouds of heaven."

⁶⁵Then the high priest tore his robes and said, "He has blasphemed! Why do we still need witnesses? Look, now you've heard the blasphemy! ⁶⁶What is your decision?"

They answered, "He deserves death!" ⁶⁷Then they spit in His face and beat Him; others slapped Him ⁶⁸and said, "Prophesy to us, Messiah! Who hit You?"

*J*esus is led, bound, back across the valley and up the hill to Caiaphas's palace for an illegal night meeting of the Sanhedrin. Peter follows at a safe distance. Matthew does not mention it, but the young disciple John is with him. They sit together in the courtyard along with members of the temple guard.

The temple guard was chosen only from the tribe of Benjamin, the fiercest warriors in Israel. The battle cry of Israel was "After you, Benjamin!" (Hos 5:8). This was an effective cry owing to the fact that the Benjaminites were always first in battle. They were known to be fearless.

From the beginning, the trial does not go well for the Pharisees and chief priests. The false witnesses cannot seem to agree until finally two witnesses (everything must be established by the mouths of two witnesses, even if they're both liars) recall hearing Jesus say he could demolish the temple and rebuild it in three days. They are referring to an incident that occurred at the very opening of Jesus' ministry, an incident that is recorded only in the Gospel of John. John tells us that after Jesus tore up the temple market for the first time he had said, "Destroy this sanctuary, and I will raise it up in three days" (2:19). Jesus' words, which were misconstrued as an attack on the temple (although they had nothing to do with the temple) will hound his disciples for decades. They are one reason Stephen is stoned (Acts 6:14).

Jesus sees this all as pointless. It is impossible to defend yourself in court against lies, and he isn't interested in defending himself in the first place. Caiaphas challenges Jesus to swear an oath as to whether he is the Messiah or not. He does not understand that Jesus forbid his followers from taking oaths (Mt 5:33-37).

Finally Jesus admits, without the oath, who he truly is: the Son of Man whom they will all see seated at the right hand of the Power. (Jesus avoids using the word *God* in their presence.) This was all they needed. In pretended disgust, they tear their robes upon hearing what they regard as blasphemy.[57] The decision is made. The sentence is passed. They spit in Jesus' face and begin beating him up (see Is 50:6). Mark and Luke tell us Jesus is blindfolded.

REDEMPTIVE TEARS

[69] *Now Peter was sitting outside in the courtyard. A servant approached him and she said, "You were with Jesus the Galilean too."*

[70] *But he denied it in front of everyone: "I don't know what you're talking about!"*

[71] *When he had gone out to the gateway, another woman saw him and told*

those who were there, "This man was with Jesus the Nazarene!"

[72] And again he denied it with an oath, "I don't know the man!"

[73] After a little while those standing there approached and said to Peter, "You certainly are one of them, since even your accent gives you away."

[74] Then he started to curse and to swear with an oath, "I do not know the man!" Immediately a rooster crowed, [75] and Peter remembered the words Jesus had spoken, "Before the rooster crows, you will deny Me three times." And he went outside and wept bitterly.

*I*t is not clear just how much Peter could see or hear from the courtyard. Luke tells us he and Jesus looked at each other across the courtyard at one point (Lk 22:61). One of the servants recognizes Peter as a Galilean who had been with Jesus. Peter denies for the first time. Later a woman recognizes him as someone who had been with the "Nazarene." In disobedience, Peter swears an oath that he does not know Jesus.

Finally, a full hour later, Luke says someone notices Peter's thick Galilean accent. Only Matthew, with his Galilean audience, gives the specific detail that Peter was recognized by his accent. Once more Peter begins to call curses on himself and make oaths that he does not know Jesus. Amid his loud protestations, he hears a rooster crow in the distance. It is the very sign Jesus had foretold. Peter, the rock, breaks down in tears.

Both Peter and Judas betrayed Jesus that night. Judas never wept; he tried to fix things (Mt 27:4-5). Like the rich young man who an eternity ago asked, "What good must I do?" (Mt 19:16), Judas thought he could do something to accomplish his own redemption. Peter, with his remarkable spiritual intuition, seemed to understand that in light of what he had just done, the only thing he could do about it was weep.

MATTHEW 27

THE SICKNESS UNTO DEATH

27:1–10

BEFORE PILATE

27:11–26

A VEGETATIVE CROWN

27:27–31

JESUS CRUCIFIED

27:32–44

JESUS "DISMISSES" HIS SPIRIT

27:45–56

A RICH MAN'S TOMB

27:57–61

"MAKE THE TOMB SECURE"

27:62–66

THE SICKNESS UNTO DEATH

¹When daybreak came, all the chief priests and the elders of the people plotted against Jesus to put Him to death. ²After tying Him up, they led Him away and handed Him over to Pilate, the governor.

³Then Judas, His betrayer, seeing that He had been condemned, was full of remorse and returned the 30 pieces of silver to the chief priests and elders. ⁴"I have sinned by betraying innocent blood," he said.

"What's that to us?" they said. "See to it yourself!"

⁵So he threw the silver into the sanctuary and departed. Then he went and hanged himself.

⁶The chief priests took the silver and said, "It's not lawful to put it into the temple treasury, since it is blood money." ⁷So they conferred together and bought the potter's field with it as a burial place for foreigners. ⁸Therefore that field has been called "Blood Field" to this day. ⁹Then what was spoken through the prophet Jeremiah was fulfilled:

They took the 30 pieces of silver, the price of Him whose price was set by the Israelites, ¹⁰and they gave them for the potter's field, as the Lord directed me.

*T*he Jewish leaders must get Jesus before the Roman governor at daybreak, because that is when aristocratic Romans took care of business. Pilate has an organized day of "Roman leisure" centered on eating and the baths waiting for him (see Acts 3:13).

Judas realizes the impact of his actions when he sees that Jesus has been condemned to death. Though he is remorseful, there are no tears; there is no true repentance. He sets about trying to fix things by returning the money. But his former fellow conspirators, the priests and elders, want nothing to do with him. Judas has served his purpose. He throws the thirty coins back into the temple; five thousand dollars' worth of silver clatters on the stone floor. Then Judas goes and hangs himself; literally he was "strangled" (see Acts 1:16-20).

As we have consistently seen, the old orthodoxy makes you blind. As the priests stoop down and gather the coins, they feel no guilt for manipulating Judas, and they feel no guilt for condemning an innocent man by means of an illegal trial. According to the old orthodoxy, it had to be done. And they are careful with what they do with the money. It was "blood money" (Deut 23:18; 27:25). They cannot simply put it back into the treasury. Instead, they use it to buy a field to bury foreigners. Oddly, they feel guilty about the money being tainted, not themselves. Matthew sees it as a fulfillment of Jeremiah 32:6-9; Jeremiah bought a similar field during the first siege of Jerusalem. With all the Old Testament passages in the remaining chapters that will be meticulously fulfilled in Jesus' death and resurrection, this is the last time Matthew uses his fulfillment formula.

Søren Kierkegaard called despair the "sickness unto death." It is the sin that leads to all other sin. Of the multiple sins that weigh down on Judas, it is despair that finally kills him. In his twisted imagination, he realizes that there is nothing left he can do but end it all. There was nothing left to do because he had denied the only thing a person can do when faced with a mountain of sin and pain: return to Jesus.

BEFORE PILATE

[11]Now Jesus stood before the governor. "Are You the King of the Jews?" the governor asked Him.

Jesus answered, "You have said it." [12]And while He was being accused by the chief priests and elders, He didn't answer.

[13]Then Pilate said to Him, "Don't You hear how much they are testifying against You?" [14]But He didn't answer him on even one charge, so that the governor was greatly amazed.

[15]At the festival the governor's custom was to release to the crowd a prisoner they wanted. [16]At that time they had a notorious prisoner called Barabbas. [17]So when they had gathered together, Pilate said to them, "Who is it you want me to release for you—Barabbas, or Jesus who is called Messiah?" [18]For he knew they had handed Him over because of envy.

[19]While he was sitting on the judge's bench, his wife sent word to him, "Have nothing to do with that righteous man, for today I've suffered terribly in a dream because of Him!"

[20]The chief priests and the elders, however, persuaded the crowds to ask for

Barabbas and to execute Jesus. ²¹The governor asked them, "Which of the two do you want me to release for you?"

"Barabbas!" they answered.

²²Pilate asked them, "What should I do then with Jesus, who is called Messiah?"

They all answered, "Crucify Him!"

²³Then he said, "Why? What has He done wrong?"

But they kept shouting, "Crucify Him!" all the more.

²⁴When Pilate saw that he was getting nowhere, but that a riot was starting instead, he took some water, washed his hands in front of the crowd, and said, "I am innocent of this man's blood. See to it yourselves!"

²⁵All the people answered, "His blood be on us and on our children!" ²⁶Then he released Barabbas to them. But after having Jesus flogged, he handed Him over to be crucified.

*P*erhaps at the same moment, Jesus is standing before Pilate. Pontius Pilate is another dark historical shadow in the Gospels. Even the references to him in ancient secular literature are despairing. He had been named prefect in A.D. 26 due to the influence of his patron, a man named Lucius Sejanus. Sejanus is perhaps the most important historical character who has a direct influence on the gospel and yet whose name most of us do not know. It is not an exaggeration to say that, from a strictly historical point of view, he is the reason Pilate handed Jesus over to be crucified.

Sejanus secured the governorship for Pilate in A.D. 26. During that same period, he was seeking to overthrow Tiberius, who had retreated to the Isle of Capri to live a life of pornographic indulgence. Sejanus's plot was finally uncovered, and he was executed in A.D. 31.

Pilate and Sejanus were well-known anti-Semites, and upon Sejanus's execution, Tiberius issued an order that hostilities against the Jews would cease throughout the empire. This background helps us understand Pilate's position. As the patron of a condemned traitor, he is on extremely thin ice and cannot afford any more attention from Rome at this moment. When a voice from the crowd shouts, "If you release [Jesus], you are not Caesar's friend" (Jn 19:12), he has no choice but to let them have their way so his position can remain secure. Because of atrocities against the Samaritans, Pilate was recalled to Rome to answer for his crimes in A.D. 36. He disappeared along the way and is believed to have killed himself. So Judas and Pilate both succumb to that "sickness unto death"; they see no other choice but to end their own lives.

Standing before Pilate, Jesus is asked if indeed he is the king of the Jews, as he has been accused of claiming. "Yes," he responds, sealing his fate.

But Pilate cannot simply let the Jewish leaders have their way. In all the Gospels, he protests the innocence of Jesus. In verses 12-14, he challenges Jesus to defend himself. Jesus' silence amazes Pilate.

In a custom about which we have no other historical reference than the Gospels, Pilate tries another approach to secure Jesus' release. He offers the completely unacceptable alternative of releasing Barabbas, a convicted criminal, in the place of Jesus. (There is a variant text of Matthew that says Barabbas's name was also "Jesus.")

At the instigation of the priests, the crowd accepts the unacceptable choice of Barabbas. The guilty man goes free while the sinless One is convicted. It is a snapshot of how the gospel works.

Amid the confusion, only Matthew reports that Pilate receives a message from his wife. She has been suffering a daylight dream about Jesus and warns her husband to have nothing to do with this "righteous" man. Divine disclosure through dreams has been a uniquely Matthean theme. Her dream is the last dream of the Gospel.

Meanwhile the crowds are screaming, "Crucify Him!" Pilate shouts over the noise, "What has He done wrong?" As compromised as his moral life may be, Pilate is still Roman enough to deplore the legal conviction of an absolutely innocent man. But the mob wins the shouting match. It always wins shouting matches.

Jesus is innocent, Pilate insists, and so is he, so he washes his hands as a public gesture—not a Roman gesture, but a Jewish one.

The response of the crowd in verse 25 is an example of calling a curse down upon oneself. Peter had done it in Caiaphas's courtyard.

Matthew gives only an abbreviated version. A fuller statement would be "If this man is innocent, let his blood be on us and our children."

Jesus is flogged by the Romans, who do not count the lashes, as the Jews must by law. (The movies about Jesus are wrong. He did not receive thirty-nine lashes.) Flogging almost always preceded a Roman crucifixion, though they were so severe, sometimes the criminal died from the flogging itself.

A VEGETATIVE CROWN

[27] Then the governor's soldiers took Jesus into headquarters and gathered the whole company around Him. [28] They stripped Him and dressed Him in a scarlet military robe. [29] They twisted together a crown of thorns, put it on His head, and placed a reed in His right hand. And they knelt down before Him and mocked Him: "Hail, King of the Jews!" [30] Then they spit on Him, took the reed, and kept hitting Him on the head. [31] When they had mocked Him, they stripped Him of the robe, put His clothes on Him, and led Him away to crucify Him.

*J*esus is in Roman hands now. The mockery and torture he receives are uniquely Roman. The cohort, a group of two to six hundred men (although the term might not be taken literally here) gathers around Jesus within the confines of the Praetorium, the residence of the praetor, a high-ranking magistrate. This is probably Herod's old palace.

First, they strip Jesus—something Jews would not have done, since nakedness was particularly offensive to them. Next, they placed one of their scarlet military robes on him. Roman soldiers borrowed from the Greeks the custom of wearing red robes to hide their blood in battle.

The crown of thorns is particularly Roman, for they traditionally utilized vegetative crowns, usually made of laurels. At Corinth, the winners of the athletic games wore crowns of withered celery. The soldiers' cruel innovation would have been particularly funny to them.

A mock scepter is placed in Jesus' hands as they kneel before him, shouting the particularly Roman "Hail." It was all a sick joke, but a particularly Roman joke.

Then the Jews spit in Jesus' face (Mt 26:67). And the pagan Roman soldiers spit on him as well. He is covered in his own blood and their spit. Tired of their games, they take off the valuable robe. It can be washed later.

Jesus is led out to be crucified.

JESUS CRUCIFIED

³²As they were going out, they found a Cyrenian man named Simon. They forced this man to carry His cross. ³³When they came to a place called Golgotha (which means Skull Place), ³⁴they gave Him wine mixed with gall to drink. But when He tasted it, He would not drink it. ³⁵After crucifying Him they divided His clothes by casting lots. ³⁶Then they sat down and were guarding Him there. ³⁷Above His head they put up the charge against Him in writing:

> *THIS IS JESUS*
> *THE KING OF THE JEWS.*

³⁸Then two criminals were crucified with Him, one on the right and one on the left. ³⁹Those who passed by were yelling insults at Him, shaking their heads ⁴⁰and saying, "The One who would demolish the sanctuary and rebuild it in three days, save Yourself! If You are the Son of God, come down from the cross!" ⁴¹In the same way the chief priests, with the scribes and elders, mocked Him and said, ⁴²"He saved others, but He cannot save Himself! He is the King of Israel! Let Him come down now from the cross, and we will believe in Him. ⁴³He has put His trust in God; let God rescue Him now—if He wants Him! For He said, 'I am God's Son.'" ⁴⁴In the same way even the criminals who were crucified with Him kept taunting Him.

*J*esus is stumbling toward the place of execution, along the most public route, and all of the Synoptic Gospels tell us about a man along the way named Simon from Cyrene, a city of North Africa that had a large Jewish population. It is always assumed that Jesus stumbled and needed Simon's help, yet there is nothing in the Gospels that says this actually happened. It was probably the soldiers' decision to commandeer Simon before Jesus collapsed. Roman soldiers were given the authority by the Julian code to impress any person to carry a burden the distance of one mile. Jesus, referring to the law of impressment, told his followers that if they were commandeered, they were to carry the burden two miles (Mt 5:41). They arrive at the execution site, Golgotha—commonly known as Calvary—where the upright stakes are already planted in the ground. The Hebrew word for "skull" is *gūlgōlet*, hence Golgotha. The Latin word for "skull" is *calvaria*, hence Calvary.

In verse 34, Jesus is offered a drink of wine mixed with what is usually referred to as myrrh. Besides being a perfume, myrrh is also a narcotic. The majority view on this passage is that it represents a custom whereby the righteous women of Jerusalem, in an act of compassion, provided the mixture to ease the pain of condemned criminals. But the Aramaic words for "myrrh" and "gall" are virtually identical. In Psalm 69:21, which prophetically portrays the scene, the word *gall* is used. Matthew uses *gall* as well.

It is important to realize that gall is not the same thing as myrrh. Gall, in fact, is poison. There is at least a chance that this offer of a drink was Satan's last attempt to kill Jesus before the cross. After all, he had tried to kill Jesus as an infant (Mt 2:16). He had tried to convince Jesus to jump off the roof of the temple (Mt 4:6). He had tried to drown Jesus in the storm (Mt 8:24). He had tried to have Jesus stoned by the crowd (Jn 11:8). Is it too much to believe that a drink, perhaps with poison gall, was Satan's last attempt to kill Jesus before he made it to the cross? The fact that Jesus spits the drink out after he tastes it might be an indication that he realized it was poisonous.

None of the Gospels give the details of the actual crucifixion. The first readers did not need the details. Everyone knew what it meant to be crucified. There is not a single word of his hands and feet being nailed. But after the resurrection he will show them the wounds. His clothes are divided into four lots (Jn 19:23-24), which the soldiers gamble for, indicating a detachment of four soldiers was assigned the crucifixion. With such a literal fulfillment of Psalm 22:18, why does the writer of Matthew's Gospel not use his familiar fulfillment formula?

The charge hangs above his head: "the King of the Jews."

The thieves hang on either side (Is 53:12).

The people pass by and mock him (Ps 22:7; 109:25).

The priests sneer, "He saved others, but he cannot save himself." They don't understand that Jesus saves others precisely by not saving himself.

JESUS "DISMISSES" HIS SPIRIT

45From noon until three in the afternoon darkness came over the whole land. 46About three in the afternoon Jesus cried out with a loud voice, "Elí, Elí, lemá sabachtháni?" that is, "My God, My God, why have You forsaken Me?"

47When some of those standing there heard this, they said, "He's calling for Elijah!"

48Immediately one of them ran and got a sponge, filled it with sour wine, fixed it on a reed, and offered Him a drink. 49But the rest said, "Let's see if Elijah comes to save Him!"

50Jesus shouted again with a loud voice and gave up His spirit. 51Suddenly, the curtain of the sanctuary was split in two from top to bottom; the earth quaked and the rocks were split. 52The tombs were also opened and many bodies of the saints who had fallen asleep were raised. 53And they came out of the tombs after His resurrection, entered the holy city, and appeared to many.

54When the centurion and those with him, who were guarding Jesus, saw the earthquake and the things that had happened, they were terrified and said, "This man really was God's Son!"

55Many women who had followed Jesus from Galilee and ministered to Him were there, looking on from a distance. 56Among them were Mary Magdalene, Mary the mother of James and Joseph, and the mother of Zebedee's sons.

*J*esus is placed on the cross at nine in the morning (Mk 15:25). This means that by this time he has hung on the cross for three hours. Suddenly darkness descends on the scene. It hovers until three in the afternoon. It is the darkness that was "felt" in Egypt (Ex 10:21). It is the deep darkness the prophet Amos felt (Amos 8:9-11):

"In that day," declares the Sovereign LORD, "I will make the sun go down at noon and darken the earth in broad daylight. I will turn your religious feasts into mourning and all your singing into weeping. I will make all of you wear sackcloth and shave your heads. I will make that time like mourning for an only son and the end of it like a bitter day.

"The days are coming," declares the Sovereign LORD, "when I will send a famine through the land—not a famine of food or a thirst for water, but a famine of hearing the words of the LORD." (NIV 1984)

From out of the darkness a voice screams, "My God, my God, why have You forsaken me?" (see Ps 22:1). Again, there is no fulfillment formula.

In this darkness Jesus has lost touch with his Father. Now he is only "my God."

In John 19:28, Jesus asks for a drink to fulfill the final prophecy of Psalm 69:21. Matthew shows us the drink of spoiled wine being offered on the sponge, which is placed on a stick. This is our only clue that Jesus was crucified on a high cross.

After the sip of sour wine, Jesus "dismisses" his Spirit, a unique privilege he said his Father had granted him (Jn 10:18). As his loud cry echoes, another sound is heard coming from inside the temple as the massive, thick curtain in front of the Holy of Holies is ripped from top to bottom. It was one of the most precious symbols of the old orthodoxy, separating the unclean from the holiness of God. Jesus shouts, "It is finished," and the power of the old orthodoxy to separate us from God is gone, ripped in two.

Only Matthew mentions the earthquake that occurred that moment and broke open the tombs of many holy people, who were then resurrected. We are told they entered the city and appeared to many. The Pharisees, who vehemently believed in the resurrection, had asked for a sign. How about this one?

There appears to be absolutely no other reference to this amazing miracle except for one tantalizing clue in the Talmud. Yohanan ben Zakkai reports that forty years before the destruction of Jerusalem, precisely the time when Jesus was crucified, the doors of the temple somehow opened all by themselves.[58] Perhaps it was the earthquake after the crucifixion that set the doors of the temple ajar.

Centurions are always portrayed positively in the New Testament, and the one who was in charge of Jesus' execution is no different. He has seen thousands of men die, but never like this. The earthquake terrifies him and his men. Perhaps Matthew's reference to the "things that had happened" means that they also saw the resurrected saints. For the centurion to say what he said about Jesus could have resulted in his expulsion from the military or possibly even his execution. Only Tiberius was the "son of God" in his world. Yet here we have a testimony from the foot of the cross covered in Jesus' own blood, for all time.

A RICH MAN'S TOMB

⁵⁷When it was evening, a rich man from Arimathea named Joseph came, who himself had also become a disciple of Jesus. ⁵⁸He approached Pilate and asked for Jesus' body. Then Pilate ordered that it be released. ⁵⁹So Joseph took the body, wrapped it in clean, fine linen, ⁶⁰and placed it in his new tomb, which he had cut into the rock. He left after rolling a great stone against the entrance of the tomb. ⁶¹Mary Magdalene and the other Mary were seated there, facing the tomb.

*A*mong the members of the Sanhedrin was at least one man who had objected to all of this. He was actually a disciple of Jesus. He was rich. He was from the nearby village of Arimethea. And his name was Joseph (see Mk 15:43; Lk 23:51; Jn 19:38-39). Mark tells us he went "boldly" to Pilate to ask for the body of Jesus. As a member of the Sanhedrin, he would have had access to the governor. To publicly identify with an executed criminal by claiming the body was indeed a bold move.

The body is prepared for stage one of the two-stage burial process. It is wrapped in expensive linen and placed on a bed of seventy-five pounds of spices (Jn 19:39). Then it is placed in Joseph's own rock-cut tomb. Normally the body would have rested there for a year, allowing the flesh to rot, so that the bones could be washed and placed in an ossuary. But Jesus didn't require step two of the process. Indeed he hardly needed step one.

A massive circular stone is rolled across the entrance of the tomb while the two Marys watch. You cannot enter into their suffering until you realize that, for them, it is all over. Jesus is gone. He is never coming back. None of his followers ever heard him say he would rise again on the third day.

"MAKE THE TOMB SECURE"

[62] The next day, which followed the preparation day, the chief priests and the Pharisees gathered before Pilate [63] and said, "Sir, we remember that while this deceiver was still alive He said, 'After three days I will rise again.' [64] Therefore give orders that the tomb be made secure until the third day. Otherwise, His disciples may come, steal Him, and tell the people, 'He has been raised from the dead.' Then the last deception will be worse than the first."

[65] "You have a guard of soldiers," Pilate told them. "Go and make it as secure as you know how." [66] Then they went and made the tomb secure by sealing the stone and setting the guard.

*T*he next day" is Saturday, the day the Judean Jews are making preparations for Passover. Galilean Jews, following the tradition of the Diaspora community, celebrated their Passover meal on Thursday, one day early.

Even though they have a multitude of other matters before them, the priests and elders are still worried about Jesus. Though his followers did not seem to hear what Jesus had said about rising from the dead, they did and are worried that Jesus' prediction might come back to haunt them. After all, his disciples could easily fake it by stealing the body.

Oddly enough, their extra caution would ultimately work against the priests. By making sure there was no chance of a ruse by the followers of Jesus, they provided one of the best pieces of evidence we have that it all happened just as Jesus said it would. It was impossible now to fake the resurrection. They had made sure of that. Everything that could humanly be done had been done to make sure it was not, could not, be a lie.

MATTHEW 28

THE RESURRECTION

¹After the Sabbath, as the first day of the week was dawning, Mary Magdalene and the other Mary went to view the tomb. ²Suddenly there was a violent earthquake, because an angel of the Lord descended from heaven and approached the tomb. He rolled back the stone and was sitting on it. ³His appearance was like lightning, and his robe was as white as snow. ⁴The guards were so shaken from fear of him that they became like dead men.

⁵But the angel told the women, "Don't be afraid, because I know you are looking for Jesus who was crucified. ⁶He is not here! For He has been resurrected, just as He said. Come and see the place where He lay. ⁷Then go quickly and tell His disciples, 'He has been raised from the dead. In fact, He is going ahead of you to Galilee; you will see Him there.' Listen, I have told you."

⁸So, departing quickly from the tomb with fear and great joy, they ran to tell His disciples the news. ⁹Just then Jesus met them and said, "Good morning!" They came up, took hold of His feet, and worshiped Him. ¹⁰Then Jesus told them, "Do not be afraid. Go and tell My brothers to leave for Galilee, and they will see Me there."

*I*t is Sunday morning. The two Marys, who had seen the body of Jesus laid into the tomb, have come back. Matthew does not tell us that they have come to anoint a dead body. The fact is, they have. The other Gospels make this clear. That they have come with spices reveals the level of their expectation. No one is waiting outside the tomb for Jesus' resurrection.

Only Matthew tells us of the second earthquake and of the angel coming to roll back the stone and sit on it. Angels appear differently throughout the Bible; sometimes they simply look like men. Here we are told this angel is luminous. Matthew tells us the fierce Roman guards "shook and became like dead men" (Mt 28:4 NIV 1984); today we would simply say they fainted.

The message of the angel is paralleled in both Mark 16 and Luke 24. They are the first words so often heard from the lips of angels: "Do not be afraid." He understands that they're looking for Jesus—that is, they are looking for the *dead body* of Jesus. To their amazement, the women hear the angels say, "He is not here, for He has been resurrected." As in all the accounts, the women are invited to come and look at the evidence. Realize, however, that the empty tomb is not proof, only evidence. Only Jesus alive, standing before them, is conclusive proof.

They are told to go and tell the disciples the good news. It is significant that the women have the privilege of being the first witnesses of the empty tomb. The disciples forfeited that privilege because of their cowardice. Jesus' word to them is, "I will go ahead of you to Galilee" (Mt 26:32)—which is to say, he's going back home to meet them. Back to the Galilee of his boyhood. Back to the Galilee of Matthew's first listeners. As in Mark's abbreviated version of the resurrection, we are told that the women are afraid. But Matthew adds an important detail: he tells us that they were filled with joy.

As they are on the way, Jesus himself meets them. As a response of pure joy and amazement, the women clasp Jesus' feet and for the first time worship him. Whenever Jesus reveals himself in a new way, he consistently has to say, "Do not be afraid." Of all those occasions, this is the most dramatic. It must have been an important message for Jesus to have repeated it. The angel already told them that he would meet them in Galilee. But here again he reiterates, "Tell My brothers to leave for Galilee."

THE BRIBE

[11]As they were on their way, some of the guards came into the city and reported to the chief priests everything that had happened. [12]After the priests had assembled with the elders and agreed on a plan, they gave the soldiers a large sum of money [13]and told them, "Say this, 'His disciples came during the night and stole Him while we were sleeping.' [14]If this reaches the governor's ears, we will deal with him and keep you out of trouble." [15]So they took the money and did as they were instructed. And this story has been spread among Jewish people to this day.

Only Matthew gives us the detail of the soldiers being bribed. He lets us know that it happened at the same instant the women were on their way to tell the disciples the good news. Apparently the soldiers have "come to" after having fainted from fear. To have deserted one's post or to have fallen asleep was one of the most serious military offenses. The penalty could be extreme, even death.

The guards go back into Jerusalem and report everything that happened to them. Even when the old orthodoxy hears the truth, its commitment to the old doctrine supersedes the new reality. In spite of the evidence, in spite of the testimony of the soldiers, the priests devise a plan; they fabricate a lie. The soldiers are bribed with a large amount of money; we are not told how much. They are to lie and say that Jesus' disciples had stolen the body while they were asleep. If this report had reached Pilate, he could have very well crucified the soldiers himself; if a soldier who was watching a convict allowed him to escape, he would suffer the same penalty planned for the convict.

The obedient soldiers do everything they are told. They take the money. They spread the lie that is still told all over Israel and indeed all over the world to this day.

JESUS MEETS THEM BACK HOME

16 The 11 disciples traveled to Galilee, to the mountain where Jesus had directed them. 17 When they saw Him, they worshiped, but some doubted. 18 Then Jesus came near and said to them, "All authority has been given to Me in heaven and on earth. 19 Go, therefore, and make disciples of all nations, baptizing them in the name of the Father and of the Son and of the Holy Spirit, 20 teaching them to observe everything I have commanded you. And remember, I am with you always, to the end of the age."

We are not told exactly how long it took the disciples to make it back up to Galilee. Even if they traveled quickly, it would have taken at least a week. Scholars debate over the location of the mountain where they met the resurrected Jesus. The truth is, we simply don't know. And the truth is, Matthew doesn't think we need to know. Gathered around the risen Savior, like the women who clasped his feet, the disciples worship him.

The Gospels specifically and the Bible in general are always painfully honest. At this supreme moment, you and I enter into the story at the level of our imaginations. We are worshiping at the feet of Jesus as well. But it's not that simple; it is never that simple. Matthew tells us that even then, as they gazed upon the face of the risen Lord and saw the scars in his hands and feet, *some doubted*. The persistence of doubt is a consistent theme in all the Gospels.

In John, at the second miraculous catch of fish, we have the enigmatic statement that as the disciples stood around Jesus on the shore of the Sea of Galilee, "none of the disciples dared ask him, 'Who are you?' They knew it was the Lord" (Jn 21:12 NIV). Doubt is a perniciously persistent thing. But if indeed, as Blaise Pascal says, doubt is necessary in order for us to truly believe, perhaps it is a good thing. Perhaps even persistent doubt can be used by God to make faith more real—and stronger.

Initially Jesus had discipled his followers in this familiar setting. Here he gives them their final charge. I would love to have heard the tone of his voice. I would love to know if its tone was somehow different now after the resurrection or if Jesus still sounded like the same simple servant he'd always been. He tells the disciples that authority has been given to him in all of heaven and on the earth. On the basis of that authority, he then sends them to go and make disciples. He instructs them to baptize in the name of the Father and of the Son and of the Holy Spirit. All that he had taught them for three years on the slopes of these same green Galilean hillsides, all the truth that he had lived out in their presence, he authorizes them to use to turn the world upside down.

The final words of any character in any novel are almost always their most important words. Perhaps this is no exception. Jesus' final word is his perfect and most reassuring word. It expresses the deepest desire of his Father. It perfectly fulfills his incarnation name: Immanuel. It is the desire that led to his incarnation. It is the deep desire that sustained him throughout his ordeal on the cross. Perhaps it is even the desire that empowered his resurrection. That desire is simply to be with us.

Imagine these words being read to those first Christians who did not yet know they were Christians. They were the faithful Jewish followers of Jesus, still living out their faith in the synagogues of Galilee. Today, as we hear those words while sitting together in the pew or at home alone reading Matthew's Gospel, they can resonate just as powerfully and comfortingly.

In the end Jesus defines himself as the One who is with us. That is his identity, and it gives birth to a new identity in us. We are now the ones who are not alone, who will never—can never—be alone. In a world that seeks to isolate and discourage us, they are the perfect words. They are the perfect words, if for no other reason than the fact that Jesus spoke them.

"And remember, I am with you always, to the end of the age."

APPENDIX A

The Five Blocks

In Matthew's Gospel, the teachings of Jesus are divided into five major sections. These five sections are probably the collection of sayings (*logia*) referred to Papias in A.D. 130. The number five is also significant in that it echoes the five books of Moses.

1. 5:1–7:29—the Sermon on the Mount

2. 10:5-42—instructions to the Twelve

3. 13:1-52—parables of the kingdom

4. 18:1-3—instructions to the gatherings

5. 23:1–25:46—Olivet Discourse

APPENDIX B

Unique to Matthew

As we seek to engage with each Gospel, we need to consider what content is unique to each book. Next we must begin to seek to understand why each author included each unique section.

1:18—the nativity through Joseph
2:1-12—the magi
2:13-15—the flight to Egypt
2:16-18—the slaughter of innocents
4:15—Jesus moves to Galilee
5:13—"you are the salt of the earth"
5:14—"you are the light of the world" (see also John 8:12)
5:17—"I did not come to destroy but to fulfill . . ."
5:17-20—uniquely Jewish
5:33—the demand to abstain from taking oaths
6:1-4—giving alms in secret
6:5-6—praying in secret
6:16-18—fasting in secret
7:6—"don't . . . toss your pearls before pigs"
8:17—". . . be fulfilled"
11:28-30—"come to Me . . . and I will give you rest"
12:18—the fulfillment formula from Isaiah
13:24-30—the parable of the weeds
13:44—the parable of the hidden treasure
13:47—the parable of the net
13:51-52—new and old treasures
14:33—after Jesus walks on the water, they worshiped him
16:6—the yeast of the Pharisees and Sadducees

17:24—the payment of the temple tax

18:19-20—"where two or three are gathered together"

18:23—parable of the unforgiving servant

19:11-12—"eunuchs"

20:1-16—parable of the workers in the vineyard

23:1-36—woes to the scribes and Pharisees

25:35—"for I was hungry . . ."

27:3-10—the death of Judas

27:24—Pilate washed his hands

28:11-15—the false report and bribing the guards

28:16-20—the Great Commission at Galilee

APPENDIX C

A Synagogue Flogging

In order to understand what sort of punishment Matthew's first listeners were facing, as well as developing an appreciation for the differences between a Roman flogging (which Jesus suffered) and a Jewish flogging, here is a description of a Jewish flogging from the Mishnah.

"10. How many stripes do they inflict on a man? Forty save one, for it is written, *By number forty;* that is to say, a number near to forty. R. Judah says: He suffers the forty stripes in full. And where does he suffer the added one? Between his shoulders.

"11. When they estimate the number of stripes that he can bear, it must be a number divisible by three. If they had estimated that he could bear forty, save one, and after he had suffered these only in part they said, 'he cannot bear forty [save one], he is exempt [from the rest]. If they had estimated that he could bear eighteen, and after he had suffered them they said, 'he can bear forty [save one], he is exempt [from the rest]. If he had committed a transgression whereby he offended against two prohibitions, and they had made for him one estimate [for them both], he suffers them and is exempt [from more stripes]; but if not, he must suffer [the first estimate], be healed again, and then be scourged the second time.

"12. How do they scourge them? They bind his two hands to a pillar on either side, and the minister of the synagogue lays hold on his garments—if they are torn they are torn, if they are utterly rent they are utterly rent—so that he bares his chest. A stone is set down behind him on which the minister of the synagogue stands with a strap of calf-hide in his hand, doubled and redoubled, and two [other] straps that rise and fall [are fastened] thereto.

"13. The handpiece of the strap is one handbreadth long in one handbreadth wide; and its end must reach to his navel. He gives him one third of the stripes in front and two-thirds behind; and he may not strike him when he is standing or when he is sitting, but only when he is bending low, for it is written, 'the judge shall cause him to lie down.' And he that smites, smites with his one hand with all his might.

"14. And the reader reads, 'if thou wilt not observe to do . . . the Lord will make thy stripes wonderful and the stripes of thy seed . . .' and he returns again to the beginning of the passage. If he dies under his hand, the scourger is not culpable. But if he gave him one stripe too many and he died, he must escape into exile because of him. If he [that was scourged] befouled himself whether with excrement or urine, he is exempt [from the rest of the stripes]. R. Judah says: A man [is exempt only if he befouled himself] with excrement, and the woman [if she befouled herself] with urine."[59]

APPENDIX D

Josephus and John the Baptist

Besides the New Testament, Josephus is the only important source of information on John the Baptist. Here is his statement regarding John in the *Antiquities of the Jews* (XVIII, v. 2).

"Now, some of the Jews thought that the destruction of Herod's army came from God, and that very justly, as a punishment of what he did against John, who was called the Baptist; for Herod slew him, who was a good man, and commanded the Jews to exercise virtue, both as to righteousness towards one another, and piety towards God, and so to come to baptism; for that with washing with water would be acceptable to him, if they made use of it, not in order to the putting away, or the remission of some sin only, but for the purification of the body: supposing still that the soul was thoroughly purified beforehand by righteousness. Now, when many others came to crowd about him, for they were greatly moved by hearing his words, Herod, who feared lest the great influence John had over the people might put it into his power and inclination to raise a rebellion, (for they seemed ready to do anything he should advise,) thought it best, by putting him to death, to prevent any mischief he might cause, and not bring himself into difficulties, by sparing a man who might make him repent of it when it should be too late. Accordingly he was sent a prisoner, out of Herod's suspicious temper, to Macherus, the castle I mentioned beforehand, and was there put to death. Now the Jews had an opinion that the destruction of this army was sent as a punishment upon Herod, as a mark of God's displeasure against him."[60]

APPENDIX E

Definitions for Forbidden Sabbath Work

In order to appreciate the world of Matthew's first listeners, here is a statement from the Mishnah regarding the classes of work that were forbidden on the Sabbath.

"The main classes of work are 40 save one: sowing, plowing, reaping, binding sheaves, threshing, winnowing, cleansing crops, grinding, sifting, kneading, baking, shearing wool, washing or beating or dyeing it, spinning, weaving, making two loops, weaving two threads, separating two threads, tying a knot, loosening a knot, sewing two stitches, tearing in order to sew two stitches, hunting a gazelle, slaughtering or flaying or salting it or curing its skin, scraping it or cutting it up, writing two letters, erasing in order to write two letters, building, pulling down, putting out a fire, lighting a fire, striking with a hammer or taking aught from one domain into another. These are the main classes of work: 40 save one."[61]

NOTES

[1]Eusebius, *The Church Histories* 3.39.

[2]Josephus, *The Life of Flavius Josephus* 235.

[3]Talmud 15d.

[4]See also Suetonius, *Lives of the Caesars*, Claudius 5:25.

[5]See P. H. R. Van Houwelingen's article, "Fleeing Forward: The Departure of Christians from Jerusalem to Pella," *Westminster Theological Journal* 65, no. 2 (Fall 2003): 182-200.

[6]*Babylonian Talmud Berakot* 28b.

[7]*Babylonian Talmud Berakot* 29a.

[8]There are multiple versions of the eighteen benedictions. This example of the twelfth benediction is the oldest known and comes from the Cairo Geniza, a collection unearthed in Egypt in 1896.

[9]One unique feature of the Gospel of Matthew is angelic disclosure through dreams (Mt 2:12, 13, 19, 22).

[10]Suetonius, *Lives of the Caesars*, Vespasian 4.

[11]Macrobius, *Saturnalia* 2:4, 1.

[12]Josephus, *Jewish Antiquities* 15–17 and *Jewish Wars* 1:347–673 provide the most extensive primary source material on Herod's life. For a good summary, see Geza Vermes, *Who's Who in the Age of Jesus* (London: Penguin Reference Library, 2005), pp. 103-111.

[13]Vermes, *Who's Who*, p. 104.

[14]In Mark we have only twenty-two minutes with Jesus, in Luke fifty-three, and in John only forty-four.

[15]*1QWar Scroll* 14:7.

[16]Pliny, *Natural History* 31.102.

[17]Stanley Hauerwas, *Matthew* (Grand Rapids: Brazos Press, 2006), p. 70.

[18]*1QRule of the Community* 1.9-11.

[19]Compare Baal worshipers in 1 Kings 18:26 or Diana worshipers in Acts 19:34.

[20]C. K. Barrett, *The New Testament Background: Selected Documents* (San Francisco: Harper & Row, 1987), p. 206.

[21]*Babylonian Talmud Sabbat* 13a.

[22]*Babylonian Talmud Sanhedrin* 47a.

[23]Clint Arnold, *Zondervan Illustrated Bible Backgrounds Commentary*, vol. 1 (Grand Rapids: Zondervan, 2002), p. 55.

[24]Tacitus, *Annals* 4.5.

[25]See discussion of Hanina ben Dosa in Vermes, *Who's Who*, pp. 99-102.

[26]See the excellent discussion of the role of scribes in Matthew's Gospel in Aaron M. Gale, *Redefining Ancient Boundaries: The Jewish Scribal Framework of Matthew's Gospel* (London: T & T Clark, 2005), p. 87ff.

[27]*Babylonian Talmud Berakot* 31a.

[28]Compare Mark 1:25 and 4:39, where Jesus even uses precisely the same word when casting out a demon in Mark 1 and when stilling the storm in Mark 4.

[29]See Gordon Franz, "Ancient Harbors of the Sea of Galilee," *Bible and Spade* 4, no. 4 (Autumn 1991): 112-22, for a description of the harbor at Gadara.

[30]"Lying on the grave" was looked upon as a sign of demonic possession in Judaism.

[31]See Josephus, *Jewish Antiquities* 8.48.

[32]*Jewish Antiquities* 17.11.4 in William Whiston, *Josephus: The Complete Works* (Grand Rapids: Kregel, 1960), p. 373.

[33]See Vermes, *Who's Who*, p. 254.

[34]Pirke Avot, electronic version loc. 193-94.

[35]Compare Mark 6:34, where the same statement comes before the feeding of the five thousand.

[36]Herbert Danby, trans., *The Mishnah* (Oxford: Oxford University Press, 1933), p. 449.

[37]*Shaliakh*: "a delegate appointed to a mission or task." Ernest Klein, *A Comprehensive Etymological Dictionary of the Hebrew Language for Readers of English* (Jerusalem: Carta Jerusalem, 1987), p. 661. "Even Judaism had an office known as 'apostle' '*shaliakh*.'" William Arndt and F. Wilbur Gingrich, *A Greek-English Lexicon of the New Testament* (Chicago: University of Chicago Press, 1957), p. 99.

[38]In Greek the word for "dance" rhymes with the word for "mourning."

[39]*Mishnah ʾAbot* 3.5 in Danby, *Mishnah*, p. 450.

[40]See *Yoma* 8.6: "When ever there is doubt whether life is in danger this overrides the Sabbath." Danby, *Mishnah*, p. 172.

[41]See *Mishnah Berakot* 6:1 in Danby, *Mishnah*, p. 6.

[42]See Josephus, *Jewish Wars* 3.10.74 for a picturesque description of this area at the time of Jesus.

[43]*Mishnah ʾAbot* 1.1 in Danby, *Mishnah*, p. 446.

[44]See Josephus, *Jewish Antiquities* 13.10.6.

[45]Compare the Mishnah, "If ten men sit together and occupy themselves in the Law, the Divine Presence rests among them." *Mishnah ʾAbot* 3.6.

[46]Compare *Babylonian Talmud Yoma* 86b, 87.

[47]See *Mishnah Giṭṭin* 9.10.

[48]The modern notion that Jesus was really referring to a gate called the "needle" is misinformed. That gate did not exist in Jerusalem until medieval times.

[49]The vineyard is always a symbol for Israel. See Jeremiah 2:21 and Hosea 10:1.

[50]*Jerusalem Talmud Berakot* 2.5.

[51]The chapter divisions were not inserted into the text of Scripture until early in the

thirteenth century by Archbishop Stephen Langton. They are not a part of Holy Scripture and occasionally interrupt the flow of the text.

[52]Arnold, *Zondervan Illustrated*, p. 147.

[53]Eusebius, *Church Histories* 3.5.3.

[54]Waiting for the bridegroom was one of the metaphors John the Baptist used to understand his own relationship to Jesus, as he was "the groom's friend" (Jn 3:29). Like the bridesmaids waiting in the dark, John saw himself waiting outside the bridal chamber, straining to hear the familiar voice of his friend, the bridegroom.

[55]Craig S. Keener, *The Historical Jesus of the Gospels* (Grand Rapids: Eerdmans, 2009), p. 118.

[56]Hauerwas, *Matthew*, p. 222.

[57]See Acts 14:14; also *Mishnah Sanhedrin* 7.5.

[58]See *Babylonian Talmud Yoma* 39b.

[59]*Mishnah Makkot* 3.10-14 in Danby, *Mishnah*, p. 407.

[60]Josephus, *Jewish Antiquities* xviii, v. 2.

[61]*Mishnah Sabbat* 7.2 in Danby, *Mishnah*, p. 106.

RESOURCES

COMMENTARIES

Arnold, Clint E. *Zondervan Illustrated Bible Backgrounds Commentary.* Vol. 1. Grand Rapids: Zondervan, 2002.

France, R. T. *Matthew.* Tyndale New Testament Commentaries. Downers Grove, IL: IVP Academic, 2008.

Gale, Aaron M. *Redefining Ancient Boundaries: The Jewish Scribal Framework of Matthew's Gospel.* London/New York: T & T Clark, 2005.

Green, Michael. *The Message of Matthew.* Downers Grove, IL: InterVarsity Press, 2000.

Hauerwas, Stanley. *Matthew.* Grand Rapids: Brazos Press, 2006.

Keener, Craig S. *The Gospel of Matthew: A Socio-Rhetorical Commentary.* Grand Rapids: Eerdmans, 2009.

————. *The Historical Jesus of the Gospels.* Grand Rapids: Eerdmans, 2009.

————. *Matthew.* Downers Grove, IL: InterVarsity Press, 1997.

Martin, George. *Bringing the Gospel of Matthew to Light.* Frederick, MD: The Word Among Us Press, 2008.

LIFE SITUATIONS AND BACKGROUND STUDIES

Barnett, Paul. *The Birth of Christianity: The First Twenty Years.* Grand Rapids: Eerdmans, 2005.

Barrett, C. K. *The New Testament Background: Selected Documents.* San Francisco: Harper & Row, 1987.

Bell, Albert A. *Exploring the New Testament World.* Nashville: Thomas Nelson, 1998.

Boring, M. Eugene, Klaus Berger and Carsten Colpe. *Hellenistic Commentary to the New Testament.* Nashville: Abingdon Press, 1995.

Bruce, F. F. *New Testament History.* New York: Doubleday-Galilee, 1972.

Charlesworth, James H., and Loren L. Johns. *Hillel and Jesus: Comparative Studies of Two Major Religious Leaders.* Minneapolis: Fortress, 1997.

Cohen, Shaye J. D. *From the Maccabees to the Mishnah*. 2nd ed. Louisville: Westminster John Knox, 2006.

Connolly, Peter. *Living in the Time of Jesus of Nazareth*. Oxford: Oxford University Press, 1983.

Danby, Herbert, trans. *The Mishnah*. Oxford: Oxford University Press, 1933.

Donfried, Karl, and Peter Richardson, eds. *Judaism and Christianity in First Century Rome*. Eugene, OR: Wipf and Stock, 1998.

Edersheim, Alfred. *Sketches of Jewish Social Life in the Days of Christ*. Grand Rapids: Eerdmans, 1979.

Ferguson, Everett. *Early Christians Speak: Faith and Life in the First Three Centuries*. Abilene, TX: ACU Press, 1981.

Fitzmeyer, Joseph A. *The Semetic Background of the New Testament*. Grand Rapids: Eerdmans, 1997.

Gianotti, Charles R. *The New Testament and the Mishnah: A Cross-Reference Index*. Grand Rapids: Baker Books, 1983.

Gower, Ralph. *The New Manners and Customs of Bible Times*. Chicago: Moody Press, 1987.

Instone-Brewer, David. *Traditions of the Rabbis from the Era of the New Testament*. Vol. 1 and 2. Grand Rapids: Eerdmans, 2004.

Lawrence, Paul. *The IVP Atlas of the Bible*. Downers Grove, IL: IVP Academic, 2006.

Leon-Dufour, Xavier. *Dictionary of the New Testament*. San Francisco: Harper & Row, 1980.

Lohse, Eduard. *The New Testament Environment*. Nashville: Abingdon Press, 1976.

Maier, Paul L. *Eusebius: The Church History*. Grand Rapids: Kregel, 1999.

Magness, Jodi. *Stone and Dung, Oil and Spit: Jewish Daily Life in the Time of Jesus*. Grand Rapids: Eerdmans, 2011.

Matthews, Victor H. *Manners and Customs in the Bible*. Peabody, MA: Hendrickson, 1991.

McReynolds, Paul R. *Word Study Greek-English New Testament*. Carol Stream, IL: Tyndale, 1966.

Mealy, Webb. *The Spoken English New Testament: A New Translation from the Greek*. Oakland, CA: Sent Press, 2008.

Overman, J. Andrew. *Matthew's Gospel and Formative Judaism: The Social World of the Matthean Community*. Minneapolis: Fortress, 1990.

Pick, Bernhard. *Jesus in the Talmud, His Personality, His Disciples and His Say-*

ings. Forgotten Books, 2012.

Richardson, Peter. *Herod: King of the Jews and Friend of the Romans.* Minneapolis: Fortress, 1999.

Saldarini, Anthony J. *Pharisees, Scribes and Sadducees in Palestinian Society.* Grand Rapids: Eerdmans, 1988.

Schurer, Emil. *The Jewish People in the Time of Jesus.* New York: Schocken Books, 1978.

Scott, J. Julius. *Jewish Backgrounds of the New Testament.* Grand Rapids: Baker, 1995.

Skarsaune, Oskar. *In the Shadow of the Temple: Jewish Influences on Early Christianity.* Downers Grove, IL: InterVarsity Press, 2002.

————, and Reidar Hvalvik. *Jewish Believers in Jesus.* Peabody, MA: Hendrickson, 2007.

Throckmorton, Burton H. *Gospel Parallels.* Nashville: Thomas Nelson, 1967.

Vermes, Geza. *Who's Who in the Age of Jesus.* New York: Penguin Reference Library, 2005.

Walsh, P. G., trans. *Pliny the Younger: Complete Letters.* Oxford: Oxford University Press, 2006.

Whiston, William. *Josephus: The Complete Works.* Grand Rapids: Kregel, 1960.

Wilken, Robert L. *The Christians as the Romans Saw Them.* New Haven, CT: Yale University Press, 1984.

Zeitlin, Irving M. *Jesus and the Judaism of His Time.* Boston: Polity Press, 1988.

Articles

Brindle, Wayne A. "The Origin and History of the Samaritans." *Grace Theological Journal* 5, no. 1 (Spring 1984): 49-75.

Campbell, Ken M. "What Was Jesus' Occupation?" *Journal of the Evangelical Theological Society* 48, no. 3 (September 2005): 502-20.

Carson, D. A. "The Jewish Leaders in Matthew's Gospel: A Reappraisal." *Journal of the Evangelical Theological Society* 25, no. 2 (June 1982): 162-75.

Catto, Stephen. "A Critical Analysis of the Present State of Synagogue Research and Its Implications for the Study of Luke." *Tyndale Bulletin* 57, no. 2 (2006): 314-16.

Couch, Mal. "The Importance of the Book of Matthew." *Conservative Theological Journal* 3, no. 9 (August 1999): 220-28.

Cunningham, Scott. "Is Matthew Midrash?" *Bibliotheca Sacra* 144, no. 574 (April 1987): 158-81.

Ferngren, Gary B. "Internal Criticism as a Criterion for Authorship in the New Testament." *Bibliotheca Sacra* 134, no. 536 (October 1977): 330-43.

Franz, Gordon. "Ancient Harbors of the Sea of Galilee." *Bible and Spade* 4, no. 4 (Autumn 1991): 112-22.

―――. "Does Your Teacher Not Pay The [Temple] Tax?" (Mt 17:24-27). *Bible and Spade* 10, no. 4 (Autumn 1997): 82-88.

―――. "The Tyrian Shekel And the Temple of Jerusalem." *Bible and Spade* 15, no. 4 (Fall 2002): 114.

Hendriksen, William. "The Beauty of Matthew's Gospel." *Westminster Theological Journal* 35, no. 2 (Winter 1973): 116-21.

Hertig, Paul. "The Galilee Theme in Matthew: Transforming Mission through Marginality." *Missiology: An International Review* 25, no. 2 (April 1997): 161-75.

Hopkins, Ian W. J. "Gethsemane and the Gardens of Jerusalem." *Bible and Spade* 8, no. 4 (Autumn 1979): 114-28.

Hutchison, John C. "Was John the Baptist an Essene from Qumran?" *Bibliotheca Sacra* 159, no 634 (April 2002): 188-200.

Loffreda, Stanislao. "Capernaum—Jesus' Own City." *Bible and Spade* 10, no. 1 (Winter 1981): 2-19.

Longenecker, Richard N. "Christianity and the Piety of Pre-Destruction Hebraic Judaism." *Journal of the Evangelical Theological Society* 5, no. 2 (Spring 1962): 52-61.

Maier, Paul L. "History, Archaeology, and Jesus." *Bible and Spade* 16, no. 1 (Winter 2003): 22-28.

―――. "The Infant Massacre." *Bible and Spade* 6, no. 4 (Autumn 1977): 98-105.

Mare, W. Harold. "Teacher and Rabbi in the New Testament Period." *Grace Journal* 11, no. 3 (Fall 1970): 12-18.

Meisinger, George E. "Judas." *Chafer Theological Seminary Journal* 3, no. 1 (Summer 1997): 3-8.

Overstreet, R. Larry. "Difficulties of New Testament Genealogies." *Grace Theological Journal* 2, no. 2 (Fall 1981): 304-27.

Reddin, Lester. "Jesus the Rabbi." *Bibliotheca Sacra* 69, no. 276 (October 1912): 694-707.

Runesson, Anders. "Behind the Gospel of Matthew: Radical Pharisees in

Post-War Galilee?" *Currents in Theology and Missions* 37, no. 6 (December 2010): 36-44.

Sanchez, Steven H. "Jesus' Use of the Title 'Son of Man' in Matthew 26:64." *Emmaus Journal* 9, no. 2 (Winter 2000): 194-203.

Sihombing, Batara. "Wealth and Wisdom in Matthew 6:19-34." *Tyndale Bulletin* 57, no. 1 (NA 2006): 156-57.

Silva, Moises. "The Pharisees in Modern Jewish Scholarship: A Review." *Westminster Theological Journal* 42, no. 2 (Spring 1980): 396-405.

Van Houwelingen, P. H. R. "Fleeing Forward: The Departure of Christians from Jerusalem to Pella." *Westminster Theological Journal* 65, no. 2 (Fall 2003): 182-200.

Varner, Will. "Another Look at the Pharisees." *Bible and Spade* 3, no. 1 (Winter 1990): 25-28.

Weiss, Harold. "Recent Work at Capernaum." *Bible and Spade* 10, no. 1 (Winter 1981): 20-27.

Wenham, D. "The Resurrection Narratives in Matthew's Gospel." *Tyndale Bulletin* 24, no. 1 (NA 1973): 22-25.

Wright, G. Frederick. "The Term 'Son of Man' As Used in the New Testament." *Bibliotheca Sacra* 44, no. 176 (October 1887): 576-602.

ABOUT THE AUTHOR

For many years Michael Card has struggled to listen to the Scripture at the level of his imagination. The result has been thirty-two albums and twenty-four books, all examining a different element of the Bible, from the life of the apostle Peter to slavery in the New Testament to Christ-centered creativity.

He has a master's degree in biblical studies from Western Kentucky University as well as honorary Ph.D.s in music (Whitfield Seminary) and Christian education (Philadelphia Biblical University).

He lives with his wife, Susan, and their four children in Franklin, Tennessee, where together they pursue racial reconciliation and neighborhood renewal.

www.michaelcard.com

ABOUT THE BIBLICAL IMAGINATION SERIES

The Biblical Imagination Series is made up of four elements: commentary, music, on-site experience and community discussion. The series overviews the Gospels by means of a commentary on each of the four books, a collection of songs and a video teaching series from Israel as well as a touring conference series. For more information go to the Facebook page for "Biblical Imagination with Michael Card" or visit

www.biblicalimagination.com

Now Available:

Matthew: The Gospel of Fulfillment
Mark: The Gospel of Passion
Luke: The Gospel of Amazement

Forthcoming:

John: The Gospel of Wisdom (2014)

ALSO AVAILABLE FROM INTERVARSITY PRESS:

Mark: The Beginning of the Gospel	**Luke: A World** Turned Upside Down	*A Violent Grace:* Meeting Christ at the Cross	**Matthew: The** Penultimate Question
music CD	music CD	music CD	music CD
ISBN: 978-0-8308-3802-8	ISBN: 978-0-8308-3801-1	ISBN: 978-0-8308-3771-1	ISBN: 978-0-8308-3803-5

   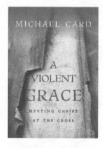

Scribbling in the Sand: Christ and Creativity	*A Fragile Stone:* The Emotional Life of Simon Peter	*A Better Freedom:* Finding Life as Slaves of Christ	*A Violent Grace:* Meeting Christ at the Cross
168 pages, paperback	192 pages, paperback	168 pages, paperback	182 pages, paperback
ISBN: 978-0-8308-3254-5	ISBN: 978-0-8308-3445-7	ISBN: 978-0-8308-3714-4	ISBN: 978-0-8308-3772-4